Public issue television

MANCHESTER
1824

Manchester University Press

Public issue television
World in Action, 1963–98

Peter Goddard, John Corner and Kay Richardson

Manchester University Press
Manchester and New York
distributed exclusively in the USA by Palgrave

Published by Manchester University Press
Oxford Road, Manchester M13 9NR, UK
and Room 400, 175 Fifth Avenue, New York, NY 10010, USA
www.manchesteruniversitypress.co.uk

Distributed exclusively in the USA by
Palgrave, 175 Fifth Avenue, New York,
NY 10010, USA

Distributed exclusively in Canada by
UBC Press, University of British Columbia, 2029 West Mall,
Vancouver, BC, Canada V6T 1Z2

British Library Cataloguing-in-Publication Data
A catalogue record for this book is available from the
British Library

Library of Congress Cataloging-in-Publication Data applied for

ISBN 978 0 7190 6255 1 *hardback*
ISBN 978 0 7190 6256 8 *paperback*

First published 2007

16 15 14 13 12 11 10 09 08 07   10 9 8 7 6 5 4 3 2 1

Typeset
by Florence Production Ltd, Stoodleigh, Devon
Printed and bound in Great Britain
by Cromwell Press, Trowbridge, Wiltshire

To Martha and Ben, who might now have a better idea of what Dad does when he's 'working'. And with thanks to my co-authors for all their support. (P. G.)

Contents

Acknowledgements

Our first acknowledgment must be to Steve Boulton who, as Editor of *World in Action* in 1997, responded enthusiastically to the idea of our undertaking this study and met us to discuss the requirements for getting it started. We did not know then that the series would end little more than a year later, giving our ambitions a stronger historical character than we had envisaged. When Steve left Granada, Ian McBride, currently Managing Editor and Director of Compliance at ITV.plc, became our indispensable point of liaison with the company during the securing of the research funding and the establishing of the project, and we owe a large debt of gratitude for his interest in the whole enterprise and his role in getting us access to the archives.

In parts of this book, our account of events and our own analyses draw heavily on formal interviews with four former members of the *World in Action* team: Professor Brian Winston, Ray Fitzwalter, Peter Heinze and Stephen Peet. We are enormously grateful for the time and support that they gave to the project and it is our great regret that the last two named have not lived to see its completion. Conversations with a wide variety of other *World in Action* personnel have also shaped our understanding of the series. We thank all of them for their time and their interest in the project and, in particular, the following people who have contributed directly to the preparation of this book in patiently responding to our e-mails or answering questions on the telephone: Simon Albury, Nick Davies, David Hart, Brian Lapping and Liz Sutherland.

We have also received invaluable help from numerous people at Granada Television who helped us to obtain tapes or information, facilitated access to archives and generally made us feel so welcome. We wholeheartedly thank David Wanless, Sheila Fitzhugh and Sue Nicholas, all of whom made Granada Yorkshire seem like a second home at one stage, and Adrian Figgess, Lynsey Wilkinson and Matt Sharp at Granada Manchester. We were also able to obtain access to the archives of the ITA and IBA and we owe a debt of thanks to the various reference library and information services staff who gave their time so freely in helping us to find what we were looking for. Principal among these were Simon McKeon, Kathy Daly, Karen Firmin-Cooper and Jan Kacperek.

We also wish to thank the many academic colleagues who have encouraged our research, invited us to speak at conferences, given of their time to discuss our work and to share findings of their own in similar fields and taken such an interest in the progress of the project. We hope that we have done justice to their expectations.

The ESRC funded the work required to produce this book (Awards R000238010 and R000239438) and we are happy to acknowledge this absolutely invaluable support.

Finally, Matthew Frost at Manchester University Press has not lost his interest in the project despite the years between contract and delivery and we offer him a full measure of authorial gratitude.

World in Action: some key names

Bernstein, Cecil	Joint managing director (to 1971) and chairman (1971–75), Granada Television
Bernstein, (Lord) Sidney	Founder and chairman (to 1971), Granada Television. Chairman, Granada Group (to 1979)
Birt, John (Lord)	*World in Action* producer (1967–69) and joint editor (1969–70)
Boulton, David	Presenter, producer (1969–84) and editor (1974–75) of *World in Action*. Head of current affairs (1980–82), Granada Television
Boulton, Steve	Researcher and producer (1983–94) and editor (1994–98) of *World in Action*
Fitzwalter, Ray	Researcher and producer (1970–76), joint editor (1976–81), editor (1981–86) and executive producer (1986–88) of *World in Action*. Head of current affairs (1988–93), Granada Television
Forman, (Sir) Denis	Joint managing director (to 1975) and chairman (1974–87), Granada Television
Fraser, Sir Robert	Director general, ITA (1954–70)
Hayes, Nick	*World in Action* editor (1989–92)
Heads, Barrie	Producer and executive producer, current affairs (to 1966)
Hewat, Tim	Executive producer of *Searchlight* (1959–60), *World in Action* (1963–64) and *The World Tonight*/*The World Tomorrow* (1965–66)
Charles Hill, Baron Hill of Luton	Chairman, ITA (1963–67)
Lapping, Brian	Current affairs producer and executive producer (1970–88), Granada Television. Executive producer (1976–78), *World in Action*

Littler, Lady Shirley   Acting director general and director general, IBA (1989–90)

McBride, Ian   *World in Action* researcher and producer (1977–91). Head of drama-documentary and further posts at Granada Television (1991 on)

Macdonald, (Lord)   *World in Action* researcher and producer
Gus   (1967–69) and joint editor (1969–71). Executive producer (1971–75) and head of current affairs/features (1975–86), Granada Television

Nelmes, Diane   *World in Action* researcher (1985–87) and executive producer (1992). Head of factual programmes and further posts at Granada Television (1992 on)

Peers, Victor   General manager, Granada Television (to 1967)

Plowden, Lady   Chair, IBA (1975–80)
Bridget

Plowright, David   Executive producer of *The World Tomorrow* (1966–67) and *World in Action* (1967–68). Head of current affairs (1968–69), head of programmes (1969–71), programme controller 1971–80), joint managing director (1976–82), managing director (1982–87) and chairman (1987–92), Granada Television

Prebble, Stuart   Producer (1982–87) and editor (1987–89) of *World in Action*

Quinn, Andrew   General manager (1977–87), managing director (1987–92) and chief executive (1992), Granada Television. Chief executive, ITV Network Centre (1992–95)

Robinson, (Sir) Gerry   Chief executive (1991–96), Granada Group

Scott, Mike   Presenter, *World in Action*. Executive producer, current affairs (1977–78), deputy programme controller (1978–80), programme controller (1980–87)

Segal, Allan   Producer (1972–78) and joint editor (1979–81), *World in Action*

Sendall, Bernard   Deputy director general, ITA/IBA (1955–77)

Thomson, George,   Chairman, IBA (1981–88)
Baron Thomson
of Monifieth

Valentine, Alex	Producer (1963–64) and executive producer (1964–65) of *World in Action*
Wallington, Jeremy	Head of 'Investigations Bureau' (1967–68) and joint editor of *World in Action* (1968–69). Executive producer, current affairs (1969–71) and head of programmes (1971–77), Granada Television
Woodhead, Leslie	Producer for *The World Tomorrow* (1966–67) and *World in Action* (1967–90), joint editor of *World in Action* (1968–69), executive producer of drama-documentary (1972–81)
Young, Sir Brian	Director general, ITA/IBA (1970–82)

Note: although this list is as accurate as possible, job titles and areas of responsibility at Granada Television tended to be quite fluid at times.

A note on referencing

Where references in endnotes are marked with an asterisk (*), they refer to documents from the Granada Television archive. Please see p. 6 for more information.

1

Introduction

This book is an historical account of how one television series, *World in Action*, celebrated for its tough journalism, visual directness and public impact, functioned and developed over its run across 35 years, from 1963 to 1998. Based on detailed examination of the written and audio-visual archives, supplemented by a range of other documents and interviews, it is an attempt to get inside the making of factual television and to explore the various dynamics of 'documentary journalism' – technological, professional, aesthetic, institutional, economic, social and political.

Our account is necessarily premised on a belief in the values of history and historical engagement, values that go beyond the scholarly imperative to record and debate the past. We believe that opening up the archives of television and, with all the hazards attendant on interpretation, looking at the detailed interplay of programme-making and society in earlier periods can illuminate and inform a more general sense of the medium. It offers the possibility of contributing to public debate about how television works and about its further social potential within changed technological contexts.

We are pleased to have this book published at a time when there is a clear growth of interest in the historical study of television, something of an 'historical turn'. Our primary reference point here is Britain, but we also welcome developments in the more established media historiography of many nations in Europe and of the United States.[1] Of key importance is the move towards 'going inside' the process of television-making rather than remaining at the level of a primarily institutional study in which much of value is noted but the local practices and the interconnections of 'programme culture' tend to escape. Of course, good levels of access to archives, restrictions on which have been a longstanding obstacle to serious academic work on television, is a requirement for this move to be made. Another requirement is a research design that is able to operate at the 'case-study' level, limiting by its programme foci as well as its time period the amount of data that is brought into the frame and thereby giving the opportunity for depth and a tracing of interconnection that eludes broader approaches. 'Case-studies' are not all that television history is about, of course, but only when a number of them are undertaken is progress on broader themes made possible.

Our own study limits itself to one series, in the process gaining strength of continuity at the same time as requiring increased care for the precise level of generality that can be supported. Historical method has longstanding challenges, among which is that of not making the mistake of reading the part for the whole but, nevertheless, of requiring some provisional, working sense of the whole in order adequately to 'read' the part at all. In running its account across four decades, our project puts pressure on the range of 'significant context' it can bring into the analysis, the latitudinal spread being limited by the sheer scale of the chronology involved. However, as we indicate more fully below, we think we offer an account in which the selectivity introduced works to organise a coherent study without too many distortions or foreshortenings.

The programme

World in Action was chosen for our inquiry because of its pivotal position in British television across its run from the early 1960s through to the late 1990s. It was, in a sense, a kind of 'hub' where questions of appropriate documentary form, journalistic value, the commitment to making the serious popular, the belief in television as a power for social and political good, became interlinked. We had variously written about these issues before, both in historical work and in studies of contemporary television, and we all agreed that a sustained examination of a single series would be a rewarding and valuable undertaking. Our own selection does not ignore other major series where the 'hub' function could be seen to be at work, notably other current affairs series like the BBC's *Panorama* (1953–) and Associated Rediffusion/Thames Television's *This Week* (1955–92), both of which have now been the subject of excellent studies to which we have referred where appropriate.[2] However, as a result largely of regional contacts from our own base in Liverpool, we were able to secure the agreement of Granada Television to have access to the written and film archives of *World in Action*. This allowed us to proceed successfully with a bid for research funding and to the work that eventually led to this volume.[3]

World in Action was a weekly series, made by Granada but broadcast nationally through the ITV network, with a standard length of 30 minutes and a format which, across its several changes, committed each edition to the exploration of just one issue. It thus differed from the variety of magazine programmes where several issues were treated in each edition. These programmes inevitably worked with a reduced research period and time allocation for each topic that made them convergent with the kinds of 'news feature' emerging at different points in the development of television news journalism.

By contrast, *World in Action*, despite the pace of its production schedule, had useful amounts of 'journalistic space' in which to develop its accounts of each chosen topic. It also had what we can see as an important amount of 'documentary space' too, space to develop a visual narrative, which gave a sense of the depth and context of the topic as well the force of its significance for the current moment and evidence of its presence, as kinds of action, in the world. The series went out for most its run in Monday evening prime-time,[4] so it was inevitably part of the broader commitment, both by BBC and Independent Television journalism, to attract a popular audience, a commitment which became fiercer in its external determinants as a consequence of shifts in the character of the television economy by the 1990s. The topics chosen varied across the domestic and the international but throughout its run the series retained a strong sense of its 'world' as being much broader than national and a sense, too, of how much that which was national needed to be seen in an international setting to be properly understood. As we shall show in the chapters that follow, the series employed a range of approaches and methods to get across its accounts and to project what was often a kind of challenge to its viewers ('look at this, and be concerned'). It sometimes took its cue from the news headlines and went behind them but it also worked from its own agenda, visiting and revisiting issues that its production team thought important and often showing a good eye for the neglected topic and the topic to which attention had been deliberately discouraged. It quickly developed a familiar identity both within the weekly schedules and the discourses of British public debate. Its title music (introduced from 1969[5] through to its finish in 1998), a strident organ riff repeated with falling intervals over a brisk groove, and the humanistic motif provided by the use later in its run of Da Vinci's 'Vitruvian man' as a titles logo (outstretched limbs giving the diameter of a traced circle) effectively became national symbols. It has been at times an exhilarating, as well as fulfilling, job to try to do justice to its history.

The organisation of the book

In planning the structure of this book we have recognised the importance both of offering a chronological commentary, crucial to a sense of development and change, and providing an analysis of those aspects of the series which we thought needed a more intensive attention. This play-off between narrative and thematic elements is endemic to historical writing, of course. Our solution has been to lead with four chapters strongly organised in terms of specific periods and the key developments within them. We then follow with three chapters, each of which focuses on an aspect of the series deserving of deeper analysis across the whole run. These chapters look at the organisation and culture of production, at the series' use of language and visual form and at the vexed issue of regulation. There were other candidates for this kind of special attention but, within the overall constraints of the volume, these seemed to be the most useful to work with, rich in their interconnections both with each other and the earlier chapters that look at specific periods. Finally, in a short conclusion we offer a summary, overview commentary. While recognising the risks of an introduction saying too much by way of outlining for the reader what is to come, we think it useful to offer here a little more on the character and kinds of emphasis to be found within the broad scheme outlined. A few sentences to sketch out the primary content of each of our seven principal chapters will provide a map of the historical territory, the transitions and the interconnections, that we explore.

Chapter 2 is about 'origins', looking at the emergence of the series from within a specific context of preceding and concurrent work against which innovation and originality can be assessed. As well as including what was always a significant point of reference, the BBC's *Panorama*, this context involves the Granada series *Searchlight*, an important forerunner of *World in Action*. We examine the key ingredients in the design of the new series as it gradually came together from 1961. Here, we bring out particularly the important role played by Denis Forman and one of his appointees, Tim Hewat, in shaping the approach to the kind of 'critical reportage' that the series would provide.

After a brief consideration of an 'interim' period between 1965 and 1967 when *World in Action* gave way to another series building upon its success, *The World Tomorrow*, we concern ourselves in Chapters 3 and 4 with what we can call 'classic' *World in Action*. The first of these chapters runs from 1967 to 1975 and covers the re-establishment of the series (with a revised brief reflecting shifts in television culture and journalism since 1963) both as a 'routine' contributor to British public debate and as a success with audiences. In its chronological survey, it looks at, among other things, varied approaches to investigation and debate about the changing role of 'film-making' in relation to the journalistic commitments of the series. A range of examples is offered to indicate the mix of national and international topics covered, to illustrate key developments and to show how the series became engaged in controversial public issues, often leading to serious clashes with authorities.

The second of these linked chapters, Chapter 4, runs from 1975 to 1988 and it continues the job of illustrating by example the series' strong involvement in public debates and its capacity to 'break' stories as well as to follow them up aggressively. In documenting further shifts in the nature both of British society and of television during the period, it shows how the regulatory context, specifically the working ideas and practices of the Independent Broadcasting Authority (IBA), became increasingly a factor in *World in Action*'s activities. Once again, where appropriate, detailed citations from the written archive are given.

Chapter 5 is also a linked chronological chapter but in developing the story of the series through to its finish in 1998, increasing emphasis is placed on changes in the television economy and the stronger commercial pressures to which *World in Action* had to respond. We look at the implications for the series of the 1990 Broadcasting Act and the setting up of centralised scheduling through the ITV Network Centre. Although we also document continuing achievement and innovation (programmes often picking up adaptively on generic developments across the full range of television output in an attempt to strengthen popular appeal), our account finally becomes one about economic imperatives and, eventually, about the closure and replacement of the series.

Chapter 6 examines the structures and processes of production and particularly the way in which these shape and display the work of the series 'team'. Much of the distinctiveness of the series, as well as its quality, inevitably stems from team-based practice. Television is inevitably a co-operative affair, of course, and all studies of production are required to recognise this when assessing questions of 'authorship' and development. What we seek to establish in this chapter is, first of all, the range of working procedures that *World in Action* established and frequently revised for getting the programme made across its different research, investigative and production roles, often in situations of considerable pressure. Then, beyond that, we review the kind of 'team culture' that gave the series its confidence and self-critical energies, paying attention to the issues of leadership and accountability that arose in this specific, institutional context. Here, some of the outstanding individuals who contributed to the series' reputation are given attention.

In Chapter 7, we move from a primarily narrative account of developments across the series as a whole to look in more detail at the sub-generic idea of 'documentary journalism' and at *World in Action*'s specific approaches to programme design. First of all, we suggest the basic categories in relation to which editions of the series were variously organised (e.g. analysis, discussion, biography, ethnography) and then we pursue further the particular formal strategies (e.g. commentary, interviews, interventions, reconstructions) used to develop and project the material. Taking examples from across the run of the series, we hope to bring out in this chapter something of the range, complexity and energy of its discourses.

In our third 'theme' chapter, Chapter 8, we explore an aspect of the series running as a strand through our entire account, the question of regulation. What does 'being fair' mean in the context of investigative journalism? How did the national bodies charged with regulating television understand their obligations to the 'public interest', particularly in situations of political dispute or where private and corporate interests were sharply implicated? By opening up selected case-studies in greater depth than the chronological chapters would easily allow, involving programmes on, for instance, foreign policy, Northern Ireland, the pharmaceutical industry and municipal corruption, we provide here what we think is a documented account unprecedented in its tracing of the actual operation, the imposition and also the challenging, of regulatory measures. This takes us to the centre not only of *World in Action*'s project, but also of the relationship, shifting in its precise nature but invariably tense, between television journalism and the State.

In our conclusion, providing a short Chapter 9, we attempt to bring together and summarise some of the principal themes to emerge from the volume, in relation to our understanding of this outstanding series, the broader pattern of television's development as a medium with a unique social and public character and the further development of 'television studies' internationally.

In developing our account, we have employed a note system of referencing, one in which for, ease of use, a full rather than abbreviated reference is given on the first citation in each chapter. Our footnotes refer to a variety of sources, including the Granada files, which are indicated with an asterisk (*). Here, we have specified the relevant box file (bf.) numbers to aid further research. In the preliminary pages of the book, after the acknowledgements, we have provided a list of some of the principal figures involved in the *World in Action* story. As an appendix, we have listed with dates each edition of the programme that we mention.

We believe that readers of several different kinds, some knowing a lot about British television already and some knowing very little, will find value in the critical record we offer. Our hope is that our organisation of the materials provides for a clear and engaging passage through the book.

Notes

1   As this book goes to press we would appear be on the edge of a quite impressive increase in published historical scholarship on television, resulting in part from doctoral studies. Much work is in progress but of the recent work to appear we might mention Catherine Johnson and Rob Turnock's collection *ITV Cultures: Independent Television Over Fifty Years* (London: Open University Press/McGraw Hill, 2005). Two significant studies in the area of this present volume are indicated in the next note. A range of articles of varying breadth and approach is appearing in academic journals, including *Screen* and the new *Journal of British Cinema and Television*.

2   R. Lindley, *Panorama: Fifty Years of Pride and Paranoia* (London: Methuen, 2003) and P. Holland, *The Angry Buzz: This Week and Current Affairs Television* (London: I. B. Tauris, 2006). We have kept up a good level of contact with Patricia Holland throughout. Although her book was published as ours was reaching a final draft, we have tried to make comparative reference to its instructive account where appropriate.

3   The work involved visits to the archives in Manchester (Granada) and then in Leeds (Yorkshire Television) following their transfer there quite soon after our work began. Extensive transfer to VHS enabled viewings at Liverpool and many documents were photocopied to allow closer scrutiny and citation than consultation only in the archive would allow. As our data about the series developed and informed a provisional sense of its contexts, achievements and challenges, interviews with selected former team members were undertaken and other institutional sources, including the archives of the ITA/IBA, were used.

4   The series began on Mondays (10.30pm, later 10.10pm), moved to Tuesdays in October 1963 (10.05 or 10.10pm) where it and *The World Tonight/ The World Tomorrow* remained until September 1966. *The World Tomorrow* then ran on Fridays (10.05pm) until the end of its run in March 1967. *World in Action* returned to Mondays on its re-launch in July 1967 – either at 8pm (1967–March 1973; September 1973–February 1974; January 1996 to end of run) or 8.30pm (March–September 1973; February 1974–December 1995).

5   The distinctive 'Jam for *World in Action*' was actually introduced sometime between Summer 1968 and February 1970. Editions in the period 1963–65 used a brassy, big band theme and then from the re-launch onwards to the arrival of the distinctive 'Jam' the programme used no title music at all.

2

Origins: technology, innovation and social purpose

The distinctively British notion of the television current affairs series, of which *World in Action* was to become such a dominant example, can be thought of as combining elements from three earlier media. In part, current affairs had its origins in the documentary cinema pioneered by John Grierson in the 1930s. Its audiences were shown and informed about actual events or activities in a manner that derived both from a liberal sense of social responsibility and a filmic concern with the aesthetics of realism. Particularly in the 1960s and 1970s, current affairs film-makers at *World in Action* and elsewhere maintained a close interest in developments in film and television documentary and sought to locate their own work, in part at least, within those traditions. A second source is to be found in BBC radio's development of Talks and Features. Talks became one of the three programme divisions of the BBC in 1946, responsible for bringing to the microphone speakers on a vast range of subjects thought to be of interest to listeners. Significantly, Talks was thought of as distinct from News. The first use of the term 'current affairs' in broadcasting was as the name for a sub-category of the Talks division particularly concerned with talks or discussions on topical matters.[1] The radio Feature, made within the BBC's Entertainment division, was more imaginative, offering an approach to factual broadcasting not unlike documentary-in-sound. Since the 1930s, features had employed innovative combinations of speech, sound and dramatisation to produce fresh insights into areas as diverse as literature, the 'human condition' and social affairs.[2] Later, as television current affairs developed into a distinctive strand concerned with topical enquiry and the scrutiny of public affairs, a third source – journalism – became increasingly significant. Few journalists were involved in documentary or radio Talks and Features, but as television current affairs found its feet during the 1950s, it drew increasingly on personnel from Fleet Street who, in turn, helped to foster new and distinctively visual forms of television journalism.

In another sense, television current affairs is a product of the British public service broadcasting ethos. From its inception, a central role of the BBC was to inform, which gave a strong impetus to the development of factual forms of broadcasting. Radio News, Talks and Features served to ensure that the BBC made a significant contribution to the 'public sphere'. From the early 1950s, BBC Television also began to take on a meaningful role in contributing to the circulation of ideas and information with the initiation of topical debating programmes such as *In the News* (BBC, 1950–56) and *Press Conference* (BBC, 1952–61). *Panorama* is generally supposed to be Britain's first television current affairs series. At its inception, however, it was thought of as a topical magazine – a product of the Talks Division – in which experts offered 'informed comment on the contemporary scene' and its development of high quality pictorial journalism took place gradually as the decade continued.[3] Of equal significance, however, was *Special Enquiry* (BBC, 1952–57), which married the BBC's Features experience to the visual traditions of social documentary to produce lengthy location reports on single issues. Narration was largely absent and the series sought out ordinary people rather than experts to describe and illustrate the conditions in which they lived. *Special Enquiry* consciously aimed to produce 'a new form of journalism' and its thematic agenda was close to that adopted in current affairs series, especially in the early years of *World in Action*.[4] When competition was introduced to television in 1955, current affairs programmes had already taken on a role in documenting society, placing items on the agenda of public affairs and offering viewers access not only to abstracted discussions of policy but to some of the people affected by it.

Independent Television's own public service obligations – enshrined by statute – meant that serious factual programming was a significant element in its output, too. Its programmes were required to 'maintain a proper balance in their subject-matter'[5] and companies produced 'balancing programmes' to offset their reliance on popular entertainment. As inexperience, loose networking arrangements and financial crises began to be overcome, the emerging pattern of ITV scheduling challenged BBC Television in the extent of its factual output, with *This Week*, networked from Autumn 1956, as its prestige current affairs series.[6] ITV extended the range of current affairs programming but initially its output differed from the BBC less in form than in its adoption of a more populist address to viewers. In both *Panorama* and *This Week*, 'personality' anchors led or linked interviews, discussions and film reports on topical social and political events. By the end of the decade, both were thriving and had developed a harder edge as a result of competition and the recruitment of fresh, able production teams.

Current affairs at Granada Television

Elsewhere within ITV, other forms of current affairs programming developed, including ITN's news feature *Roving Report* (1957–64). However, the company most committed to the spirit of public service broadcasting and to expanding the social and political contribution of Independent Television's output was Granada. Granada was an anomaly among ITV contractors: it remained a family firm; Sidney Bernstein, its guiding light, had been staunchly opposed to commercial television and remained a Labour supporter; his vision was that the company should have a 'social mission'; its management was also closely involved in programme-making. Granada produced a wide range of programmes, many popular and often unashamedly populist, but by the end of the decade it was established as a specialist in factual programming. Here, it adopted a more radical and irreverent approach than the patrician BBC and its ITV competitors, summed up in its submission to the Pilkington Committee in 1961: 'We believe that programmes in public affairs should stimulate original thought and should not reflect, however brilliantly, only the accepted attitudes (or platitudes) of political and social life'.[7]

One key series in the development of this approach was *Under Fire* (Granada, 1956–59), in which authority figures in London were subjected to a lively interrogation by a studio audience in a regional centre, normally Manchester. The spectacle of politicians or industrialists confronted by ordinary people rather than professional pundits was completely new and, whilst the political classes found it shocking, its confrontational approach made it popular with viewers. *Under Fire* was intended to reflect popular disillusionment with politicians. It was conceived as 'the Country v. Westminster and Whitehall' and had 'distinct aspects of circus'.[8] Granada relished the political controversy it caused. But the platform that it gave to ordinary people to tilt at authority also made it a democratic departure for television. Another significant Granada programme was *What The Papers Say* (Granada/Channel 4/BBC, 1956–), in which a leading journalist gave a weekly review of the daily papers. This too was a programme that aroused controversy, partly among newspapers, which were quick to criticise a programme in which their failings were exposed to public ridicule, and partly at the ITA, who were continually concerned at any appearance of political partisanship: 'Our worries [about *What The Papers Say*] have been just about chronic', wrote the ITA Director-General Sir Robert Fraser in 1960. Speakers have 'used the programme as a means of highly controversial personal political advocacy ... Far too often it turns out to be a programme of teasing and sneering'.[9] Lord Hill, the ITA Chairman, saw Granada's radicalism and dislike of authority as deep-seated: 'I came to doubt whether Sidney Bernstein, its presiding genius, really accepted the constraints of the Television Act', he wrote. But he also acknowledged Granada to be 'the most enterprising of [the ITV] companies' – it was 'live, vigorous and imaginative'.[10]

These and other series contributed significantly not only to the establishment of a radical reputation for Granada but to the liberalisation of public affairs coverage on television generally. Both routinely breached the Fourteen Day Rule, an agreement which served to prevent the broadcast discussion of any issue to be debated in parliament in the coming fortnight, and in so doing helped to overcome the deferential approach to politics and parliamentary debate which had been inherited from the BBC. The Rule was eventually suspended in December 1956. Through these series, Granada also challenged regulatory strictures, helping to liberalise, if only slightly, the ITA's interpretation of 'impartiality'. Independent television could not be seen to be partisan (although this remained a frequent criticism of both programmes from the Conservative party and sections of the press), but it could at least be critical in its coverage of public affairs.

Despite its success in public affairs and political programming, before 1959 Granada had not had a current affairs series involving location filming and reportage. Where such an approach, then becoming common in *Panorama* and *This Week*, was used it had been in 'specials' – single documentaries on contemporary issues. Although these covered a range of subjects, Granada again took a radical line, earning a reputation as 'the company with the social conscience'.[11] By 1960, 'specials' had been devoted to such taboo subjects as homosexuality, euthanasia, mental health, cancer and venereal disease, all subjects to which *World in Action* was later to return. Granada's attitude, and its first foray into current affairs reportage, however, is best explained through an examination of two of its key figures.

In the haphazard months immediately before and after the launch of Granada Television, Denis Forman emerged as its Head of Programmes (he never held the title formally), initiating much of its early programming. 'Serious' programming was Forman's principal area of interest and he believed strongly that ITV's contribution to national life in this field should be as significant as in entertainment and drama. Essentially, Granada's early factual programming reflected Forman's world view: *Under Fire, What The Papers Say* (which he also produced, uncredited, for its first year) and many of the 'specials' were his creations. Over the next 30 years, Forman was to play a hugely important role both at Granada, where he defined and oversaw its contribution to serious programming, and in helping to mould ITV, where he fought to shape the network, contested regulatory constraints on the development of television journalism and wrote many papers on the public role of television and of current affairs in particular.[12] In later years, as Chairman of Granada, he became one of the foremost guardians of public service broadcasting within ITV: 'In many ways', he wrote, 'I had more in common with the BBC's attitude to broadcasting than with some of my more commercially minded colleagues in ITV'.[13] It was also Forman who, during the late 1950s, recruited a group of able lieutenants, mostly print journalists, who were to become leading figures in the development of Granada's serious programming in the 1960s and beyond. These included Barrie Heads, David Plowright, Bill Grundy, Mike Scott (initially a floor manager on *Under Fire*), Derek Granger, Jeremy Isaacs and Tim Hewat.

Hewat was Granada's other key current affairs innovator of the time. A high profile journalist at the *Daily Express*, then at the height of its popular success, he had been Northern Editor and London Assistant Editor when he left to join Granada in May 1957, realising both that the path to the *Express* editorship was blocked and that television offered huge, untapped potential for journalism. The term 'phenomenon' is often used to describe Hewat,[14] and his character and work rate were certainly important factors in his influence at Granada. He was colourful, brash, shocking, rude, and very un-British – 'a headlong ruffian son of the Australian earth' who posed as 'a movie version of a newspaper man'.[15] Hewat lacked television experience on joining Granada, but learned quickly in regional programmes, on *What the Papers Say* and even in variety. Sheer force of personality, energy and, above all, journalistic flair soon set him apart. Essentially, Hewat was a popular journalist in the *Express* tradition of strong headlines and breezy, campaigning style. He was single-minded and decisive in sizing up the aspects of a story that could grab and hold viewers and his programmes were direct, lively and pioneering.

Searchlight

Hewat quickly sought a vehicle for his style of journalism. By March 1958 he had already engaged Sydney Elliott, formerly editor of the *Evening Standard* and *Daily Herald*, to produce preliminary research briefs for a reportage-based series which Hewat described as a 'social *Panorama*'.[16] While the format of studio presentation with filmed inserts may have been modelled on *Panorama*, Hewat's approach to his series could not have been more different: 'The aim of these programmes', his original brief stated, 'is to raise hell about things that are wrong – wrong because they are unjust, unfair or inefficient'.[17] The new series – initially to be called 'Probe', 'Attack' or 'Search' – was to be 'critical and aggressive': 'There will be a strong flavour of "J'accuse" in our treatment'.[18] *Searchlight* (Granada, 1959–60), as it was finally entitled, was also to adopt a much bolder style. Each programme opened on three searchlights against a dark background, accompanied by drums and clashing cymbals as the shot tightened until the middle searchlight filled the screen to dazzle the viewer. Provocative verbal and visual tasters followed. A programme on the nation's schools opened thus:

> Five hundred of our schools were condemned more than a quarter of a century ago – and they are still in use today. Only one child in three goes to a school built within the last ten years. Tonight *Searchlight* writes a report and says 'Room for improvement'.[19]

'Crawling highways', on traffic congestion, opened with a rapid montage of traffic signs: 'Slow dangerous bends', 'Halt at major road ahead', 'Road narrows', 'Drive slowly through village', 'Double bend', 'Hill 1 in 9', 'No overtaking for 150 yards', and so on.[20] Although tame by modern standards, these attention-grabbing devices were wholly at odds with the measured, gentlemanly technique of *Panorama*. The same brash, populist approach was apparent throughout the series. Illustrative gimmicks were frequent: in 'Slaughter on the avenue', footage of 'corpses' laid out in a London street was used to show the incidence of road deaths; 'Appointment at Aintree', about the Grand National steeplechase, was anchored by presenters on horseback. Studio sequences were shot in stark black 'limbo', with life-size graphics that presenters could walk up to. *Searchlight* was 'tabloid journalism brought for the first time to television'.[21]

Despite Sidney Bernstein and Denis Forman's support for innovative and provocative current affairs programming, it took several internal battles to get *Searchlight* on the air. Cost was the main obstacle and, when the series was first proposed, film had recently been banned outright at Granada as too expensive. Forman found himself launching a 'campaign' for the programme to be commissioned. He demonstrated that it could be made for 30 per cent less than *Panorama* and *This Week* and, with the compromise that it should be fortnightly and include no overseas shooting, *Searchlight* was finally given the go-ahead in

February 1959, by which time two 'dry-runs' had been made.[22] Such was Hewat's confidence in the idea, however, that in April 1958 he wrote that 'we are on to biggest thing to hit commercial television – or BBC television – yet.'[23] He even treated the dry-runs as programmes for transmission and showed them almost unchanged in the early weeks of the series.

Searchlight finally began on 2 March 1959, replacing *Under Fire*. It ran fortnightly for 27 programmes until 6 June 1960, with five programmes repeated in the 1959 summer break. Each programme investigated a single issue. The objects of its 'attacks' included contaminated food, child cruelty and the commercialisation of Christmas, but these 'knocking' programmes were 'balanced' by wholly celebratory programmes on breakthroughs such as the Comet airliner and penicillin at a ratio of about two to one. Programmes consisted of about ten minutes of film footage, often mute with voiceover, with the remainder of the half-hour slot filled by studio explanation and discussion with prominent figures. Each was produced either by Hewat or Jeremy Isaacs and directed by Mike Wooller. Kenneth Allsop was brought in as a high profile presenter but later replaced by Bill Grundy, a Granada regular. Hewat's control, however, was total. A succession of researchers were dispatched to write 'scripts' and these were used as the basis for location shooting, but Hewat himself wrote every word that appeared on screen, usually in the hours immediately before recording.[24] Towards the end of the series, film was used more – for links and location interviews with experts – and the programme became less studio-based. There were also some thematic departures, notably a profile of Nikita Khrushchev and a one-hour special, 'Crisis in South Africa' (AKA 'The divided union').[25]

The latter, instigated by Sidney Bernstein and giving a snapshot of South African politics following the Sharpeville massacre, provides a vivid illustration of Granada's commitment and ingenuity in current affairs. Bernstein's response to South Africa's refusal to let the world's press enter the country to investigate the massacre was to assemble an unofficial commission of four British 'observers' including Labour and Conservative MPs and the Vice-Chancellor of Cambridge University. Unwilling to refuse entry to such an illustrous group, South Africa permitted the observers, accompanied by Hewat and his crew, an interview with Prime Minister Verwoerd and a visit to Sharpeville. Despite run-ins with the secret police, Hewat also managed to obtain interviews with outlawed black leaders and riot victims. Back in Manchester, Bernstein and Forman themselves participated in editing the rushes and Bernstein had a stand-up row with Hewat over whether the finished programme would portray the South African regime as sufficiently evil.[26] Such editorial involvement in serious programming from the Chairman himself would have been unheard of elsewhere in ITV. Nevertheless, 'Crisis in South Africa', revealing and condemnatory, was a journalistic scoop for which the ITV companies pre-empted their early evening schedules. Characteristically, Hewat was particularly concerned it should be scheduled to 'counterblast' *Panorama*.[27]

Searchlight was an effective challenge to the 'staid' hegemony of *Panorama* and *This Week* but, in Denis Forman's recollection, 'not a distinguished show'.[28] Its forthright, high-impact style led to charges that topics were approached for their sensational appeal rather than in a spirit of public service and that they were treated superficially. Hewat himself preached the virtues of simplification without acknowledging the potential trade-off between popular appeal and depth of enquiry that his approach to programme-making could entail.[29] Hewat also had little interest in visuals unless they carried some pictorial gimmick. As a print journalist, words were his principal medium and visuals were to be used, where possible, for impact. Otherwise their role was solely to illustrate commentary. Despite his desire for 'control', in *Searchlight* and at the opening of *World in Action*, Hewat left 'the pictures' largely to Mike Wooller, often with instructions as dismissive as: 'Get me some crap to go with that'.[30]

Searchlight had a much more serious flaw, however, as Hewat quickly appreciated. In a briefing document produced in the 1959 summer break, he wrote:

Searchlight always has a point of view . . .

   Searchlight has one big snag. By its nature it sails close to the Television Act and is under the closest scrutiny by the Independent Television Authority.[31]

Searchlight's 'point of view', so central to Hewat's conception of it, was irreconcilable with the Television Act's requirement for 'due impartiality . . . in matters of political or industrial controversy or relating to current public policy'.[32] The hasty inclusion of celebratory programmes alongside 'attacks' was Hewat's first sop to ITA criticism.[33] Even these, however, were unashamedly one-sided. Another was '*Searchlight* on *Searchlight*' (AKA '*Searchlight* under attack'),[34] in which critics of the first series and its attitude were given a programme in which to respond. At the time, the ITA interpreted its obligations under the Act very strictly and 'editorialising' of any kind was prohibited. As Sir Robert Fraser put it: 'Ideally at the end of any edition of *Searchlight* I should be unable to say what is Granada's attitude on the issue'.[35] Other ITV programme contractors were equally critical, having themselves been refused permission by the ITA to mount one-sided current affairs programmes.[36] Granada did not share this interpretation of the Act, nor of the journalism it would produce. For the *Searchlight* team, such strictures were absurd. Facts were at the heart of the programme, supported by 'intensive deep x-ray research', and the conclusions to which such facts inexorably led were surely preferable to the 'over-conscientious neutralism that is endemic in so many television programmes.'[37] Hewat, ever the popular journalist, 'was never so happy as when a *Searchlight* caused some sort of commotion'.[38] But throughout the company a more radical agenda was at work, colouring its whole approach to television journalism. Unlike the BBC, Granada maintained little deference towards the established order in society. As Forman explains: 'A good story we defined as something that someone didn't want you to publish'.[39]

Fraser judged that almost every edition of *Searchlight* was in breach of the Television Act, but none were banned. Instead the ITA made various attempts to guide the series away from editorialising. Letters and telephone calls were exchanged, and a meeting between Fraser and the team arranged in December 1959 at which he made it clear that he approved of the series and especially its 'penetrating reporting'.[40] These had little effect, however, and in June 1960 the final disagreement arose in a letter from Fraser over the 'Crawling highways' programme. Ironically, this was one of *Searchlight*'s least controversial programmes and Fraser's tone was almost apologetic:

> As no one can be found to say that the roads do not need improvement, it might seem excessively stiff to complain about the billing and presentation of last Monday's *Searchlight*. Just because this is so, it is as good an example as I can give you to show how far-reaching is the prohibition placed on opinionated programmes by the Television Act ... This was a programme of opinion on a matter of public policy. The billing proudly proclaimed it to be so, and it proved true of the billing ... It was meant to take a line and I should be staggered if anyone said it was not.[41]

Granada disputed whether the topic could have been tackled in any other way, and noted that the Minister of Transport had raised no objection to the script and had replied on air to the programme's supposed 'point of view', but the company's difference of opinion with the Authority seemed irresolvable.[42] That the press tended to back Granada in such disputes cannot have helped matters either. Finally, Granada conceded defeat, announcing to the ITA that it would take off the air five of its 'serious' programmes which had received the authority's criticism, including *Searchlight*. Whilst acknowledging that the programme 'has often been the most excellent television', Fraser did not mourn its passing: 'It was one long torment to us, so how can we do other than breathe a sigh of relief.'[43]

The *Searchlight* affair was one of the earliest exchanges in a dispute over journalistic impartiality that was to dominate Granada's relations with the regulator over many years, especially in relation to *World in Action*, and to become almost a personal crusade for Denis Forman (see Chapter 8). Granada's stance, however, was essentially quixotic. The company was aware that the structure of Independent Television ensured that the Authority was the only arbiter of the Act. Granada, however, was continually pushing to extend the scope of television current affairs and this at least was broadly welcomed by the ITA itself.[44]

After *Searchlight*

Despite its problems, *Searchlight* was immensely significant in the development of *World in Action* and current affairs television more generally. Its pursuit of a single subject per programme was then an unusual departure and its 'critical' approach to rooting out wrong-doing was thoroughly innovative. It was Tim Hewat's first attempt at a series embodying the kind of current affairs reportage that he felt strongly that television ought to be doing. In this, *Searchlight* has been widely acknowledged as the direct precursor to *World in Action*. Hewat made immediate plans to institute a successor and to retain the existing team, which had by then stabilised to comprise three regular researchers (including Elliott) and Philip Oakes as scriptwriter.[45] However, perhaps because Granada feared further trouble with the ITA, there was to be no successor until Hewat finally launched *World in Action* two-and-a-half years later.

In the intervening period, Granada's belief in the value of current affairs remained undiminished and Hewat turned instead to innovative 'specials' and short series in which he built upon the lessons of *Searchlight*. Notable amongst these was *45 Cranley Drive* (Granada, 1961), tracing and reconstructing the events leading to the trial of the Portland spy ring. *45 Cranley Drive* was made by the *Searchlight* team of Hewat, Wooller and Oakes but was innovative in several respects. All of the standard *Searchlight* techniques of current affairs reportage were used – direct address to camera, narration voiced over stills or actuality footage, location interviews – but the programme also used dramatic reconstruction to illustrate elements in the story. This represented the first use at Granada of a technique that was still rare in current affairs programming but which the company were later to develop as a major current affairs tool.

Hewat's approach to the programme was informed strongly by his experience of newspaper coverage of stories of this kind. For him, it was:

> the most old-fashioned piece of journalism imaginable. In newspapers, whenever there was a big trial, the reporters, the photographers, the picture-snatchers, are assigned to get a story ready for the last day of the trial – full background. Incredibly, it was the first time that this simple technique had been applied to television.[46]

Prepared weeks in advance, *45 Cranley Drive* was shown with a live introduction at 8.30pm on the day that the trial verdicts were given, pre-empting the ITV network's planned variety programme. It was a considerable achievement for Granada, especially given the risk that a different verdict would have left a costly programme untransmittable, and its interviews with those who had informed on them yielded considerable new information about the spy ring. Hewat was particularly proud that he had scooped the newspapers: 'They all came out with big centre-page articles, and you didn't need to read 'em, because you'd seen it all on TV the night before'.[47]

A Sunday in September (Granada, 1961) was another, very different, Hewat achievement. It was a languid, observational half-hour film illustrating the events of Battle of Britain Sunday in central London, the day of a sit-down protest against nuclear weapons. With only the briefest narration to set the scene, the programme placed the mounting drama of parades and protests among shots of ordinary scenes of Sunday London life to produce a documentary in the Griersonian mould climaxing in a brawl in Trafalgar Square. *A Sunday in September* was a pleasing film made newsworthy by its depiction of the protest, but its principal achievement was a logistical one. The decision to make it was taken only on the previous Friday, but by the Sunday Hewat and his director James Hill had assembled 12 film crews involving more than 40 technicians, each with instructions down to the last detail. Editing began at midnight on the Sunday and the completed programme was shown at 6.30pm on the following day. Hewat described it as 'the most ambitious film coverage that television had yet seen'.[48] This time, however, other ITV companies could not be persuaded to pre-empt their schedules and the programme was never shown in London.

Hewat was also keen to pursue a more international agenda, influenced by his experience as a foreign correspondent and perhaps reacting against *Searchlight*'s domestic confinement. At a meeting to 're-start' Granada's current affairs in September 1960 it was noted that 90 per cent of its output had covered home affairs.[49] His proposal for another 'survey type' show in the *This Week* mould having been turned down, Hewat devoted much of 1961 to making foreign-based programmes. Four programmes on India and one on Paris at the height of the Algerian crisis won praise, but the four-part *Cuba Si!* (Granada, 1961), the first Western programmes to examine Castro's Cuba from the inside, proved much more controversial. It had to be made surreptitiously and Hewat and James Hill had numerous brushes with the Cuban authorities. Hewat returned with a programme that he saw as an accurate assessment of the state of the country ('Cuba probably needed a hefty dose of Marxism', he wrote. 'The country has been outrageously and stupidly exploited by the Americans').[50] The ITA disagreed, accusing the programme of lacking impartiality and being 'slanted unfairly against the United States', a reading endorsed by Granada's lawyer. Even Granada's American advertisers attempted to put pressure on the company over the series. Sidney Bernstein was called to the ITA to be given a reprimand in person, but by then it already been transmitted.[51] Characteristically, Granada continued to stand up for *Cuba Si!*, with Bernstein comparing his role to that of a newspaper editor: 'Once settled, the programme became a Granada programme and I was prepared to defend it, and the people who made it, against attack'.[52]

Establishing *World in Action*

The impetus for the series that was to become *World in Action* originated at a meeting in December 1961 of Granada senior producers and executives to discuss current affairs programme ideas. One Denis Forman proposal, for a 'Northern *Panorama*', examining world affairs from a Northern viewpoint, led to the establishment of a working party which met several times in the early months of 1962. The working party decided to re-use the *World in Action* title, coined by John Grierson for two documentary film series and purchased from him by Granada in 1961 to be used as a unifying title for unrelated 'specials'.[53] It also drew up a document outlining the programme's intentions which may be read as a wish list for a programme keen to develop a new, less Establishment-oriented approach to television reportage. It emphasised the value of thorough research, of freshness, simplicity and clarity of presentation and of assuming that viewers shared a modern, 'enlightened' view of the world. Interestingly, it identified and rejected what it saw as the two existing 'formulae' of television reportage – the treatment of topics in the news through interview or discussion, and the personal report.[54] By mid-February, however, its twin objectives of offering a Northern perspective and of maintaining aspirations towards international reportage were proving difficult to combine and Forman no longer had time to be closely involved. After a lull, the 'Northern' aspect was hived off to form the basis of planning for the *Scene at 6.30* regional magazine (Granada region only, 1963–66). Tim Hewat, who had not been involved in the working party, assumed responsibility for the international reportage dimension.

In July 1962, Hewat produced a detailed outline for consideration by Granada's Programme Committee. Retitled 'Granada Reports' or 'Horizon', the programme was to be weekly and had gained a home affairs agenda, a clear sense of its purpose and a commitment not to use reporters in shot. In characteristic style, he wrote:

> This will be critical reportage. We will investigate topical themes.
>
> Our parish will be Britain, but our diocese will be Europe. These programmes must reflect, indeed foster, the fundamental changes which must sweep over Britain when we become part of Europe economically and, later, politically . . .
>
> Think of any subject which we might have tackled in *Searchlight* and it can be done in this broader context.[55]

Interestingly, the succession from *Searchlight* is here made explicit, and Hewat seems to follow that programme's controversial approach in proposing a pro-active, campaigning role for 'Granada Reports'.

The accompanying budget for the programme reveals another very significant innovation not mentioned in the main text – shooting on 16mm synch sound film. Hitherto, location footage for current affairs programmes had almost always been shot on 35mm stock with full crews – a cumbersome and costly process. 16mm had already been adopted in television news, but it appears to have been Hewat at the December 1961 current affairs meeting who persuaded Granada that it could be used for current affairs and that costs could thus be halved with little diminution of quality. Cryptically, the surviving minutes merely state: '16mm to be considered (faster to shoot, slower to edit)'.[56]

16mm was a key aspect in Hewat's broader vision to transform the practices of current affairs television. Essentially, this rested on speed and mobility of equipment, and clarity and simplicity in presentation. Giving a paper in early 1964, he criticised established techniques of television journalism in the studio and on location as slow and old-fashioned, and demonstrated how lighter, more mobile 16mm equipment could enable a unit to travel in a single car, greatly increasing its flexibility and speed of response.[57] From his *Express* training, he took the axiom 'Be brief' and attempted to apply it to his presentation of current affairs, in contrast to the 'waffle and non-conclusion' that he believed to be the guiding principles of *Panorama* and *This Week*: 'You've probably only got one real contribution to make in any field you go into', he wrote later. 'I felt that the contribution worth making to television journalism was to cut out the chicken shit.'[58]

Hewat also attempted to challenge the rigid separation of roles that marked television journalism. He insisted that journalists coming into television learned the techniques of film-making, even if they themselves did not operate the camera. Experience in journalism alone was not considered sufficient to make proper use of the medium.[59] His initial *World in Action* team also contained film-makers with little direct journalistic experience who were encouraged to develop a journalistic eye for film-making. Furthermore, he sought to use multi-skilling to reduce the size of travelling crews. In his single car unit he envisaged a producer/writer, a cameraman/director, a sound-man and a researcher, one of whom would drive. A separate director, he believed, would simply be: 'a time-consuming go-between; I think there should be a two-way development of directors who learn to handle the camera and cameramen who learn to direct shots.'[60] For *World in Action*, he also dispensed with the travelling production assistant except on rare occasions.

Indirectly, Hewat's adoption of 16mm filming was crucial to these endeavours too. Shooting on 35mm film, programmes such as *Panorama* and *This Week* had been subject to union agreements drawn up for feature film production and specifying a crew of twelve. But the technicians' union (ACTT) operated a different agreement for 16mm news-gathering, giving Granada grounds to negotiate for smaller crews. Agreement was reached in November 1962, effectively allowing for a crew of between ten and twelve to function as two independent units when filming for *World in Action*. For most shoots, Hewat's vision of a single car unit remained unfulfilled, but lighter crewing gave *World in Action* an advantage over its competitors in cost, flexibility and deployment of personnel. It offered other advantages too, including the promise of a new relationship between crew and subject. As Granada's negotiator put it, a crew of twelve would have been 'a positive disadvantage, since it was unwieldy and slow, and had an inhibiting effect on interviews with people unaccustomed to film appearances.'[61] Hewat believed that 16mm equipment could mean that 'it was almost never necessary to arrange events for the camera – the camera should be able to arrange itself round the event'.[62] Furthermore, 16mm was inexpensive enough for *World in Action* to be the first regular current affairs series made entirely on film.

World in Action 1963–65

In the latter months of 1962, Hewat assembled a team for *World in Action* (the title was re-adopted in October) at Granada's London offices in Golden Square and set about detailed pre-planning. The first Monday of 1963 was settled on as a launch date. Two pilot programmes were shown to Granada Television ancillary staff shortly before Christmas and their responses discussed with Forman and with Sidney and Cecil Bernstein. As a result, captions were re-shot and the pace quickened.[63] Hewat's initial team consisted of six producer/directors, including Hewat himself, Mike Wooller, Bill Grundy and Alex Valentine (recruited by Hewat for a 1962 Granada series). Together with four researchers, this group devised, planned and produced each programme. Wilfrid Thomas and Derek Cooper were brought in to speak the series' distinctive voiceover commentaries. Crews and equipment were hired from Samuelson Bros on a contract basis with David Samuelson himself as Chief Cameraman. Since each programme idea that was pursued was given a production number, the extent of the team's pre-planning can be deduced from the fact that the first programme transmitted – 'Atomic arms race', an assessment of the nuclear arms race and Britain's part in it in the aftermath of the Cuban missile crisis – was given number 22. Thirty numbered ideas had been abandoned by the end of the first season in June 1963.

Styles and techniques

Despite its innovative use of visual devices and teaser questions, this first edition of *World in Action* is a digest of existing deeds and opinions, offering no new information nor even interviews with experts.[64] It is mostly compiled from stock footage and visuals (newspaper articles pictured, for example) which merely illustrate the voiceover text and there is no sign of the hand-held camera-work that came to be characteristic of the series' look. The decision to close with the reading of a James Thurber story (at the suggestion of Sidney Bernstein) is an experiment not repeated in the series. However, the use of two authoritative male voices speaking a script packed with information already suggested the pace and urgency that became associated with *World in Action*'s presentation of public affairs. *World in Action*'s wordiness set it apart, as Brian Winston, a researcher in the early years of the programme, recalls:

> The scripts . . . went from eleven or twelve pages – foolscap pages, standard television format – which everybody thought were going like a train; they were finishing up as sort of sixteen, eighteen page scripts.[65]

Hewat was also insistent about World in Action's mode of address to its viewers:

> There was a sense of 'you'd better make this absolutely clear what this is about' and people have the right to have their attention tickled. But there was never any sense that there was any subject that was too complicated, there was never any sense that you talked down, never any of that.[66]

To a modern-day viewer, the pace and density of the information being given in these early programmes is so striking that it can seem hard to absorb all of it.

Quickly, other hallmarks of the series became apparent too. Interviews were common but, in contrast to the 1960s conventions of television presentation, they were generally filmed as direct statements to the viewer and with no hint of the presence of an interviewer. Winston points to the novelty of this technique and also that it was 'amazingly powerful', even though it often occurred simply because there was no interviewer to be addressed. Like the decision not to use reporters, it gave the impression that viewers were brought closer to the subject, rather than having their access to actuality mediated through the presence and personality of television professionals.

As a direct consequence of shooting on 16mm, of Hewat's journalistic approach and of enormous pressures of time, *World in Action* also developed a particular 'look' that distinguished it from its competitors. 'Gritty-looking' was a common description, but '*World in Action* was actually appallingly badly made', explains Winston. As we have seen, Hewat's prime concern was with the programme's scripts: 'It was idea-led, and you then had to find the pictures to illustrate it. It was always the idea which came first', recalls its first film editor, Peter Heinze.[67] There seems to have been little interest in aesthetics besides what Winston describes as 'a positive anti-aesthetic':

> There was a real sense of not wanting the thing to look well, whereas I suspect that the crews elsewhere were actually trying to establish their *bona fides* as news documentary-slash-documentary film-makers. Tim was almost determined.[68]

In fact, normal 'filmic' qualities seem to have been condemned. Winston recalls a *World in Action* producer-cameraman returning from Africa to be mocked for shooting what Hewat described as: 'back-lit begging bowls! Bet you wasted hours waiting for the light, didn't ya?'

But the production process itself was the principal cause of *World in Action*'s 'fast and dirty' look. Each programme normally involved a period of careful research and its shape would be plotted out prior to shooting, but Hewat insisted that scripting and editing should wait until the last possible moment, ostensibly for maximum topicality. In this way, he worked to tight deadlines that mirrored the routines of press production. For most programmes, Hewat worked throughout the night before transmission, writing each word of the script himself. As a page was completed, the editor would cut the film to it:

> I can only see him sitting there scribbling and as he finished each page he'd throw it to me ... And then I would go to my cutting-room door and I'd finish the last one and I'd say 'where's the next page, Tim?' ... I mean, he knew that he couldn't have me standing there doing nothing. So he would say, 'when you're free, tell me.' And I'd say, 'look, I need more paper', you know.[69]

Peter Heinze was recruited by Hewat as senior film editor from ITN where speed was essential. Hewat's last-minute scripting gave him no alternative but to apply the same approach for *World in Action*. Winston recalls Heinze cutting to a script simply by measuring out film by the yard. In the process, there was little time to seek out the best quality takes. For Stephen Peet, an early *World in Action* producer with extensive experience in documentary film-making, 'it was heartbreaking watching him at work ... I said, "Look, I shot a much better shot of a plane landing than that". "Haven't got time, haven't got time". You know, it was like that'.[70] Hewat would apply the same rough and ready approach to adding a music track. Winston recalls him running a Beethoven symphony and 'simply punching it up when the sound went a bit dead'.

A consequence of this self-imposed rush-to-deadline was that films were often not properly finished. There was rarely time to produce a clean transmission copy. Prints were made on grey-based stock so as to 'wash out' the dirt. Often the cutting copy itself was transmitted, complete with joins. For transmission, the film had to be taken across London to ATV's telecine machine at Foley Street. It was not uncommon for it to arrive minutes before it was due on air. So, despite Hewat's pronouncements about the importance of film-making alongside journalism, the source for the series' 'anti-aesthetic' lay in a much greater respect for journalistic values than for film. As Winston puts it: 'Of course it was a very 'gritty-looking' series. We'd been stomping over the show-print with hobnailed boots really.'

In approach and style, *World in Action* had much in common with *Searchlight*. Its use of rhetorical visual and verbal devices aimed at grabbing and holding the audience's attention continued an approach begun in that programme, as did its employment of 'stunts' – visual metaphors – including illustrating British troop deployments by having 10,000 toy soldiers laid out on a world-map painted on a studio floor (in 'The thin red line') or, most famously, showing coffins carried out of houses in a Salford street to illustrate deaths from bronchitis (in 'Bronchitis'). In some cases, *World in Action* presented near-remakes of *Searchlight* enquiries, the most obvious being a programme in which the reliability and integrity of repairers of household goods is tested by having them repair items with known faults (an investigative technique still being used by the series in 1997).[71] It had a similar populist tone too, determinedly accessible in its manner (by intention, the television equivalent of the press doctrine 'on every page a surprise'[72]) and in its choice of subjects, although carefully researched. For Heads, its approach was 'as informed as the main story in *The Economist* yet as briskly and interestingly written as the cover story of *Time*'.[73]

Also similar to *Searchlight* was *World in Action*'s willingness to 'editorialise', as the ITA described it. Of course, Hewat was well aware of the obligations imposed on programme-makers by the Television Act. But the ITA's interpretation of 'balance' suited neither his journalistic instincts nor his vision for a livelier current affairs television. From his July 1962 description of the series as 'critical reportage' and his subsequent comments, it is clear that Hewat retained his convictions about how current affairs ought to be regardless of the regulator. For him, *World in Action* was: 'declamatory and aggressive, inquiring and insubordinate, trying to bludgeon the audience into thinking for themselves'.[74] And he was proud that it was: 'the first Current Affairs series to get rid of those dreary anchor men, to state a case which made no more than a genuflection towards balance, to sock the story to 'em, baby, as hard and as true as we could'.[75] Almost every programme drew complaints from parties who felt they had been wronged by it, although this is not an uncommon occurrence for current affairs series. Many complainants wrote first to the ITA, with which, not surprisingly, Granada and *World in Action* had numerous conflicts, including two early programmes effectively banned outright. Hewat characteristically accused the ITA of 'nit-picking', but after a programme on Southern Africa ('The guns') had drawn complaints of one-sidedness from sources including the Foreign Office and the governments of Portugal and South Africa, the ITA took the unprecedented step of requiring each *World in Action* script to be vetted prior to broadcast. No other television series provoked more discussion between the Authority and a programme contractor.[76] In this respect, the later version of *World in Action* that began in 1967 was no less controversial.

Team and production routine

At the centre of *World in Action*'s production routine was the team meeting. On the day after transmission, as many of the team as were available – technicians as well as producers and researchers – would gather to review the previous night's programme, discuss progress on existing programme ideas and put forward fresh ones. Accounts suggest that the tone of these meetings was inclusive and consensual and that discussions were lively and wide-ranging. Although Hewat was a strong leader, even junior members of the team like Brian Winston felt that the apparent democracy of team meetings gave them considerable influence over the series' direction. Certainly ideas were accepted whatever their source. Hewat maintains that: 'the projectionist must have come up with a larger number of starting notions for shows than anyone else'.[77]

In addition, the team were separated physically from the remainder of the Golden Square building, but worked at close quarters in an open plan office, often drinking together at night. 'Every conversation and every phone call could be heard by everyone', Hewat later recalled. 'It was a newspaper office technique of working.'[78] These arrangements, of course, helped to foster a strong team ethic, a sense of shared purpose and massive self-confidence – Forman describes the team as 'a private army within Granada'.[79] The willingness of Hewat and Granada's management to stand by the team whatever they did also contributed to this group identity. Winston speaks of a sense of being 'protected':

> I really felt, very strongly, that if I fouled up, Tim would put up a haze of blue language and drive all but the very strongest on earth away defending our editorial rights, and then put the phone down and give you the most almighty bollocking. But there was no question of Tim using your failings to, as it were, defend himself. And that level of loyalty and that sense of absolute integrity, even for some fairly outrageous stunt, was why I loved them.

For Winston at least, no other series that he worked on came close to matching *World in Action*'s team ethic. While acknowledging that it may have been intangible to viewers, Barrie Heads claimed that the 'internal, self-generated excitement about *World in Action*' was essential to the aura of success that it generated.[80]

This initial incarnation of *World in Action* ran until August 1965 and comprised 100 programmes. Two of these were bought in and re-edited, but the remainder were made by the team, including one (*Yeah! Yeah! Yeah! New York Meets The Beatles*, 1964) shown under its own title and made in colour. Several others were made but not transmitted.

The series was a rapid success, quickly attracting ratings among the top twenty, higher than *This Week* and double those for *Panorama*.[81] Press comment was also almost universally favourable, and sometimes lavish: 'a true innovation in television journalism', 'the most outstanding new programme on television this year'.[82] Despite the acclaim, many early programmes were technically poor and lacked the directness of thematic focus that the series was later to acquire. As David Boulton recalled:

> Soft profiles of Stanley Matthews and Jean Shrimpton, features on ballroom dancing and Paris fashions, essays enigmatically entitled 'Beef', 'Roads' or 'Sundays' now seem all the emptier for the drum-backed urgency with which they were presented.[83]

World in Action was also too expensive. Examining the causes, Granada's finance officer pointed to the number of programmes aborted and to Hewat's 'last-minute' working methods ('trying to complete a film quickly means overtime, taxis and possibly not enough time for polished editing or writing'). In sharp contrast to the public hyperbole of Hewat, his support for the series' continuation seems lukewarm: 'Personally [I] think this programme will gradually improve with experience and is still worthwhile'.[84] Experience did ensure that fewer programmes were aborted but Hewat's working methods remained unchanged, although *World in Action* moved to Tuesday in October 1963, partly to reduce weekend overtime.

Programme subjects

Duncan Crow proposes a typology of *World in Action* programmes involving *profiles* of people in the public eye, lengthy *inquiries* revealing the 'changing characteristics of our social and economic life', and *exposés* uncovering 'the "springs of motion" behind the news' at home and abroad.[85] Certainly occasional profiles of people in the news were shown, including Charles De Gaulle, Stanley Matthews, Lord Denning and Jim Clark, but there were fewer than a dozen of these programmes. Not all were gentle either – the team went ahead with 'Lord Denning' 'in the public interest' despite his refusal to co-operate and attempts to have the programme stopped.[86] But the distinction between 'inquiries' and 'exposés' is hard to determine, especially in an era before investigative journalism was commonplace on television. Neither Winston nor Heinze recall this typology being employed in selecting programme ideas at team meetings. Winston is clear that enquiry and revelation were the main motivations for the team.

A substantial number of programmes examined subjects, domestic or international, with on-going news significance – sites of conflict such

as the Congo, Southern Africa, Vietnam or Cyprus, political developments in Britain and abroad or specific incidents including pirate radio
stations, a shipping disaster and various industrial disputes. There were
general programmes on a wide range of social issues – slum housing,
for example, race relations, venereal disease (updating Granada's earlier
documentary on the subject) or gentler targets such as job of the nanny.
Similarly, a wide range of institutions were scrutinised, ranging from
the Church of England and the 'Keep Britain Tidy' campaign to
Voluntary Service Overseas and the newly-launched *Sun* newspaper.

Of more significance for the development of current affairs journalism,
however, are those programmes with a stronger investigative element.
A programme comparing supermarket prices with those in high street
shops ('Supermarkets') has been described as *World in Action*'s first
'investigation',[87] but a number of more revelatory investigative programmes were produced in the course of the series. Among topics explored
in this way were the background to Soviet diplomat Sergei Ivanov's
involvement in the Profumo affair, cross-border smuggling (in which a
crew accompanied a smuggling expedition between Andorra and Spain),
the Moral Rearmament movement, the causes of the sinking of the
cruise liner *Lakonia*, the bankruptcy of self-made industrialist John Bloom
and exploitation in the record industry. Programmes such as these rarely
involved headline-making revelations of the sort associated with later
periods of *World in Action*, but most uncovered information that had
not been reported widely if at all and involved substantial research.

Subjects were often selected for their topicality. In many cases, the
appearance of topicality was the product of careful pre-planning with
programmes made in advance to coincide with predictable events such
as the release of government reports. But the team also prided itself
on its ability to respond rapidly to breaking stories. On various occasions,
stories emerged that were deemed to warrant the pre-empting of existing
plans and a new programme was hastily assembled. An outbreak of
typhoid in Zermatt and protests against the Queen of Greece during
a visit to London provide the earliest such examples. A crew was
dispatched immediately to Switzerland to cover the former ('Typhoid
– Zermatt'); for the latter ('Greek royal family'), one crew left for Greece
while another followed the Queen in London to catch the final day of
her visit. In both cases the programmes were transmitted six days later.[88]
The assassination of President Kennedy provided another cause for
programmes to be assembled hurriedly. A crew, led by Hewat, left for
Dallas immediately after the shooting and returned with two programmes
– one on the city and its reaction to the shooting; the other a profile
of President Johnson assembled from footage of his speeches – to be

transmitted in consecutive weeks. 'Dallas', the first of these, shown eleven days after the shooting, won the 1964 Television Guild Award for Best Factual Programme.[89]

World in Action also established itself as a site for innovation in various ways. Hewat repeated his journalistic scoop over *25 Cranley Drive* by commissioning Granada's second drama-documentary, a reconstruction of the 1963 Great Train Robbery. Exactly like its predecessor, the programme was made months in advance and shown as a hurriedly-scheduled *World in Action Special* on the day of the trial verdict, despite the risk of action for contempt of court.[90] Peter Heinze recalls it as the simplest *World in Action* programme he worked on – no rhetorical devices to maintain the attention of viewers, 'almost entirely narrative'. '7 up' was a significant innovation in a different way – a remarkable social document suggested by the old nostrum 'Give me a child until he is seven and I will show you the man'. It brought together twenty children from varying social and geographical backgrounds and recorded their views on home, school and life in general to offer: 'a glimpse of England in the year 2000' – because 'the union leader and the business executive of the year 2000 are now seven years old'.[91] '7 up' became one of Granada's most significant documentary projects, giving rise to sequels at seven-year intervals in which the children were revisited and the patterns of their lives traced. The original programme and its successors have been sold, and garnered awards, all over the world. The format has also been sold, leading to versions tracking children in territories as diverse as America and Russia.

Programme subjects were not always chosen solely for their significance as public issues. On occasions the choice could be strategic, as with a wholly uncritical programme about Oxfam. Stephen Peet, its producer, recalls it as arising out of 'Charities', an investigation into the high proportion of donations diverted by leading charities to cover administration and hospitality costs. Oxfam, who were wrongly implicated in the resulting programme, complained. As a form of restitution, Hewat agreed to a favourable programme on the charity's work worldwide ('Oxfam'). His real motivation, though, was to obtain permission to film in South Africa, which would normally have been denied but for Oxfam's support. In this way, the crew that made 'The guns', exposing South Africa's involvement in Angola, were able to enter the country legitimately. Winston recalls a similar arrangement with HM Customs, whose work was featured in a programme entitled 'Smuggling', partly in order to enable *World in Action* crews taking equipment overseas to obtain more favourable treatment. An arrangement like this, despite its journalistic benefits, raises serious issues of

editorial independence for current affairs television and perhaps reveals
the naivety of the era. Whilst it remained common for *World in Action*
to film undercover in unwelcoming territories, there is little evidence
in later periods for the practice of making uncritical programmes to
appease institutions that might be hostile to the series.

Tim Hewat remained as *World in Action*'s Executive Producer only
until February 1964, before moving on to develop new programme
ideas. But he continued to have a supervisory role and, with its tone,
approach, working practices and team ethic already well established,
the series retained its basic principles under his successors Derek Granger,
Alex Valentine and, at the very end of its run, David Plowright and
Barrie Heads. There was some development as the series wore on,
however. With the growing prominence of youth culture, the series
made several programmes recording its rise. The impetus for this came
largely from Dick Fontaine and Mike Hodges, who emerged as the
producers most in touch with popular trends. It was Fontaine who
promoted *Yeah! Yeah! Yeah! New York Meets The Beatles* as a programme idea, and Peet recalls Hewat dismissing his earlier suggestions at
production meetings for films about the phenomenon of the Beatles at
the Cavern Club in Liverpool, and about the growth of men's boutiques
in Carnaby Street. Granger and Valentine seem to have been more
open to ideas reflecting developments in popular culture, with the
result that Fontaine and Hodges later made films about pirate radio
('Radio pirates') and Jean Shrimpton ('Models') for the series. 'The flip
side', Hodges' investigation of the record industry featuring footage
from a live performance by the Rolling Stones and interviews with pop
stars, was also shown.

Another significant development involved the style of shooting. The
initial interest at Granada in experiments in New York with very
lightweight, hand-held equipment came perhaps from Sidney Bernstein
himself, but by early 1964, *ciné-vérité*, as it was known, was causing
a 'stir'. 'As a style, this has caught professional peoples' imagination
as nothing since the sensational first impact of Eisenstein & Co.', wrote
Forman.[92] At *World in Action*, Fontaine again seems to have been the
prime mover in employing these techniques, although it is clear that
much of the team had a professional interest in developments in
documentary technique. Fontaine persuaded Hewat to hire David and
Alan Maysles, leading practitioners in the emerging American Direct
Cinema movement, to shoot the American sequences in *Yeah! Yeah!
Yeah! New York Meets The Beatles*.[93] Derek Granger, who had replaced
Hewat by the time the Beatles film was shown, was impressed with
the effects of its shooting style. He wrote:

As a documentary I think it achieved a most unusual quality – and I was sure it caught the Beatles in a way which revealed their unique, personal qualities more than any other filmed record there has been of them . . . Having to submit to this kind of very close camera scrutiny can be a gruelling business. But . . . I think that the charm and truthfulness of this record will have a real effect in promoting a wider interest in this kind of documentary film reporting.[94]

Granger decided that the involvement of film-makers like the Maysles brothers could be invigorating for the programme:

It seemed to me that *World in Action* was the place for new techniques . . . What perhaps happened during my tenure was that form became more important than content . . . I did tend to go for more soft subjects than one would have done otherwise, but mainly it was to experiment with these new techniques.[95]

As a result, D. A. Pennebaker was engaged to shoot a programme about a tin strike in a small Ontario town ('Timmins, Ontario') and the Maysles brothers were used again to cover the presidential election campaign of Barry Goldwater. Hodges, producer of 'Goldwater', was delighted at the new opportunities offered by their technique. With the Maysles filming continually and unencumbered by heavy lights, he found that: 'it was just like taking a notepad out with you because you just went . . . You know, you could film anything actually'.[96]

The effect of Granger's formal radicalism on the series was significant. It led to some of the techniques of Direct Cinema being adopted by *World in Action*'s own film-makers. The Maysles brothers had modified the standard Arriflex camera by moving the magazine to make it more suitable for hand-held use. David Samuelson also began to experiment with camera modifications, including a device by which the zoom lens could be controlled with one finger while the camera was hand-held.[97] Producers were also given greater licence to experiment with shots and the Maysles' technique was much copied. One of the most noteworthy examples was 'Models', whose New York sequences were shot by the Maysles while Fontaine shot the British sequences in a similar style. Whilst noting Hewat's disapproval of the choice of subject (it 'was thought very, very flossy, a reprehensible thing to do on *World in Action*'), Granger defends it as 'germinal', capturing the spirit of the times:

When Antonioni came to England to make *Blow Up* not long after, he asked to see 'Models'. It was that influential in its day . . . People like Dick Fontaine wanted their head, and the freedom to put together something which told a story of a different kind; something which might tell a slightly more significant story of the Sixties.[98]

Essentially, it was the character and approach of *World in Action*, rather than its thematic agenda, that set it apart from its competitors. Like them, its selection of topics was based essentially on a broadsheet news agenda, aiming either to expand understanding of stories already reported or to engage with issues of public significance that were felt to deserve coverage. It is possible, however, to discern some trends in story selection. Winston explains: 'One of the things that Tim was doing, it seems to me in retrospect, is that within the broad, broadsheet political agenda ... he was always looking for angles that would be fresh and give him some mileage'. This may explain why *World in Action* had a particular fondness for consumerist and internationalist topics. Consumerism was a little-explored programme area at the time (Winston says: 'my feeling is that the *Panorama* lads and *This Week* would not have dealt with consumerism'), but it chimed with the *World in Action* approach, being significant publicly but also part of a populist agenda that was close to the lives of the audience. Notable examples were 'Supermarkets', 'Repairs' and programmes investigating value for money in the funeral business and debunking the idea that petrol brands contained different ingredients. The series was also remarkably international, as Hewat's initial plans had suggested. No fewer than 43 programmes were wholly or partly filmed overseas. Filming covered an enormous range of countries (Heads' estimate of 'more than 30' seems conservative),[99] but the USA figured above all – in 15 programmes, with two more examining its involvement in Vietnam and one its influence on British culture. This is explicable in two ways: firstly by reference to Hewat's own pan-national world view ('he really thought the world was shrinking', notes Winston) which he was to develop further in *The World Tomorrow*, his successor to *World in Action*. Secondly, this was an era in which developments in the USA seemed to offer so much more global significance than those in Britain, given its lead in technology and popular culture, but also its involvement in Vietnam, the emergence of the civil rights movement and the political uncertainty wrought by Kennedy's assassination. It was the knack of Hewat and his team to recognise the importance of such topics early and to present them in a manner attractive to a mass audience – in David Plowright's description, as 'rock and roll current affairs'.[100]

Notes

1 See A. Briggs, *The History of Broadcasting in the United Kingdom, Vol. IV: Sound and Vision* (Oxford: Oxford University Press, 1979), pp. 78, 581–6. An earlier usage was in the title of the Army Bureau of Current

Affairs, established in 1941 to promote public education and to raise morale in wartime.

2 See R. Lindley, *Panorama: Fifty Years of Pride and Paranoia* (London: Politicos, 2002); Briggs, *Sound and Vision*, pp. 701–5.

3 See Briggs, *Sound and Vision*, pp. 993–4.

4 For a thorough account of *Special Enquiry* and its relation to documentary and radio Features, see J. Corner, 'Documentary voices', in J. Corner (ed.), *Popular Television in Britain* (London: British Film Institute, 1991), pp. 42–59.

5 Section 3(1) (b), Television Act, 1954, 2 & 3 Eliz. 2, c. 55.

6 B. Sendall, *Independent Television in Britain – Vol. 1: Origin and Foundation, 1946–62* (London/Basingstoke: Macmillan, 1982), pp. 252–5; see P. Holland, *The Angry Buzz: This Week and Current Affairs Television* (London: I. B. Tauris, 2006).

7 Granada Television, 'Memorandum submitted to the Committee on Broadcasting, 1960', in E. Buscombe (ed.), *BFI Dossier 9: Granada – The First 25 Years* (London: British Film Institute, 1981), p. 119.

8 D. Forman, *Persona Granada* (London: Andre Deutsch, 1997), pp. 76–8; *Mike Scott, quoted in N. Chanan, 'Granada Television – The Early Years', ch. 9 (unpublished ms., 1977) (bf. 1438).

9 *Fraser, Letter to V. Peers, 16 August 1960 (bf. 1090).

10 Baron Hill of Luton, *Behind the Screen: The Broadcasting Memoirs of Lord Hill of Luton* (London: Sidgwick & Jackson, 1974), p. 20.

11 B. Paulu, *British Broadcasting in Transition* (London: Macmillan, 1961), p. 77.

12 See P. Goddard, '"Improper liberties": Regulating undercover journalism on ITV, 1967–1980', *Journalism*, Vol. 7:1 (2006).

13 Forman, *Persona Granada*, p. 273.

14 See, for example, Forman, *Persona Granada*, p. 125; D. Robinson, 'The wild man of Manchester – A profile of Tim Hewat', *Contrast*, 1:2 (1961), 118.

15 *Derek Granger, quoted in Chanan, 'Granada Television – The Early Years', ch. 25.

16 *Elliot, letter to Hewat, 12 March 1958 (bf. 1581).

17 *Hewat, undated memo (March 1958) (bf. 0539).

18 *Hewat, memo to Stuart Griffiths, undated (c. May 1958) (bf. 0539); *Hewat, memo to senior executives, 29 October 1958 (bf. 0855).

19 *Searchlight*, 'Sixties child', tx. 4 January 1960.

20 *Searchlight*, 'Crawling highways', tx. 6 June 1960.

21 *Bill Grundy (*Searchlight* presenter), quoted in Chanan, 'Granada Television – The Early Years', ch. 15.

22 Forman, *Persona Granada*, p. 132.

23 *Hewat, letter to Elliott, 8 April 1958 (bf. 1581).

24 See Robinson, 'The wild man of Manchester'.

25 Tx. 11 April 1960.

26 *Hewat, draft memoir for unpublished history of Granada Television, *c.* 1976 (bf. 1437).

27 *Hewat, cable to Granada Television, 4 April 1960 (bf. 1138).

28 Forman, *Persona Granada*, p. 132. In comparison to *Searchlight*, he describes *Panorama* and *This Week* as 'ponderous' and 'aimless' respectively.

29 Robinson, 'The wild man of Manchester'.

30 Forman, *Persona Granada*, p. 133.

31 *Hewat, '*Searchlight*. What is it all about and why?', undated (*c.* July 1959) (bf. 0539).

32 Section 3(1)(f), Television Act, 1954, 2 & 3 Eliz. 2, c. 55.

33 *Hewat, quoted in Chanan, 'Granada Television – The Early Years', ch. 15.

34 Tx. 11 September 1959.

35 Quoted in Forman, *Persona Granada*, p. 215.

36 *Peers, memo to Hewat, '*Searchlight*', 5 March 1959 (bf. 1130).

37 *K. Allsop, unpublished article about *Searchlight*, April 1959 (bf. 0536). See Chapter 8 for a more detailed discussion of these issues.

38 Robinson, 'The wild man of Manchester'.

39 Forman, *Persona Granada*, p. 215.

40 *Hewat, memo to Granada executives, 'Luncheon at Scotts Restaurant, Piccadilly', 4 December 1959 (bf. 1130).

41 *Fraser, letter to Peers, 17 June 1960 (bf. 0971).

42 *Peers, letters to Fraser, 20 June, 1 July, 19 July 1960; *Fraser, letters to Peers, 24 June, 11 July, 22 July 1960 (all bf. 0971).

43 *Fraser, letters to Peers, 16 August 1960, 5 December 1960 (bf. 1090).

44 Sendall, *Independent Television in Britain – Vol. 1*, pp. 354–5.

45 *Hewat, memo to Granada executives, 'Goodbye *Searchlight*', 13 June 1960 (bf. 1138).

46 *Hewat, quoted in Chanan, 'Granada Television – The Early Years', ch. 15.

47 Quoted in Robinson, 'The wild man of Manchester'.

48 Quoted in Chanan, 'Granada Television – The Early Years', ch. 15.

49 *A. Suudi, 'Current affairs programmes – Agenda for a meeting on 13th September 1960' (bf. 1140); *D. Crow, 'History of Granada Television', ch. 26 (unpublished ms., 1969) (bf. 0978,).

50 Letter to S. Bernstein, quoted in Forman, *Persona Granada*, pp. 214–15.

51 Sendall, *Independent Television in Britain – Vol. 1*, p. 354; *A. Leighton Davis, memo to S. Bernstein, 5 February 1962 (bf. 1436); *S. Bernstein, quoted in Chanan, 'Granada Television – The Early Years', ch. 15.

52 *S. Bernstein, quoted in Chanan, 'Granada Television – The Early Years', ch. 15.

53 *Crow, 'History of Granada Television', ch. 26.

54 *Appendix to Minutes of Current Affairs Meeting, 11 January 1962, quoted in Crow, 'History of Granada Television', ch. 26.

55 *Hewat, 'An outline of Granada Reports', 24 July 1962 (bf. 1154).
56 *Minutes of Current Affairs Meeting, 6 December 1961 (bf. 1148).
57 *Hewat, '1965 and all that', paper presented at Granada Television 'Avanti' conference, 20 January 1964 (bf. 1010).
58 *Hewat, quoted in Chanan, 'Granada Television – The Early Years', ch. 25.
59 *Hewat, quoted in Chanan, 'Granada Television – The Early Years', ch. 25.
60 *Hewat, '1965 and all that'.
61 *B. Floud, letter to G. Elvin (ACTT) 28 September 1962 (bf. 1228).
62 *Crow, 'History of Granada Television', ch. 30.
63 *Hewat memo to S. Forman and C. Bernstein, 28 December 1962 (bf. 1154).
64 'Atomic arms race' and its visual style are discussed in Chapter 7.
65 Brian Winston, interview with the authors. Further comments in this chapter attributed to Winston are drawn from the same interview.
66 Brian Winston.
67 Peter Heinze, interview with the authors. Further comments in this chapter attributed to Heinze are drawn from the same interview.
68 Brian Winston.
69 Peter Heinze.
70 Stephen Peet, interview with the authors. Further comments in this chapter attributed to Peet are drawn from the same interview.
71 *Searchlight*, 'The repairs muddle', tx. 16 March 1959; *World in Action*, 'Repairs'; *World in Action*, 'House of horrors'.
72 T. Hewat, 'Introduction', in D. Crow, *World in Action* (London: Mayflower, 1965), p. 9.
73 *B. Heads, untitled account of Granada current affairs, 16 September 1966 (bf. 1015).
74 *Hewat, quoted in Chanan, 'Granada Television – The Early Years', ch. 25.
75 *Hewat, draft memoir for unpublished history of Granada Television, c. 1976 (bf. 1437).
76 B. Sendall, *Independent Television in Britain – Vol. 2: Expansion and Change, 1958–68* (London/Basingstoke: Macmillan, 1983), p. 301. For a detailed discussion of these events and of regulatory intervention over *World in Action*, see Chapter 8.
77 *Quoted in Chanan, 'Granada Television – The Early Years', ch. 25.
78 *Quoted in Chanan, 'Granada Television – The Early Years', ch. 25.
79 Forman, *Persona Granada*, p. 134.
80 *Quoted in Chanan, 'Granada Television – The Early Years', ch. 25.
81 *Heads, untitled account of Granada current affairs, 16 September 1966 (bf. 1015); Forman, *Persona Granada*, p. 134.
82 *Sunday Telegraph*, 17 February 1963; *Brighton Evening Argus*, 15 January 1963.

83 D. Boulton, *World in Action: The First Twenty-One Years* (booklet to accompany retrospective programme) (Granada Television, 1984), p. 4.

84 *Litchfield, memo to S. Bernstein, 18 April 1963 (bf. 1244).

85 D. Crow, *World in Action '63* (London: Consul, 1963), p. 10.

86 *Peers, letter to B. Sendall (ITA), 22 August 1963 (bf. 1228).

87 Boulton, *World in Action: The First Twenty-One Years*, p. 4.

88 Crow, *World in Action '63*, pp. 23–4, 135.

89 Crow, *World in Action*, p. 35.

90 'The great train robbery' was in production as early as August 1963 (*Hewat memo to S. Bernstein, Forman, 28 August 1963 (bf. 1244)).

91 *World in Action*, '7 up'.

92 *Granger, quoted in Chanan, 'Granada Television – The Early Years', ch. 25; Forman, paper presented at Granada Television 'Avanti' conference, 20 January 1964 (bf. 1010).

93 Winston.

94 *Granger, letter to B. Epstein, 24 February 1964 (bf. 0039).

95 *Granger, quoted in Chanan, 'Granada Television – The Early Years', ch. 25.

96 Mike Hodges, interview with Rodney Geisler, 3 March 1998, for BECTU History Project.

97 *Hewat, quoted in Chanan, 'Granada Television – The Early Years', ch. 25.

98 *Quoted in Chanan, 'Granada Television – The Early Years', ch. 25.

99 *Untitled account of Granada current affairs, 16 September 1966 (bf. 1015).

100 Speaking in the *World in Action: 30 Years* retrospective programme.

Interlude: *The World Tomorrow*

World in Action's one-hundredth edition, on 3 August 1965, was its last. Its creator, Tim Hewat, already had plans in place for an even more hard-hitting, international replacement. *World in Action*'s half-hour Tuesday slot was allocated by the network for Granada to provide a 'balance' programme – a programme of 'serious' content to balance the entertainment programming offered for much of the rest of the evening – so the scheduling of a successor presented no difficulty for the company.

The World Tonight, was a grandiose, meticulously-planned idea typical of Hewat and reflecting his convictions about the role of television current affairs. Not only did it take over *World in Action*'s slot but also its offices in London and Manchester, its crewing arrangements (the contract with Samuelsons continued) and many of its staff. Its premise was the establishment of 'bureaux' around the world, each staffed by Granada producers who could familiarise themselves with the territory, initiate stories based on knowledge of the region and respond swiftly to give a regional angle to international stories. The existing British/American practice of despatching crews from home 'leads to well-intentioned but ill-informed reporting', wrote Hewat when first proposing the idea to Denis Forman in January 1965.[1] His initial idea went further: Hewat hoped to exploit new opportunities offered by Eurovision and satellite links to co-ordinate and transmit live a current affairs programme linking contributions from around the world. Subjects were to be 'similar to those presently covered by *World in Action*'.[2] By April, Hewat was establishing and staffing his bureaux and had despatched the first in a series of 'All Bureaux' reports through which the series was managed and its production process explained. His plans were costlier than *World in Action*. Bureaux in London, New York, Tokyo, Rome and Paris were each to be established and staffed by a Granada reporter-producer using local crew. Reporter-producers with a roving brief were also appointed, although the need for economies caused early plans for Hamburg and Prague bureaux to be dropped.[3] In July, Hewat circulated a comprehensive 14-page guide, offering 'pointers' from his experience of current affairs production and to the particular requirements of 'round-the-world production'. It contains some classic examples of the Hewat credo, emphasising truthfulness based on research, clarity of explanation through simple language, and exhortations such as 'keep your viewers' attention glued to the screen by constant excitement'. Hewat even prescribed the series' shooting style – 'one fascinating shot' for each sequence, 'impact is always more important than prettyness or sharpness or composition' and, following his *World in Action* approach, no two-handed interviews but speakers making statements to camera.[4]

After a dry run at the end of July, Hewat was glowing with enthusiasm: 'This programme is going to work. Its potential is enormous. We are onto something new and good'.[5] But he also identified improvements: more pace, the need for iconic shots to establish location ('the Oslo segment needed a fjord badly') and a reversion to *World in Action*'s voice-over narration rather than the in-vision studio anchor that had been envisaged. On 7 September 1965, *The World Tonight*'s run began, but its opening report on Britain's money crisis – a surprisingly domestic topic in the light of Hewat's much-vaunted international approach – received poor notices and Hewat admitted to choosing an unpopular subject and to technical errors.[6] Subsequent subjects were more international, including the population explosion, the Commonwealth, exports, the rise of computers and the 1966 Olympics, and the following month Hewat could report that the series was getting a kinder press and a Top 20 rating.[7] Each edition comprised a series of mini-documentaries from the various bureaux, rigidly segmented by intertitles containing the location name and a clock-face showing the local time. But reviewers remained equivocal. In December, *The Times* described the vivid style of 'the supercharged successor to *World in Action*' in terms reminiscent of its predecessor:

> For every fresh date-line round the globe, a clock-face flashes up proclaiming the split-second timing and accuracy of the programme. Film reports are liberally garnished with murder weapons, wreckage and corpses steeped in gore. The commentators are hard-faced men, never wasting a word; at every minute, as they stand rapping out the facts against a trouble-torn background, you expect a bullet to carry them off . . . Television is a market place and those who shout loudest have the best chance of making themselves heard; particularly, as in this case, when they have a firm understanding of just how much information can be put across in such conditions. Facts received from television rarely stick in

the memory for long: the technique of the Granada production team is to select a handful of essential facts and drive them in with hammer blows.[8]

But, complained the same article: 'It scrambled evidence and artifice together . . . [O]ne might describe it as documentary melodrama.'

In one important respect, the series failed to conform to Hewat's intentions. The breathless presentation and indicators of immediacy tended to conceal reports that were at best general overviews rather than up-to-the-minute accounts of the state of world affairs. By November, Hewat was acknowledging this and attempting to make a virtue of it. He told bureaux: 'as you all know our programme is not a topical one in any news of the day sense'. Forward-looking programmes such as 'The computer age'[9] had shown 'where our strength really lies', he believed, so the emphasis on topicality was to be dropped, together with the clocks, and the title changed to *The World Tomorrow*. 'I made a mistake in the choice of the title *The World Tonight*', he wrote. 'It tied us too much and is not strictly honest. *The World Tomorrow* while being more exciting will also fit us a lot better.'[10] By January 1966, then, Granada's principal current affairs programme was occupying distinctly different territory from *World in Action* or indeed *This Week*. Its international dimension was put to the service of assessing future trends in technology, prosperity and international development, each programme now closing with a short segment making predictions. At the end of April, with the pressure of establishing a successful series easing, Hewat stepped aside, leaving Granada shortly afterwards.

The new Editor of *The World Tomorrow* was David Plowright. In early 1966, he set about reconsidering the role and format of the series, proposing that it should avoid what he saw as the predictability of existing current affairs programming and exploit the new public interest in scientific developments and predictions to concentrate largely on 'subjects which concern the future of mankind, politically, technologically, sociologically and medically'. Four-fifths of its output would be orientated in this way but, for the remainder, 'it would be unwise of us to plan a series which did not allow Granada to use its current affairs half hour to report or comment on a major national or international news story'. Its style would now be 'non-hysterical, simple, vigorous and as well-written as a James Cameron piece', though plans for studio anchors to provide flexibility and 'punctuation' were not acted upon.[11] The overseas bureaux were no longer central to conceptions of the series and Plowright questioned their continuing value. But his main interest was in its choice of subject matter and how it was to be approached.

In accordance with Plowright's intentions, *The World Tomorrow* became a series whose principal focus was scientific and future-orientated. By March 1967, reports had covered test-tube babies, credit cards, automation, techniques for mind control, for controlling the weather and for reversing the aging process, amongst others. But more mainstream social and political topics, such as student and hippie activism, LSD, and political developments in Indonesia, Singapore and America, were also covered. There was also a detectable change in style as the series cast off Hewat's legacy – 'from the pile-driving of the tabloid form' to a more 'thoughtful' approach involving 'well made and gently interesting programmes'.[12] The rigid segmentation of the programme into reports from each bureaux was abandoned in favour of a better flowing, more comprehensible whole, though some intertitles were initially retained for clarity. The bureaux were retained until the series' 1966 summer break although contributions from Tokyo, and from Rome in particular, had by now dwindled almost to nothing.[13] When it resumed, *The World Tomorrow* reverted to more familiar production methods with each programme now a single report in the hands of one producer. As bureau producers returned home, there were more wholly British-based reports but the American bureau (now an 'office') was retained, from whence John MacDonald continued to contribute about one in every six of the programmes.

The status of *The World Tonight* and *Tomorrow* as part of the history of *World in Action* is ambiguous. Its programmes are sometimes included in Granada's internal logs of *World in Action* editions and those who worked on both series rarely seem to differentiate between them in their recollections.[14] Granada's *World in Action* anniversary programmes each imply a continuous run of programming from 1963 and disregard entirely the gap between 1965 and 1967.[15] In the development of current affairs coverage at Granada, this period might be viewed as a significant transitional phase. It began with huge optimism and urgency, intended to trump the achievements of its predecessor and to construct an even more ambitious brief for current affairs. In this, it reflected its founder's ambitions and world view, perhaps at the expense of a truly significant journalistic contribution. Essentially, Hewat's *The World Tonight* was technology-led: 'They were obsessed with technological things', recalls Brian Winston, a producer on the programme. 'Speed, speeding it up, was what it was about, you know. Tim was a man of this age.'[16] Under Plowright, the emphasis changed: the obsession with speed and modernity were dropped in favour of story-telling and coherence. Clarity and authority were striven for through attention to shape, narrative and audience interest rather than through a concern for 'impact' and bullet-point simplification to 'hammer home' the message. In effect, Plowright's methods were less ambitious but more mature than Hewat's, reflecting the growing maturity of television as a journalistic medium. In this they prefigured the approach taken by the 'new' *World in Action* that was to replace *The World Tomorrow* when its run ended in March 1967. The series was transitional in another way too. Gradually, many of the remnants of Hewat's journalistic team moved on and a new band of producers, who were to produce many of the pioneering programmes in the early years of the new series, was assembled under Plowright. Among these were Brian Moser, later to found *Disappearing World* (Granada, 1970–93), Leslie Woodhead, who would establish Granada's drama-documentary strand, and Mike Ryan, producer of over 50 *World in Action* programmes between 1967 and 1980.

Notes

1 *Hewat, memo to Forman, '*The World Tonight*', 11 January 1965 (bf. 0785).
2 *Forman, letter to Bernard Sendall (ITA), 11 March 1965 (bf. 1086).
3 *Hewat, to All Bureaux, 'Report No. 4', 9 July 1965 (bf. 0785).
4 *Hewat, '*The World Tonight*' (guide for producers), 1 July 1965 (bf. 0785).
5 *Hewat, memo to bureaux, '*The World Tonight*', 6 August 1965 (bf. 0785).
6 *The World Tonight*: 'Bankruptcy', tx. 7 September 1965; *Hewat, to All Bureaux, 'Report No. 7', 13 September 1965 (bf. 0785).
7 *Hewat, to All Bureaux, 'Report No. 8', 22 October 1965 (bf. 0785).
8 *The Times*, 4 December 1965, p.12.
9 Tx. 26 October 1965, p. 12.
10 *Hewat, to All Bureaux, 'Report No. 9', 24 November 1965 (bf. 0780).
11 *Plowright, memos (to Forman but no addressee given): 'Project X – Some notes on a proposed TV programme', 17 February 1966; '*The World Tomorrow* – 1966 series' (no date) (both bf. 0774).
12 *Forman, memo to *World Tomorrow* team, '*World Tomorrow*', 16 November 1966 (bf. 1522).
13 **World Tomorrow* cost summary, marked 'final for series', 12 June 1966 (bf. 0785).
14 Peter Heinze and Brian Winston, both producers on *The World Tonight* and *The World Tomorrow*, were interviewed by the authors.
15 *World in Action – The first 21 years* and *World in Action: 30 years*.
16 Brian Winston, interview with the authors.

3

1967–75: the classic period

'Title TBA'

On his appointment to take over *The World Tomorrow* in early 1966, David Plowright immediately produced a paper in which he assessed what he saw as 'the ten-year evolution' of television current affairs. He identified three stages:

a) The magazine – based on the assumption that viewers were incapable of accepting more than a few minutes of a serious subject. The programme's identity was a presentable well-mannered link man.

b) The television reporter – initially a handsome front man for a script writer and later a story teller in his own right. Ugliness was less of a disadvantage.

c) The replacement of discussion with assertion in one subject half-hour shows which excluded the to-camera man. *World in Action* set the pattern; *This Week* followed it.[1]

Plowright concluded that 'there are too many current affairs programmes on the air broadcasting predictable stories in much the same way' and that current affairs 'often reflects rather than leads'. His paper is interesting for several reasons: in situating current affairs historically, it draws attention to its adherence to a settled formula; by extension, it demonstrates the scope and desirability for current affairs to take a further evolutionary step; furthermore, it illustrates the seriousness with which Plowright approached his role as editor of Granada's principal current affairs programme. He was not simply replacing its founding editor but questioning the very basis upon which it conducted current affairs journalism. Plowright made substantial changes to *The World Tomorrow*, but a year later he was embarking on a further reassessment exercise to determine its future. This second round of consultations led to the re-establishment of the *World in Action* title in Summer 1967 and, arguably, to a fourth stage in the development of the form, in which investigative journalism figured prominently and 'behind the headlines' reports on topical events became a lesser function.

The catalyst for reassessing Granada's current affairs contribution was an internal consultation exercise, the 'Future Outlook Group', intended to re-evaluate the company's output. Sessions on drama, comedy, children's and educational programming were held between February and May 1967 but the first, involving Denis Forman and all of the company's factual producers, was devoted to current affairs. To prepare for it, Plowright formulated some clear proposals for a new series, within which the philosophy and organisation of the new *World in Action* is already recognisable. The meeting seems to have accepted the need for a new series without debate and the discussion concerned how Plowright's proposals could be put into practice. He suggested a weekly series with an umbrella title for which three dedicated teams provided programmes of reportage, inquiry and observation. Reportage would provide the largest output and involve the quickest turnaround, responding to 'the argument and controversies of the moment', but would be selective and, where possible, innovative in treatment. As Plowright's earlier paper showed, he was conscious that such programmes competed directly with *Panorama* and *This Week*. Inquiries, described as 'television insights – well researched exposés of some racket, scandal, evil deed or momentous occasion', were to have a much slower turnaround – perhaps eight to twelve shows a year with flexible transmission dates and meticulous research at whatever length was required. Observations embraced gentler, impressionistic films about personal lives and provocative social questions. Plowright had in mind programmes in the vein of *Man Alive* (BBC, 1965–82) and *This England* (Granada, 1966–91) produced by individualistic film-makers, of which Denis Mitchell was the company's most celebrated example.[2] In Plowright's terms, these films were thought of as 'implicits', in contrast to the 'explicit' coverage of the reportage and inquiry programmes.[3]

With the new series approved, Plowright began refining his plans and making firm decisions on its form and content. *The World Tomorrow*'s production and research teams were to be retained, so each producer was asked to write a paper on the shape of a future series under the heading 'What's Next'.[4] Widely divergent formats and goals, not all of them practical, were suggested, but they provide a fascinating insight into contemporary thinking about current affairs, its past mistakes and present purposes. Some common themes are apparent, most notably a universal aversion to the 'excesses' of Tim Hewat's *World in Action*: Russell Spurr condemned 'a journalistic style which bellowed so loudly it almost drowned the sound of clattering scissors, as amateur editors butchered the film'; for Mike Murphy, such programming 'grabbed its audience by the lapels and shouted at

them, and presented the most banal truisms as "little-known facts"',
though he acknowledged that audience engagement with current affairs
grew as a result; John Sheppard professed himself 'bored' with 'the
hectoring punchy headline-type' style of 'the Granada voice'. *The World
Tomorrow*, Spurr suggests, whilst 'more reflective and certainly more
artistic', was hampered by a narrow formula that restricted producers
and was not clear enough about its goals to capture audience interest.
There was also general acceptance that the 'big causes' of earlier
television documentary ('homosexuality/abortion/drugs/colour bar',
according to Brian Armstrong) had ceased to be appropriate, a point
also made by Forman in an earlier paper noting that the 'emotional
battle' over minorities was already won.[5] Among recurring suggestions
were the need for more rigorous research, for the incorporation of
ideas and people reflecting the emergence of youth culture and radicalism,
and for the 'news magazine' approach to be abandoned as a result of
worldwide improvements in television news coverage. There are various
ideas for the development of more visual forms for current affairs,
creating a greater distance from print journalism, and for more flexible
formats in which reporters or studio settings can be used where
appropriate. In several of these areas – the need for a more visual
approach, particularly for 'implicits'; sufficient flexibility to use in-vision
reporting where appropriate – Plowright had already drawn similar
conclusions, and he seems to have shared the general distaste for the
Hewat approach: 'We will be assertive', he wrote, 'but not with the
voice of moral indignation'.[6]

Decisions over the arrangements for the new series were being taken.
Initially, it was to have occupied the slot to which *The World Tomorrow*
had moved in September 1966 (Friday at 10.05pm) but this was not
felt to be ideal. By March, agreement had been reached with the network
for it to run at 8.00pm on Mondays. Another benefit of the change
was that the start date could be put back from 5 May to 3 July,
offering more preparation time.[7] The programme budget, drawn up
in April, reflects some further telling decisions. There is provision for
the establishment of two dedicated Granada film-crews, ending the
relationship with Samuelsons that had lasted since the earlier *World
in Action* was set up in late 1962. The New York office, established
in 1965 for *The World Tonight* with its own producer and crew, is
retained but with a slightly smaller budget than for the final series of
The World Tomorrow, suggesting a reduced role. The overall budget
for the series is increased by a quarter compared with *The World
Tomorrow*, reflecting the company's expectations of the series and of
Plowright.[8]

The choice of a title for the new series presented a trickier problem. Plowright had suggested 'a title that permits blanket coverage of material discussed in Reportage, Inquiry, Observation',[9] while overseas sales suggested the benefits of an international title:

> *World in Action/Tonight/Tomorrow* has that ring of global endeavour even though the subject went no further than Manchester. This kind of title intrigues the foreign buyer (and his viewers).[10]

In the event, no fewer than 280 titles were considered and for several months the series was discussed internally simply as 'Title TBA'. For convenience, its budget breakdown was headed '*World Tomorrow* (series 3)'. *World in Action* was considered and rejected several times before, by May, it was agreed upon as the title. The confusion over the title illustrates how the new series had only a titular relationship to its predecessor and had been conceived as a wholly new venture. Nonetheless, within a few years it became common for Granada and for *World in Action* staff to consider it as having a direct link with the original Hewat series.

Of all the decisions taken prior to the launch of the new *World in Action*, that with the greatest significance for the 'evolution' of current affairs followed from Plowright's original outline, in which he had advocated separate teams for Reportage, Inquiry and Observation. This was how he described his vision for the Inquiry team:

> The people working on such a team should not be faced with a weekly or fortnightly deadline. They should be allowed time to scratch about under every stone and carefully sift what they find before being committed to a transmission date ... We should find a team capable of digging out the story, examining it and presenting it as on-screen reporters.[11]

At the 'Future Outlook Group' meeting in February 1967, it was agreed to establish 'a substantial research bureau' – the first such in British television.[12] A Head for the Investigations Unit was soon found. Jeremy Wallington had an extraordinary pedigree in the developing field of newspaper investigative journalism. He had been a founder of the *Sunday Times* 'Insight' team in 1963, moving later to the *Daily Mail*'s 'Newsnight' team where he had helped to expose Dr Emil Savundra, the notorious car insurance swindler, in one of the most celebrated examples of early British investigations. By the time he joined Granada on 17 March 1967, Wallington was Assistant Editor of the *Mail*.

Pioneered by the 'Insight' team and by *Private Eye*, investigative journalism was one of the success stories of the British press in the 1960s, justified initially by the huge profile and acres of column inches occupied by the revelation of the Profumo and Rachman scandals.

Operations similar to 'Insight' had sprung up in its wake, involving a dedicated team of specialist journalists and painstaking research, and most national newspapers now had one.[13] To transplant such methods to television was innovative but also risky. To employ a whole team to conduct open-ended investigations carrying no guarantees of success represented a considerable investment on the part of Granada. Regulatory constraints were also likely to make television a more difficult medium than the press in which to conduct investigations. And television carried with it a specific requirement to be visual. Plowright acknowledged the difficulties posed in a note to Forman: 'Getting the best out of the "investigative" stories means using techniques currently out of favour (candid camera, hidden microphones, etc.). Shouldn't we start some negotiations with the ITA?'[14] Plowright's reasons for establishing the Investigations Unit were presumably journalistic, but it is harder to see what the rewards were for Granada for a move that contained no guarantee of increased audiences (and thus revenue), would be more likely to upset than draw praise from the British establishment and which might result in costly legal cases. The decision to support it says much about the prevailing attitudes of senior figures within the company, in particular Denis Forman, but also alludes to the fashionable status that dedicated investigative units in the press were enjoying. It was already planned that the venture would one day be extended into publishing.[15]

The Investigations Bureau was established as a semi-autonomous unit in London, with Wallington – given the title of Editor – supported by three researchers enlisted from newspapers, among them Gus Macdonald, a raw recruit from *The Scotsman* in his first television job. The approach was systematic. Wallington produced a detailed set of 'standing orders' for his staff, partly to standardise working methods but also to ensure that all source materials were retrievable in the event of the legal challenges that were sure to arise. Library researches and conversations were to be written up (in triplicate!), a story library was to be established, organised methodically with subject files and ideas lists, and each researcher given a set of magazines to read for useful cuttings.[16]

World in Action in 1967 and 1968

That Granada had high hopes for *World in Action*, wishing it to be seen as innovative and chiming with the culture of the times, is apparent from the hyperbole of the press releases accompanying its launch. The programme was 'bringing fresh stimulus to broadcast journalism' in a 'popular, entertaining and significant form'. Its 'team of fifty' were 'young radical and untamed – and all have a nose for news . . . They are in love with facts, and are being given the time and money to find them'. 'The programme will travel widely and will treat its audience as intelligent citizens of the world.'[17] But in the event, the series succeeded in making the hype seem justified.

Before its official opening on the first Monday of July 1967, *World in Action* had already made a mark. Responding swiftly to the prospect of an Arab–Israeli war and using existing contacts, the series mounted two 'specials' at the beginning of June containing interviews with leaders from both sides – President Nasser of Egypt; Levi Eshkol and David Ben Gurion of Israel.[18] Both programmes contributed to the news agenda in giving the leaders platforms to explain their positions to audiences in Britain and the Western world, and garnered news coverage for Granada.[19] In the first, however, *World in Action* faced a problem that was to prove perennial: *Panorama* aired a similar interview with Nasser on the same night.

In the months following its opening, *World in Action* exceeded any hopes Granada may have had for it. Its ratings – the most quantifiable measure of success – were phenomenal. The first five programmes were placed third, sixth, fourth, fifth and seventh respectively in the week's top twenty and there were no signs of decline thereafter. In the first season of 40 programmes, no fewer than nine were watched by at least half of the possible viewing audience, with an even higher proportion in Granada's own North region.[20] The first few editions also hinted at the thematic range of the series. A brave opening programme ('A girl called Sharon'), following the latter stages in the life of a seven-year-old leukaemia sufferer and her parents, was succeeded by reports on the illegal import of heroin and cocaine ('Some grains of truth'), for which recorded telephone calls provided evidential support, and on political tensions in the West Indies following Anguilla's unilateral declaration of independence from St Kitts and Nevis ('Duel in the sun'). Plowright was delighted. In a memo to the team, he praised the variety of these first three programmes and added: 'The subjects were all relevant, their treatment was surprising and what's more they were commercially viable'.[21]

The remainder of the season maintained the standard. The range of topics and approaches is striking not only for its diversity but also for the way in which – in the era of *Sergeant Pepper*, Woodstock and anti-Vietnam War protests – *World in Action* sustained a focus on significant elements underlying the radical socio-cultural changes of the time. At *Panorama*, 'the 1960s had come and gone, yet [it] continued on its stately way as if the Beatles, Profumo and *That Was The Week That Was* had never been',[22] but in 1967 and 1968 *World in Action* devoted six programmes to drugs, and four each to the American civil rights movement and to anti-Vietnam protests. Other popular cultural themes included pirate radio, the hippie movement and student militancy. The series also contained some significant journalistic moments. In only its fifth regular programme, *World in Action* marked the freeing of Mick Jagger on drugs charges by staging a meeting between him and leading establishment figures including the Bishop of Woolwich and the editor of *The Times*. In a tranquil English garden, they discussed youth culture and morality in 'a dialogue between the generations'.[23] The idea of a fresh, Granada-trained researcher named John Birt, 'Mick Jagger' was an 'outrageous and improbable programme' that gained semi-legendary status within the series' canon as the 'the outstanding example' of a category of programming that might be termed 'stunts', in which *World in Action* itself initiated a fresh angle on a subject 'that would attract the viewers' attention and keep them hooked'.[24] Such events also provided welcome publicity for the series. Equally significant journalistically was 'End of a revolution?', in which Brian Moser, making a portrait of Bolivia, stumbled into the village in which Che Guevara had been captured and became the only newsman to film him lying in state, surrounded by the soldiers who executed him.

World in Action proved to be innovative in other ways. In an echo of *A Sunday in September* (see Chapter 2), six crews were assembled at short notice to film an anti-Vietnam war demonstration in central London, its build-up and the riot outside the American embassy in Grosvenor Square that was its aftermath. The use of multiple cameras facilitated cross-cutting between various points at the heart of the action and long-shots offering an overview of events. The core of the film was the riot itself, a brutal ten-minute sequence without commentary showing events from both sides of the police lines that is now thought of as a classic piece of *vérité* film-making.[25] Like *A Sunday in September*, editing began immediately and the complete programme was transmitted the following day. The riot had become the principal news story of the day so the film was timely, seeming to stand as raw 'evidence' of the events that had taken place in Grosvenor Square. 'The demonstration' was a one-off, however. Similar observational techniques were used sporadically in later *World in Action* programmes but rarely without a voiceover to guide viewers' interpretations of events. Less successfully, the team attempted to offer a fresh approach to the political interview by placing the Liberal leader Jeremy Thorpe alone in a studio while unseen interviewers bombarded him with questions that 'were not only pointed but offensive', in the opinion of *The Times*' reviewer.[26]

More generally, these early programmes show a marked concentration on the USA. Of the 58 editions broadcast by the end of 1968, 19 were shot in America or covered American-inspired events (no fewer than 40 programmes were wholly or partly shot overseas in this period). The most obvious reason for this was the continued existence of the New York office as an autonomous production unit. Its producer, John MacDonald, contributed eight programmes and advised on others, but other *World in Action* teams also travelled freely to the USA and by early 1968 a New York presence was being questioned: 'It may be we can find a more economical way of operating by hiring crews for specific projects'.[27] Closure came at the end of that year – the final dissolution of Hewat's ambitious 'round-the-world production' idea – although the office was retained for a time as a base for visiting producers. Earlier in the decade, America had been seen as an inspirational source for stories: 'I think in the early sixties Britain was rather dull and America was exotic, and the lightweight camera gave you the chance to see the Americans in action. America was also very accessible', explains Gus Macdonald. 'We were also the rock and roll generation, so you tended to hope the future might lie in the States.'[28] So for the young teams making *The World Tomorrow* and *World in Action* between 1966 and 1968, America was seen as a site for innovation, excitement and a burgeoning youth culture. Repeatedly, it was used as an indicator of cultural, economic and social developments that Britain might soon embrace. *World in Action*'s producers and researchers were not only young – Plowright, their senior figure, was only 36 when the series was relaunched – but attracted by the popular radicalism being exhibited in the USA, which explains the concentration of programmes on the civil rights movement and opposition to war in Vietnam in 1967 and 1968. Only five America-related programmes were shown in 1969, however, but this may be less a reflection of the closure of a production base than of a decline in the perceived salience of these subjects.

Radical attitudes on the part of the team may also have informed the series' focus on civil conflicts and state oppression during this period. Conflict zones are a common source of overseas current affairs subjects, of course, but *World in Action*'s examination of conflict or oppression in Spain, Greece, Guyana and Portuguese Guinea (now Guinea-Bissau) took distinctly pro-resistance stances that contrasted with an unarguably even-handed report from Cuba. The Portuguese Guinea programme, entitled 'A group of terrorists attacked . . .', provides the most interesting case. In filming opposition guerrillas at close quarters on raids against colonial positions, it was a brave and ground-breaking film whose purpose, as expressed by Plowright after the event, was 'reportage rather than appraisal ... to show what guerrilla warfare in this particular part of the world was really like'.[29] As such it ran 45 minutes and was scheduled as the series' first 'special'. But the programme contained no pro-Portugal statement challenging the guerillas' viewpoint, leaving it open to vehement condemnation from the Portuguese Embassy and a host of establishment figures sympathetic to Portugal. Lord Buxton, Anglia Television's Chairman, described it as 'a transparent eulogy of one faction only, which because of its lack of veracity could easily rebound on the cause it was blatantly striving to promote'.[30] In view of the response, the ITA sought and obtained an undertaking that the programme would not be repeated. But incidents like this contributed to an Establishment perception of *World in Action* as politically left-wing, building upon long-standing perceptions of Granada and embodied in Julian Critchley's description of the team as 'Granada's Guevarists'.[31]

Plowright acknowledges that part of the series' agenda was 'an interest in the underdog' and that asking direct questions of those responsible for social problems was 'a little new' in the 1960s.[32] To the extent that programme-makers believed 'that a television programme might have an effect on the way people looked at the world', *World in Action* saw itself as pioneering.[33] Two early programmes illustrate this approach well. 'Ward F13', confronting viewers with the dehumanising conditions of the female geriatric ward of a mental hospital, still makes harrowing viewing 35 years later:

> Commentary: 'There are 78 beds, only inches apart. The baths are ancient and chipped. The edge of the lavatory seat is so worn it would scrape old skin ... Some have been here 40 years. Some younger ones have 30 years or more to go before they die ... Most are incontinent. You breathe urine all the time you are there.'[34]

The programme divided its time between demonstrating the squalor and pitilessness of the hospital environment and questioning its medical administrator about his own responsibility for the scenes on display and the system he was upholding. Another programme, 'Born losers', sought to address the topic of family poverty. A single family – parents and nine children living on £16 a week – were chosen to illustrate it, and the programme described their circumstances with sympathy but sometimes took a hard line in questioning them about their circumstances. A large number of viewers' letters were received and it was clear that many were shocked to find that such poverty existed and understood little about its causes (some simply described the programme as 'nauseating', 'drivel', 'hogwash'). To illustrate by particularising is a common enough approach for a programme needing to engage viewers and provide stimulating visuals, but here such a strategy also caused problems. Numerous viewers offered financial or material help to the family, but few seemed to understand them to be an instance of a wider problem.[35] And the programme damaged its subjects: they felt that they had been 'had', relationships broke up and a 1980 follow-up was abandoned for fear that it too would become 'a rape of the family'.[36]

And so to the Investigations Bureau. For Gus Macdonald:

> The first *World in Action* exposés were infrequent but instructive. Those of us from newspapers found television investigation a much tougher trade which demanded film as evidence. Documents, second hand accounts and stills of the guiltiest of men did not make good television.[37]

On television, then, investigative journalists needed to be more proactive than their press counterparts, using set-ups, hidden cameras and impersonation to obtain evidential visuals. Three early investigations illustrate the focus of the Bureau at this time and the techniques employed to make visual and engaging investigative reports. 'Smith's back door' examined the ease with which government sanctions imposed on Ian Smith's Rhodesia could be circumvented. It revealed the contribution of British companies in providing oil to Rhodesia and in sustaining its asbestos industry through imports to Britain, but its central story involved the export of a motor axle, organised and then tracked by the Bureau team. The dramatic value of this is evident from the programme's opening:

> Tonight *World in Action* admits to commissioning a crime – the crime of sanctions-busting. The place is a street in Salisbury, the capital of Rhodesia. The man is Meb Cutlack, a *World in Action* reporter. Inside the parcel is a motor-car back axle – one of the many items Britons are specifically forbidden to send to Rhodesia under the sanctions laws. We sent the axle there as a test; to show graphically just how easy it is to beat the sanctions laws – and how delighted British firms are to help you do it.[38]

Using this approach, the programme was able to show the circuitous routes that goods for Rhodesia were following and to expose two shipping firms responsible. To meet the need for evidence, telephone negotiations with the shippers were recorded and broadcast after re-voicing, an incident viewed with displeasure by the ITA and which led to a lengthy debate within ITA committees.[39]

A comparable technique, again motivated by the need to present visual evidence, was used in 'The merchants of war', investigating the clandestine export of arms to the rebel African state of Biafra. This time *World in Action* reporters uncovered the supply chain by posing as arms dealers, giving rise to an opening and structure that again played on the drama of covert activity. Patient stake-outs, possible because of the length of research time available, were used to provide further incontrovertible visual evidence:

> We lay in the back of a car in Lisbon with clothes over our heads for a week ... We filmed mercenaries using a certain hotel and then hid out at Lisbon airport for a further week to film the guns coming in and out.[40]

Clandestine activity and the appeal of witnessing the revelation of hidden deeds, even where they have been 'set up' by the programme team, were also behind a programme exposing the techniques of industrial espionage. In 'Spies for hire', having earlier secured the permission of an electronics company, *World in Action* engaged a firm of private detectives to obtain information from the company. Hidden cameras not only filmed *World in Action* reporters, posing as competitors, instructing the detective agency but also the actual espionage work as its detectives bugged a telephone and photographed secret blueprints. With the job completed, the set-up was revealed to the spies as they presented their bill and a director was interviewed about the morality of his agency's work.

Each of these, and similar investigative editions of the period, used television techniques to expose wrong-doing and reveal the extent of hidden activity. They were significant journalistic enterprises in their own right with few television precedents at the time, but they also made for compelling television. Giving his observations on the series two years after its relaunch, *World in Action* researcher Richard Martin outlined the value of its investigations: They were 'the programmes that get talked about and remembered', he observed. 'They all shared an air of intrigue, a conspiracy between the programme-maker and the viewer which made for an impression of watching a "thriller" live and for real.' But their impact was blunted by the inability of a television programme to follow up its stories by continuing to foreground them in subsequent editions as a newspaper would have done: 'Campaigning journalism has still to be cracked on TV'.[41] In this, of course, he fails to acknowledge the impact of ITV's regulatory system – the virtual impossibility of campaigning whilst maintaining impartiality.

By the end of 1968, *World in Action* had a relatively settled team growing in experience, an approach and thematic range that was established, and ratings and reactions suggested the series was thriving. To a surprising degree, it continued to reflect Plowright's initial tripartite approach. The investigations closely adhered to his prescription for 'Inquiries'. The majority of programmes constituted 'Reportage', although most were well-removed from the type of 'news background' or 'situation report' piece more common in *Panorama* and *This Week*. In practice, they tended not to follow any breaking news agenda but to pursue fresh approaches to understanding on-going social and cultural circumstances, scientific developments, foreign conflicts and popular movements. The 'Implicits' were rarer and harder to classify ('Mick Jagger', despite its proximity to the news agenda, might be included; 'The demonstration' was essentially an impressionistic programme whose newsworthiness was fortuitous). 1968 also saw Norman Swallow's 'The long bridge', a report on the refugees crossing the Israel–Jordan border, and a Denis Mitchell feature, 'Situation vacant', illustrating the impact on the lives of ordinary Mancunians when the party machines arrive for a by-election, but such programmes were comparatively unusual. Not that the series was above criticism: In Richard Martin's view, *World in Action*'s 'liberality' and 'irreverence' had made it predictable, its house style 'smug'. 'There are better ways of skinning a cat than using a steam-roller', he wrote.[42]

Seeing out the sixties

Despite personnel changes, the pattern established for the programme was to continue over the next few years. After his promotion to Head of Current Affairs in August 1968, David Plowright retained a close involvement with *World in Action*. Day-to-day responsibility for the series was vested in Jeremy Wallington and Leslie Woodhead in the first of a series of joint editorships that reflected the series' twin bases in London and Manchester. Wallington himself took over as Executive Producer, Current Affairs, the following summer and, with Woodhead seeking a return to film-making, Plowright, now Head of Programmes, appointed Gus Macdonald and John Birt as joint editors. Aged 27 and 24 respectively, their appointment matched the times with a remarkable faith in the value of a youthful perspective. According to Birt, the idea was to ally his imagination to Macdonald's journalistic skills.[43] To judge from his regular, critical memos on the series, Plowright regarded imagination and innovation as *World in Action*'s key strengths. Praising its resourcefulness, perceptiveness and impudence, and wary of complacency, he declared in one memo that 'surprise distinguishes *World in Action* from its more cautious, reverential competitors', before urging still greater flexibility in the approach to subjects.[44]

Programmes were still thought of as comprising reportage, inquiry or observation. Only in the former category, mostly involving overseas reports, was the series felt to be unimaginative:

> With one or two notable exceptions the [reportage] shows have been competent but not extraordinary. They could have been done by anyone else and the only *World in Action* stamp they bore was a self-congratulatory commentary line here and there.[45]

Amongst the 'notable exceptions' may be included two films that reflected the editors' youthful, radical sense of the news agenda and captured from the inside key moments in the development of American protest politics. With an approach reminiscent of 'The demonstration', a team was despatched to cover the build up to and progress of the vast anti-war march in Washington in November 1969 and found themselves within its front ranks as they were tear-gassed by the National Guard. Transmitted less than two days later, 'Five days in Washington' was a timely and dramatic account of a major news event and *World in Action*'s first programme shown in colour. Three months later, and before the verdicts were even announced, *World in Action* showed 'Conspiracy', Woodhead's film about the Chicago conspiracy trial, made with unprecedented access to the defendants during the trial itself.[46]

The category of 'observations' provided the most scope for innovation, often using close observation of an individual to offer an implicit picture of a circumstance at a macro level whilst avoiding the 'worthy' dullness of a more abstract documentary addressed to the circumstance itself. The period to summer 1970 saw some notable and varied examples. In 'Ken Petty, alas no longer with us', the new 'hippie' lifestyle was examined through observation of the daily life of a self-confessed 'drop-out' who was then asked to justify his motivations to parents and former friends, while 'Death of a student', based on the public suicide of a Czech student activist, was able to say 'more about the Czech situation than a wordy report could have done'.[47] In a classic 'stunt', *World in Action* took Mary Whitehouse to Copenhagen to see for herself the operation of a more liberal moral regime ('The state of Denmark'). Plowright singled out 'Ken Petty', 'Seymour' and 'Quentin Crisp' as 'encouraging breaks with tradition', although care was taken to ensure that a worthwhile social contribution accompanied the stylistic departures that they made.[48] 'Seymour' purposefully used the observational techniques of Direct Cinema to follow a habitual criminal on the day of his release, offering an insight into criminality and recidivism.[49] 'Quentin Crisp' 'teetered on the brink of being unusable in *World in Action*' but was included as 'an exceptional one off'.[50] It was made by

Denis Mitchell, occupying an autonomous role within Granada's current affairs department, originally for a series called *Seven Men* (Granada, 1971). Mitchell also contributed 'Bannside', a chilling profile of Ian Paisley to coincide with his by-election victory. Characteristically, both films eschewed narration and relied solely on the speech of their subjects.

Under Wallington, and later Mike Ryan, the Research Bureau remained a robust and often controversial contributor to the series and its most cherished feature,[51] intended to produce about 12 programmes a year with varying gestation periods. Two programmes in this period were the subjects of particular controversy. The provocatively-titled 'A case to answer' investigated allegations of petty corruption in the Hong Kong Police, initiated by the claims of an ex-officer and investigated at length by *World in Action* journalists. But in the absence of verifiable proof, the programme relied upon testimony and circumstantial evidence alone, opening thus: 'We do not have specific proof. But after five weeks of inquiries we believe there is no doubt that the police have a case to answer'.[52] Consequently, the programme was difficult to defend against a complaint by the Hong Kong Police, supported by the ITA, which was inclined to view the case as another example of the series' willingness 'to go crusading' regardless of its statutory obligations.[53] In public Granada continued to defend the programme but privately Plowright, Wallington and Woodhead were forced to concede that it 'did not reach the normal standards of accuracy which *World in Action* has set for itself'.[54] Ironically, when the series mounted a repeat investigation into Hong Kong policing four years later ('The squeeze'), much negotiation with the ITA and some re-editing were required but, crucially, hidden cameras captured a policeman taking a bribe.

'The most widely used drug in the world', a programme on the medical dangers of excessive consumption of Aspirin provoked controversy of a different type. The team recognised that great sensitivity was required if public confidence in Aspirin taken at normal doses was not to be undermined. As a result, much trouble was taken to secure the early co-operation of the ITA, where senior figures and medical advisors were involved at various stages in previewing and suggesting amendments, and to vet the programme thoroughly within Granada, including screenings for the Programme Committee, the company Board and Lord Goodman, Granada's lawyer. But there were further complications: in the programme, pharmaceutical advertising was blamed by the Consumers Association for encouraging 'Aspirin-eating'. Both the ITA and Sidney Bernstein recognised that it would be hypocritical to continue to show commercials of the type condemned. Although the

ITA tightened its scrutiny of such commercials, it proved difficult to get ITV companies' agreement to forego revenue and risk the withdrawal of pharmaceutical advertisements.[55] To secure impartiality and keep the confidence of advertisers, the ITA also facilitated negotiations over the programme with the Proprietary Association of Great Britain, who put up a speaker to close the programme with a reassurance of the safety of Aspirin if used correctly.[56] Nonetheless, it was still necessary for Granada and the ITA to resist pressure from Aspirin manufacturers to dissuade them from transmission – Granada even received a threatening telegram from Alka-Seltzer on the Sunday morning before transmission, despite the Television Act expressly forbidding advertisers from having any control over programme content.[57] In the event, the programme was considered a success and proved a fine example of Granada/ITV co-operation. It also showed the strategic benefits of securing early ITA support, although Forman wondered darkly:

> what would have happened if a climate of opinion against the programme created by the drug industry [had] persuaded a number of influential people that the programme was exaggerated and that there was a serious threat of undermining their confidence in a harmless and useful domestic drug? Perhaps I am wrong in thinking this would have had some kind of influence on Members of the Authority.[58]

Here was a programme with clear public service objectives and demonstrable public benefits, but getting it shown represented a triumph of perseverance, such were the hurdles that had to be negotiated. Having been commissioned in January 1970 and expected to take six weeks to make, it was in production for no less than 23 months![59]

'The Monday and Tuesday Club'

With Birt's return to programme-making in 1970, a further reorganisation took place. The production of *World in Action* and of Granada's contribution to the networked Tuesday documentary slots was combined under Wallington with Macdonald and Woodhead as deputies. The following year, Macdonald himself took over as Executive Producer, Current Affairs, but he remained directly in charge of *World in Action*, aided from 1974 by David Boulton's appointment as the programme's Editor. David Plowright, however, continued to be closely involved with the series, as he would for the remainder of his Granada career.

'The Monday and Tuesday Club', as the combined operation was playfully known, seemed to offer a number of advantages. In Wallington's view, its production team were 'probably the most competent and experienced group that any current affairs unit in television has ever had' and the new arrangements offered much greater flexibility to producers:

> Many people are seeking ways of extending the range of documentary television ... A number of people who might otherwise have become frustrated and passed on remain involved as a result of the change.[60]

The difficulty of valued producers 'outgrowing' the constraints of weekly current affairs was to be a perennial one for *World in Action* and this solution – 'to allocate a number of Granada's specials slots to WIA rather than allocating a number of WIA people to special slots' – was first mooted 18 months earlier.[61] A further motivation was that it offered scope to expand the form of current affairs outwards into extended 'specials' and dramatisation. Despite the temptations of formal experimentation, however, Wallington was clear that *World in Action* was to remain the premier operation.

Only three *World in Action* programmes since 1967 had escaped the regular Monday slot to run 45 minutes – still shorter than the multi-item *Panorama*'s regular running time. The nine Tuesday slots per year that now fell within the compass of the expanded team had to accommodate *Disappearing World* and a diverse range of features, but by summer 1972 there had been six more Tuesday programmes that were closely, if not always titularly, related to *World in Action*. These included *Seven Plus Seven*, the first septennial return to the children of the 1964 '7 up' experiment,[62] and Woodhead's 'How to steal a party'. The latter followed a state delegation to observe the power struggles and deal-making on the floor of the American Democratic Convention. It was shot 'in continuous close-up, with only a minimum of explanation' and Raymond Williams was among many who praised the power of its 'dramatic closeness', contrasting it with 'ordinary' current affairs treatments of politics.[63] Also sold to various US stations, 'How to steal a party' was the most acclaimed of several observational programmes of the period described by Macdonald as 'narrative vérité', capturing political or industrial conflict and negotiation at close quarters with minimal intervention and seen internally as 'an important advance in reporting politics on television'.[64]

Of even greater significance, however, was the impetus that the extended slots gave to the development of dramatised forms for the handling of current affairs. Moments of dramatised reconstruction were not uncommon in *World in Action*, but the desire to develop full-scale drama-documentaries, still comparatively rare in television at the time, had been expressed regularly at Granada following their successes of the early 1960s. For Plowright, the impact of BBC *Wednesday Plays* like *Cathy Come Home* had shown drama-documentary's effectiveness in opening up social enquiry; he had initially proposed to include dramatisations as part of the revived *World in Action* and continued to see them as desirable.[65] One drama-documentary, *The Pueblo Affair*, recreating the Court of Inquiry that investigated the capture of a US warship and drawn from transcripts and press reports of the Court, was shown in early 1970.[66] Despite being written and researched by Mike Murphy, a *World in Action* producer, *The Pueblo Affair* was essentially a solo project with no direct successors. But Granada's next such venture derived entirely from *World in Action* and demonstrated the other main trigger for Granada's drama-documentary production – the difficulty of making programmes about events which could not be filmed using conventional current affairs documentary techniques.

That *World in Action* was unable to make well-informed programmes about the Soviet bloc as it could with the USA was a long-standing source of frustration. When the wife of improved Soviet dissident Pyotr Grigorenko smuggled out a lengthy document giving an account of his trial, the team realised that it could form the basis for 'a very constrained and puritanical form of dramatic reconstruction'.[67] Running 45 minutes in the Tuesday documentary slot, the resulting programme, *The Man Who Wouldn't Keep Quiet*, met all of the team's criteria for dramatisation: it was purposeful and journalistically relevant, its subject was not accessible by other means and it was based on evidence strong enough that its authenticity could scarcely be questioned.[68] It later drew praise for its accuracy from Grigorenko himself following his release.[69] A week earlier, the same slot had been used for *The Other Spike*, Spike Milligan's own dramatised account of his mental breakdown and treatment, told with comic exaggeration rather than journalistic accuracy.[70] Wallington acknowledged that, but for length, both drama-documentaries could have been shown in the Monday slot; each 'grew out of the WIA debate' but were seen as 'splendid examples of the new flexibility'.[71] *The Man Who Wouldn't Keep Quiet*, however, proved to be the inspiration and template for the company's extensive drama-documentary production over the next three decades. Following two more drama-documentaries for the Tuesday slot, both with Eastern European subjects and based on meticulous documentation,[72] a separate drama-documentary unit was established with the same journalistic disciplines and commitment to accuracy. Crucially, it remained within Factual Programming, depended largely on personnel drawn from *World in Action* and was intentionally located in an adjacent office to ensure that ideas, approaches and even subjects could be exchanged.[73]

1975: taking stock

By the beginning of the 1970s, the series was established as, arguably, Britain's most ground-breaking current affairs series and certainly its most popular. Ratings had declined somewhat from the heady figures in 1967, but *World in Action* maintained a steady Top 20 presence, periodically figuring in the Top 10. In the *Sun* newspaper's poll, *World in Action* was voted 'Top Current Affairs series' annually from 1970 to 1975. With a well-defined house style and still a much stronger focus on investigative journalism than any of its competitors, it had settled into a pattern that would continue with little modification for more than a decade. By the end of 1974, 'The Monday and Tuesday Club' had been abandoned and most of Granada's Manchester-based factual programmes were housed in a single open-plan office to encourage an exchange of ideas and personnel whilst retaining – notionally – their separate identities. Looking back at recent seasons from this point, Gus Macdonald offered a frank assessment that reveals much about the series' thematic agenda under his management and its sense of its own value. In it, he identifies his own 'working categories' of *World in Action* programming and emphasises the need to provide a good mix between them.[74] Macdonald's categories, outlined below, provide a good basis for an overview of the series' output since the beginning of the decade and a perspective different from the more rigid ones employed earlier by Plowright:

a) National political

Political coverage had generally been conceived of as a weakness within *World in Action* and a particular strength of its competitors, a complaint that would recur throughout its history. But Macdonald reports a 'dramatic' improvement, partly due to innovative election and referendum coverage. For the October 1974 election, Granada's regional news magazine and *World in Action* collaborated in establishing the 'Granada 500' – a representative panel of 500 voters from the marginal seat of Preston, who were polled for shifts in their opinions while participating in a regional campaign series examining election issues. Finally, for a networked *World in Action Special*, they travelled to London to put questions in turn to the three major party leaders. The 'Granada 500' idea, begun regionally at the previous election, was widely acclaimed and established a lasting formula for campaign coverage, later being taken over by the network as the 'ITV 500'. Prior to the European referendum, *World in Action* showed its first two-part Special, 'A bus round the market', in which Mike Scott took Lord George Brown, Clive Jenkins and a coach party of Britons on a tour

of Common Market countries and people. Apart from the 'narrative
vérité' programmes of the early 1970's, the series' other main party
political offerings consisted of interviews or film profiles of major
politicians. The most notable of these involved Margaret Thatcher
when a candidate for the Conservative Party leadership. The stridently-
titled 'Why I want to be leader – by Margaret Thatcher' was conceived
as a mildly tongue-in-cheek cheek idea, but its candid glimpse into her
character, background, philosophy and family life helped to establish
her 'housewife and mother' persona in the public consciousness and
was 'credited with being a substantial influence in [her] becoming Party
Leader'.[75]

b) Continuity

Television current affairs journalism has been criticised for the difficulty
it has, in comparison with the press, in 'campaigning'. Generally, once
a topic has been aired a series moves on and any pressure is released,
a point raised by Wallington in 1969:

> It is apparent that we can no longer rely on newspapers to pick up WIA's
> information and finish off the attacks we begin. We have to do it ourselves.
> We need to return to our subjects, if necessary again and again, in order
> to effect anything.[76]

In noting 'a new emphasis on continuity', Macdonald's assessment
registers *World in Action*'s success in combating this problem. By
1975, the series had developed a number of running themes to which
it had given extensive coverage. Some of these were justified by news
values, although the series often sought to avoid a reactive approach
in favour of one that could open up new perspectives on a topic. The
Vietnam war and its broader implications had been the subject of 12
editions by 1975, and Northern Ireland the subject of 17, one of which
had been banned by the IBA.[77] Of stronger campaigning significance
was the 'torture series'. In 1973, *World in Action* began to show films
cataloguing and presenting evidence of torture in different countries.
In most cases, permission to film was refused and these programmes
were often made using lightweight amateur equipment by teams disguised
as tourists, sometimes at considerable personal risk. The idea of a
series was partly retrospective: with several programmes made, it was
decided to pursue the topic more purposefully and make it a running
theme, establishing a *de facto* 'unit' dedicated to torture. This culminated
in a public event at which seven *World in Action* films on torture were
screened with the support of Amnesty International[78] and also in 'The
year of the torturer', a 90-minute networked Special drawing together

ideas and extracts from the torture series. Besides this programme and *The Man Who Wouldn't Keep Quiet*, included retrospectively in the torture series, the strand ran to nine programmes each covering a different territory and mostly made between 1972 and 1974: Turkey, South Vietnam (discussed further in Chapter 7), Spain, Czechoslovakia, Brazil, Chile, Portugal, Greece, Zanzibar, Yugoslavia, the USSR and, most controversially, Northern Ireland.

With the Investigations Bureau and the now-autonomous drama-documentary unit as models, the idea of units dedicated to particular types of programme was to resurface again in *World in Action*. Most notable was the 'economy unit' under Mike Scott, established at a time of mounting economic pressure and supposed under-performance in Britain, and amid perceptions that *World in Action* was neglecting economic affairs. In 1975, the first programme from the unit, 'The nuts & bolts of the economy', was widely praised – Granada's Programme Committee considered it 'a breakthrough in finding a way to present a complex and specialised subject in a way that held the attention and at the same time conveyed the problem' – and won a BAFTA.[79] By June 1978, Scott, acting as both executive producer and on-screen reporter, and a small team had produced 14 'Nuts & bolts' programmes appearing intermittently in *World in Action* slots with the *World in Action* logo in the opening titles. For Fitzwalter, however, the torture and economy units suffered a serious weakness compared to the Investigations Bureau in that they were anchored to subject matter rather than method. Despite the perceived benefits of specialisation, the danger was that 'you start perpetuating subjects because you are there. The ideas should come first, not the people . . . I felt he [Scott] started making repetitive programmes.'[80] Eventually, the 'Nuts & bolts' programmes moved outside the *World in Action* stable, mounting six televised economic seminars before being reincarnated in 1980 as a monthly regional strand.

On a less grand scale, *World in Action* did develop an enviable record in returning to the subjects of earlier programmes, sometimes several times. Macdonald notes five such instances in the 1974–75 season.[81] Across the series as a whole, the programmes about Thalidomide survivor Kevin Donellon represent a notable example of this. Kevin first appeared, aged 10, in 1972 in an observational programme shot in a single day and was revisited in 1981, 1987 and 1995.[82] Over a smaller time-scale, a 1973 investigation exposing suppliers overcharging the National Coal Board was followed in 1974 by a programme on the parliamentary enquiry that followed and shortly after by another on the circumstances surrounding the Board's decision to sack the man who exposed the scandal.[83] As with the '7 up' series, a distinct advantage of revisiting earlier subjects was the ability to build in a developmental context by re-showing footage from earlier programmes.

There were also subjects that *World in Action* seemed determined to place on the public agenda and, by repetition, to maintain there over long periods. Particular examples were apartheid in South Africa, the subject of 20 programmes between 1970 and 1992, and intelligence and official secrecy, the subject of 9 programmes between 1973 and 1988. In both cases, these were controversial and difficult subjects that frequently brought criticism and regulatory intervention. Of particular interest here are two films revealing the social conditions of black South Africans. In 1970, 'The dumping grounds', billed as 'an investigation', was one of the earliest programmes to show graphically the poverty, starvation and oppression of black township-dwellers, and inspired a follow-up, 'The discarded people', in which a team returned to find that little had changed 11 years later. Both programmes refuted government claims about the fair treatment of blacks and, like many of the South African programmes, both were made clandestinely with tourist equipment in response to the government's refusal to give permission to film. 'The discarded people' had to be smuggled out of South Africa after the crew was arrested and held for three days. So dangerous were such missions to South Africa thought to be that one 1976 programme, 'The law breakers', carrying interviews with victims of police brutality in Soweto, was transmitted without end credits to prevent reprisals.

In preparing 'Secrets', a wide-ranging examination of the unworkability of Section 2 of the Official Secrets Act (which a judge had declared should be 'pensioned off' as early as 1970), Granada was dismayed to be asked by the D-Notice committee, with IBA support, to remove a passage referring to GCHQ. More frustratingly still, to allude to this apparent 'censorship' in press briefings could itself be construed as grounds for prosecution under the Act.[84] The irony of this situation rankled and similar attempts at 'censorship' were to recur in relation to later 'campaigning' programmes challenging the Act and the security establishment (see Chapter 4).

c) Social/popular TV journalism

The 1974–75 season had produced ten programmes with overtly populist subjects, including a profile of boxer John Conteh ('John Conteh: Punching for a dream'), a discussion on homosexuality chaired by Jimmy Savile ('Coming out') and a report on rape in America, provocatively entitled 'Sex and violence'. However successful with audiences,

Macdonald found himself uncomfortable with such calculated attempts to make *World in Action* less austere. But, he added:

> Mindful – even fearful – of being trapped in the narrow aesthetics of one's own past and in the interests of keeping WIA straddled from A–B to Page 3, we should continue to risk an occasional pain in the crutch.[85]

The 'social and popular' area tended to be a fertile one for the sort of 'stunts' with which *World in Action* occasionally sought to cause a stir. Two in particular stand out in the first half of the 1970s, although neither was wholly successful. In 'The village that quit', 100 residents of a Staffordshire village were persuaded to give up smoking for a week and their experiences filmed as a means to highlight the health risks. The programme yielded two follow-ups, after six months and 21 years,[86] and, remarkably, Brian Blake researched the first two and produced the third – a tribute to his longevity within the series. Categorised years later as 'quality populism',[87] this experiment may be viewed now as a precursor to the 'Can you live without . . .?' strand of programming, varieties of which are commonplace within present-day factual entertainment. This may be no coincidence: the formula was repeated in 'The Luddenden experiment' in 1975, when a different village was persuaded to give up meat in the context of rising food prices, and in 1990 *World in Action* itself invented the 'Can you live without . . .?' banner for 'Can you live without your car?', involving a comparable experiment examining an extended family's reliance on their cars in the light of traffic congestion.

In the other significant 'stunt', an early example of 'social action' programming, the series attempted to anglicise the American practice of placing children for adoption by presenting them in 'commercials' fronted by Ben Hunter, presenter of such programmes in the USA. A disagreement with the IBA over the programme's ethics delayed its transmission, but it too gave rise to two follow-ups, including one in which the same approach was applied to elderly people awaiting discharge from mental health institutions.[88] Results of the adoption experiment were mixed: there were 3,760 calls to phone-lines advertised at the end of the programme, an early example of 'interactive' television, and 2,600 letters. But interest soon dissipated, few turned up at follow-up meetings and, although the profile of fostering and adoption rose generally, only one of the four featured children was placed.[89]

d) Film-making

One detrimental change noted in Macdonald's 1975 breakdown is a decline in distinctive film-making. This, he suspects, may result from an increased focus on investigative and political programming and also from qualitative changes in the nature of social and political problems, now lending themselves less to 'microcosmic treatment':

> Through the moving/vivid/aesthetic experience of this symbolic victim/ villain/demonstration you the viewer/critic/politician gets the message which implies that society should/must/could do something immediately to put things right. Somehow it doesn't seem that easy anymore, hence the demand for more 'issue' journalism and fewer troubling 'stories.[90]

For Macdonald, as this description implies, observational film-making seemed to offer the best opportunity for distinctiveness and there had been few successors to the 'narrative vérité' programmes of the early 1970s. But the warm reaction of viewers in a recent Audience Apprecia-tion Survey to 'The blood and guts shift', recording 24 hours in the casualty department of a Liverpool hospital, suggested to him that *vérité* applied to subjects in microcosm was effective not only in aesthetic terms. Formal changes were afoot in another sense too. Including Specials, Macdonald notes that in-vision reporters or anchors had been used in no fewer than 18 programmes in the past two years: 'But what about the folklore which has it . . . that WIA is the programme where nobody gets between you and the action?'[91] The reality was that *World in Action* was not averse to the use of reporters where this method was felt to be appropriate and would continue to use them periodically for the remainder of its existence.

e) Investigative programmes

Although Macdonald notes that investigative programmes are 'angst-ridden' internally and take a disproportionate amount of management time, he considered in 1975 that *World in Action*'s investigative 'momentum' and public reputation remained 'undimmed'.[92] Depending on definition, up to one third of programmes could be deemed 'investigative'. Indeed, in 1973/74 half were claimed to be, following a deliberate effort to 'harden the series journalistically' which, Macdonald acknowledges, resulted in an impression of 'coldness, inflexibility and even self-righteousness'.[93] And, in significance if not in number, 'gropes' (as they were universally known) were still the bedrock of the *World in Action* 'brand', providing its most substantial journalistic contribu-tions. The period to the mid-1970s represented their heyday, with Woodward and Bernstein's Watergate investigation making folk heroes of investigative journalists and the notorious 'Birt–Jay thesis' not yet having given ammunition to senior figures in broadcasting and politics to cast them as naïve activists.[94] Macdonald's explanation for *World in Action*'s pre-eminence is revealing:

Investigative journalism has always been the most difficult area of current affairs programme making and we have it to ourselves for the most obvious of reasons: it costs a great deal of money (Tea); one programme can wipe out experienced team members for most of a series (Dundee); there are formidable legal problems (Gozo); it strains relations with the IBA (Poulson); aggrieved people lodge complaints (lifeboats); juries make unexpected decisions (Drug Squad); powerful interest groups fight back (Ceylon); viewers protest (British agents in Ulster); civil servants put on pressure (Hong Kong); and sometimes the narrative threatens to collapse under the weight of accumulated detail (Coal Inquiries). Worst of all are the times when nobody seems to notice.[95]

This list serves not only to catalogue the difficulties of television investigative journalism, but also hints at the variety and public significance of the investigations mounted by the series in the 1970s: Granada saw them as doing more than reporting the news – its investigations sought to *make* it.[96] It also underlines the continuing need for investigations to be conducted with a tougher journalistic discipline than other forms of television reporting. Granada's view, not always shared by regulators, was that television investigative journalism was essentially comparable to that in the press:

> We feel ... that journalism is journalism whether expressed in words or in words and pictures, and that the only difference between the two media is that whereas both have to respect the law, television has to take account of more law (the Television Act being additional) than newspapers.[97]

Naturally, investigations were the area in which *World in Action* found itself most often in conflict with the IBA and some of its investigative output in this period is covered in more detail in Chapter 8. A sample of more significant investigative programmes of the period, chosen either because the scrutiny they afforded had consequences that were in the public interest or because they illustrate some of the difficulties of television investigative journalism, is given below.

'The drugs squad file' investigated conspiracy and perjury within the Metropolitan Police drugs squad and the means by which it falsified evidence to secure convictions, building upon a story first uncovered by the *Sunday Times* 'Insight' team which led to the trial of six officers. The programme drew upon evidence from interviews with those who were victims of drugs squad practices and on revelations from concealed filming. It caused particular problems legally, largely because the programme was made to be shown after the trial verdict and passed by lawyers on the assumption of a guilty verdict. In the event, a jury whose attitude was described by the judge as 'merciful' found the defendants not guilty on most of the charges and unexpectedly acquitted three altogether.[98] Amid hasty and confusing legal advice, parts of the programme which were now unusable had to be swiftly remade.

'How safe are America's atomic reactors?', filmed largely in the USA, examined the safety record of nuclear power stations of the type that Britain was about to purchase, drawing upon the testimonies of some eminent American experts. In this it was topical, revelatory and alarming, being discussed in the House of Commons on the night of transmission and causing dismay to nuclear authorities in Britain and America. Prints were later sold to pressure groups and screened to scientific conferences throughout America. Ralph Nader even showed the film to a committee of Congress 'who were said to be impressed' as part of his campaign for a moratorium on nuclear power.[99]

Prompted by concerns about workers' employment and health conditions, *World in Action* investigated British-owned Indian and Sri Lankan tea plantations in 1973 in 'The cost of a cup of tea'. Two more reports from the same team followed in 1975 to establish whether progress had been made after the revelations of 1973. The first of these follow-ups, 'Tea: the deadly cost', revealed that conditions and death-rates had worsened still further. Accompanied by a doctor, a *World in Action* team filmed and tested workers and their children in secret and at dead of night, tea companies having refused not only co-operation but access to estates. Four specialist nutritionists oversaw the results and confirmed that malnutrition was widespread. Regardless of these difficulties, the data revealed in 'Tea: the deadly cost' prompted the Foreign Office to become involved and led to plantation visits by a cross-party group of British MPs already in Sri Lanka for a conference. An early day motion congratulated Granada on the programme, but the MPs reported on their return that it was 'selective, unbalanced and biased'.[100] Granada stood by the programme's findings in the face of a comprehensive lobbying and smear operation on the part of the tea companies, which claimed that the programme started out 'with an objective in mind', that its sample was selective and that the doctor, a consultant with experience in treating estate workers and a strong track record in both Britain and Sri Lanka, had been struck off or was unqualified.[101] As an example of the problems *World in Action* faced when 'powerful interest groups fight back',[102] these events had strong resonances when the series faced much more frequent attempts to derail its investigations in the 1980s. In an interesting example of 'continuity', Michael Gillard, one of the original investigative team, returned to the subject in 'Tea – a bitter taste' in 1983, conducting very similar tests at tea estates in Bangladesh with distressingly similar findings.

Unlike some *World in Action* investigations, which involved gathering a broader or firmer body of evidence about a story already wholly or partly in the public domain, the tea programmes provided new evidence to reveal a fresh scandal. Similarly, 'The Dundee dossier' represented a painstaking and revelatory investigation into local government corruption broken wholly by the team's efforts. It also represented one of the series' longest investigations, tying up several researchers for seven months – a testament to Granada's dedication to investigative journalism even at high cost. Substantial evidence was presented that Dundee's housing policy was directed by councillors with undeclared financial interests in building and property companies. Despite claims – rejected by the journalists involved – that *World in Action* misrepresented the nature of their enquiries in gathering evidence and parliamentary accusations of 'trial by television', the programme led swiftly to the expulsion of two Dundee Labour councillors and later to a trial that was the longest in Scottish legal history.[103]

'Standards in public life' was an issue that demonstrated unambiguously the public interest role that investigative journalism could play and 'The Dundee Dossier' was neither the first nor the most celebrated intervention by the programme in this area. It had been the theme of three earlier programmes each linked, directly or indirectly, to the conduct of Reginald Maudling, Home Secretary in the Heath government until his resignation in July 1972. The first, 'The schemes of Jerome D. Hoffman', followed two years of investigations by *Private Eye* in investigating the Real Estate Fund of America, a company run by an American fraudster already banned from trading in New York, of which Maudling had been president. With Hoffman's empire already collapsing, the programme was effective in explaining the extent of his deception but Maudling's role was downplayed, largely at the insistence of the ITA. Hoffman fled the country as a result but Maudling emerged unscathed, his involvement assumed by many to be due merely to carelessness.[104] When Maudling later resigned it was over his links with the companies of the corrupt architect and developer John Poulson, although it was the conflict of interest arising from his responsibility for the police, who were prosecuting Poulson, to which his departure was attributed. The story of Poulson, involving systematic payments over a ten-year period to corrupt councillors throughout Britain and their recruitment as 'public relations consultants', was also not new. Ray Fitzwalter had investigated it for the *Bradford Telegraph and Argus* prior to his recruitment by *World in Action* in 1971, but initially the series showed no interest in it.[105] Only when Poulson's bankruptcy precipitated Maudling's resignation did it become a national story, even though the extent of his corruption and the catalogue of councillors involved was still not widely understood. Poulson's bankruptcy hearings provided the source material for what was perhaps *World in Action*'s most celebrated programme, *The Rise and Fall of John Poulson*.

Its fame arose in part from the IBA's much-criticised move to ban an earlier version 'as a matter of broadcasting policy' in January 1973, an event discussed in Chapter 8. But the programme was momentous in its own right. The team had pieced together the astonishing extent of Poulson's 'web of corruption' as revealed at the bankruptcy hearings and had sought to substantiate each fact independently so as to avoid repeating uncorroborated allegations. So whilst, notionally at least, little in the programme was not already in the public domain, Plowright was proud to proclaim it as 'a factual account of the Poulson affair told with a great deal more clarity than newspapers have been able to achieve with access to the same material'.[106] Its impact was substantial. When the banned programme was shown to the press, Fitzwalter reports:

> I could hear people gasping, hardened reporters who thought they knew a lot about this. And you could hear them saying, 'oh my God that's how it all worked' ... I mean, initially it was a huge chart on a desk, and it worked out almost like a spiders web from Poulson, his practices, his companies, and then all the ranks of people he influenced, almost invariably corruptly. And the amazing thing really was that people in authority didn't want to believe that it could be true.[107]

The programme was also well received by the police, who praised its accuracy, clarity and usefulness to the Fraud Squad in building a case against Poulson and his associates.[108]

A third programme, 'Business in Gozo', followed, revealing Maudling's role whilst in office in enabling Poulson to secure a hospital contract on the island and aid to the Maltese government to fund it, without declaring his own interest in Poulson's companies. This was a damning and hitherto unpublicised aspect of the Poulson story and virtually a *World in Action* exclusive, although the *Daily Mail* revealed aspects of it on the day of transmission. The following day, realising the magnitude of *World in Action*'s revelations, the *Mail* reprinted the script almost in full.[109] In an effort to salvage his political career, Maudling made a Commons statement on the night of transmission, condemning the programme's 'grave and evil allegations' and promising to sue. In the event, no writ was issued against Granada for four months, until the day on which the General Election was called.[110] But *World in Action*'s case was exceptionally strong, based on five damning letters acknowledging Maudling's guilt, all of which eventually came into the team's possession.[111] In the Commons, the Select Committee on Conduct of Members spent eight months investigating the allegations against Maudling only for the House to vote against acting upon its damning conclusions.[112] Meanwhile, it became clear that Maudling's libel action was tactical and that he was seeking to delay a hearing for as long as possible. Eventually, it lapsed on his death in 1979. But the effect of it on *World in Action* was profound. As the programme's principal researcher, Ray Fitzwalter found himself forced to take a year away from the series to produce evidence for Granada's defence and for the Select Committee: 'I was so busy at one point serving the lawyers I was keeping three secretaries going simultaneously, day in day out.'[113] More broadly, the suit and Maudling's litigiousness had a restraining effect on the series' investigations. Plowright told his superiors:

> At the moment we are avoiding any subject with a Maudling implication for obvious reasons but I am beginning to feel that this sort of muzzling of *World in Action* enquiries is going to be harmful to the programme's reputation.[114]

He went on to list three substantial investigations that the series had dodged because public interest concerns had been outweighed by possible links to the Maudling case. Besides revealing Maudling's own wrong-doing, however, these programmes also had a wider beneficial outcome in focussing attention on MPs' interests. Sixteen days after the transmission of 'Business in Gozo', the Commons voted to establish a compulsory Register of Members' Interests.[115]

Despite their significance, these investigations presented problems for programme-makers. In 1970, Wallington had acknowledged 'immense journalistic professionalism' to be the main requirement for investigations and that 'pictures are secondary'.[116] The two Poulson programmes, and others like them, relied upon the presentation of evidence – documents, transcripts – and upon explanatory devices such as charts, graphics and stills. This seemed to render the familiar film-report-with-voiceover approach inappropriate, and such programmes were anchored by a pair of presenters from a studio with cutaways to graphics and stills. Static interview sequences and the occasional film-clip represented the only moving pictures. Ironically, given the significance of the evidence they contained, visually these were among the dullest programmes mounted by *World in Action* and nowadays appear remarkably staid. Legal issues presented a further problem and required great care to be taken over the claims made in these programmes. *The Rise and Fall of John Poulson*, for example, was carefully structured as an argument for stronger safeguards over public officials, so that the extent of Poulson's corrupt influence emerged as justification for wider public scrutiny rather than for its own sake. Within such a framework, the implication of wrong-doing could be enough to support the argument, restricting the programme's exposure to potential, if unfounded, libel suits. Fitzwalter could scarcely have been surprised when his original title for the Gozo programme, 'Anything Gozo', was instantly blue-pencilled by the programme's lawyers.[117]

Notes

1   *Plowright, memo to D. Forman, 'Project X – Some notes on a proposed TV programme', 17 February 1966 (bf. 0774). The first two stages broadly reflect developments at *Panorama* from its inception until the mid-1960s (see R. Lindley, *Panorama: Fifty Years of Pride and Paranoia* (London: Politicos, 2002)).

2   *Plowright, 'Title – TBA', 8 February 1967; *'Notes of Future Outlook Group Meeting No. 1', 14 February 1967 (both bf. 1244).

3   *Plowright, notes for discussion with Forman, 'TBA' (6 March 1967) (bf. 1497).

4   *Papers submitted by Brian Armstrong, Jo Durden Smith, Ingrid Floering, John Sheppard, Russell Spurr, Leslie Woodhead), April 1967 (bf. 1497); paper submitted by Mike Murphy and one unattributed paper (bf. 1244)

5   *Forman, memo to Plowright, 'Project X: Some reciprocal thoughts', 17 February 1966 (bf. 0774).

6   *Plowright, 'TBA'.

7   *Forman, memo to senior current affairs producers, 'Follow-up report on FOG meeting No. 1', 20 March 1967 (bf. 1075).

8   *T. Gill, budget for '*World Tomorrow* (series 3)', 10 April 1967 (bf. 1497).

9   *Plowright, 'Title – TBA'.

10 *G. Valvona, memo to Forman, 'FOG – Minutes 14 February', 23 February 1967 (bf. 1075)

11 *Plowright, 'Title – TBA'.

12 *'Notes of Future Outlook Group Meeting No. 1'.

13 For accounts of the rise of investigative journalism in the 1960s see, for example, H. de Burgh, *Investigative Journalism: Context and Practice* (London: Routledge, 2000), pp. 48–9 and fn., and A. Doig, 'Retreat of the investigators', *British Journalism Review*, 3:4 (1992): 44–6.

14 *Plowright, 'Title – TBA'.

15 *Wallington, memo to Research Unit Staff, 'Research Unit Organisation (1)', 18 July 1967 (bf. 1533). The idea of publishing investigations in book form was never realised, with the exception of R. Fitzwalter and D. Taylor, *Web of Corruption: The Story of J.G.L. Poulson and T. Dan Smith* (London: Granada, 1981).

16 *Wallington, 'Research Unit Organisation (1)'.

17 *'Granada Programme News: *World in Action*', launch press release (no date) (bf. 1209).

18 *World in Action Special*: 'War both sides'; *World in Action Special*: 'After the war'.
19 See, for example, *The Times*, 6 June 1967, p. 4.
20 TAM ratings. *World in Action* overseas sales brochure (no date) (bf. 0721); *list of first 49 *World in Action* programmes with audience shares (no date) (bf. 1208).
21 *Plowright, memo, 24 July 1967 (bf. 1497).
22 Lindley, *Panorama*, p. 114.
23 J. Birt (2002), *The Harder Path* (London: Time Warner), p. 90.
24 *B. Blake, memo to R. Fitzwalter, etc., 'World in Action – The first 30 years', 9 November 1992 (bf. 0692).
25 See J. Corner, *The Art of Record* (Manchester: Manchester University Press, 1996), pp. 45–6.
26 *World in Action*: 'Jeremy Thorpe, you're on your own'; J. Critchley, *The Times*, 2 July 1968, p. 13. For a fuller discussion of this programme, see Chapter 7.
27 *Plowright, memo to C. Bernstein, 'New York', 23 January 1968 (bf. 0721).
28 Speaking in the *World in Action: 30 Years* retrospective programme.
29 *Plowright letter to press counsellor, Portuguese Embassy, 2 May 1968 (bf. 1208).
30 *Letter to Forman, 4 April 1968 (bf. 1208).
31 *The Times*, 17 August 1968, p. 17. See Chapter 6.
32 Speaking in the *World in Action: 30 Years* retrospective programme.
33 Leslie Woodhead, speaking in the *World in Action: 30 Years* retrospective programme.
34 *World in Action*: 'Ward F13'.
35 M. Murphy, 'Viewers on poverty', *New Society*, 12 October 1967: 505.
36 *Sheppard, memo to David Boulton, 'The Walsh family', 16 April 1980 (bf. 0720).
37 G. Macdonald, 'A short history of group gropes', in J. Wyver (ed.), Festival Programme, Edinburgh International Television Festival, 1984, p. 19.
38 *World in Action*: 'Smith's back door'.
39 *Forman, memo to senior current affairs staff, 'Note of an item taken under Any Other Business at the SCC meeting at the ITA on Wednesday 17 January 1968', 23 January 1968 (bf. 1090). 'Smith's back door' is discussed further in P. Goddard, '"Improper liberties": Regulating undercover journalism on ITV, 1967–1980', *Journalism*, 7:1, 2006: 49–50.
40 G. Macdonald, 'ITV 70: *World in Action*', *Illustrated London News*, 31 January 1970: 14–15. 'The merchants of war' is discussed in more detail and the opening quoted in Chapter 7.
41 *R. Martin, memo to Macdonald and Birt, 'Programme ideas', 15 July 1969 (bf. 1533).
42 *Martin, 'Programme ideas'.
43 Birt, *The Harder Path*, p. 100.

44 *Plowright, memo to Wallington and Woodhead, '*World in Action*: Some thoughts for the break', 17 February 1969 (bf. 1208).

45 *Plowright, '*World in Action*: Some thoughts for the break'.

46 For these programmes, see Birt, *The Harder Path*, pp. 103–4.

47 *Plowright, '*World in Action*: Some thoughts for the break'.

48 *Wallington, memo to 'The Monday and Tuesday Club', 'From now till '72', 13 August 1970 (bf. 1054).

49 Birt, *The Harder Path*, p. 104.

50 *Wallington, 'From now till '72'.

51 *In 'From now till '72', Wallington describes it as the programme's 'spine'.

52 *World in Action*: 'A case to answer'.

53 *B. Sendall (ITA), letter to Forman, 2 June 1969 (bf. 1338).

54 *Plowright, memo to Forman, '*World in Action* – Hong Kong', 7 July 1969 (bf. 1208).

55 *S. Bernstein, undated interview with N. Chanan (bf. 1435); *Forman, memo to S. Bernstein, etc., 'Aspirin – diary note of a discussion with Brian Young and Joe Weltman following screening 27 4', 28 April 1971 (bf. 0745); *Wallington, memo to Plowright, 19 January 1971 (bf. 0745).

56 *Wallington letter to A. Graham (ITA), 15 November 1971 (bf. 0745).

57 *Forman, account prepared for Granada Television Board, '*World in Action* – South of the border', 8 December 1971 (bf. 1070).

58 *Letter to Sir B. Young (Director General, IBA), 10 April 1973 (bf. 0964).

59 *Macdonald, memo to Plowright, 'Denis [sic] Woolf', 21 January 1970 (bf. 0691).

60 *Wallington, 'From now till '72'.

61 *Wallington and Woodhead, memo to Plowright, 24 January 1969 (bf. 0745).

62 *Seven Plus Seven*, tx. 15 December 1970.

63 In *The Listener*, 27 July 1972: 124.

64 *Macdonald, letter to Raymond Williams, 3 August 1972 (bf. 0742); other *World in Action* programmes identified as 'narrative vérité' included 'Labour in the raw' (see Birt, *The Harder Path*, pp. 114–15), 'The lump', 'The container row' and 'Caught in the Act'.

65 *Plowright, 'Title – TBA'; *Plowright, '*World in Action*: Some thoughts for the break'.

66 Tx. 19 January 1970 in Granada's *Playhouse* series.

67 Woodhead, speaking in *World in Action: 30 years*.

68 *Wallington and J. Powell, discussion paper, 'Some thoughts on 25-minute drama-documentaries', 10 January 1973 (bf. 0674).

69 Speaking in *World in Action*: 'General Grigorenko's new campaign'.

70 Tx. 17 November 1970.

71 *Wallington, memo to 'The Monday and Tuesday Club', 'Where we're at – 2', 18 November 1970 (bf. 0745).

72 *A Subject of Struggle*, tx. 26 September 1972; *Full Circle*, tx. 7 May 1974.

73 Ray Fitzwalter, interview with the authors. See also Woodhead's account of drama-documentary production at Granada in E. Buscombe (ed.), *BFI*

Dossier 9: Granada – The First 25 Years (London: British Film Institute, 1981), pp. 109–16.

74 *Macdonald, untitled analysis of recent *World in Action* series, 25 June 1975 (bf. 1340).

75 *'Left/right', undated/unattributed internal paper (bf. 1209); D. Boulton, *World in Action: The First Twenty-One Years* (booklet) (Granada Television, 1984), p. 13.

76 *Wallington, memo to Plowright, '*World in Action*', 4 March 1969 (bf. 0745).

77 *World in Action*: 'South of the border' – see Chapter 8.

78 'Torture and Persecution', Institute of Contemporary Arts, 6 December 1973.

79 *Minutes of Programme Committee meeting, 18 December 1975 (bf. 1061).

80 Fitzwalter, interview with the authors.

81 *Macdonald, untitled analysis of recent *World in Action* series.

82 *World in Action*: 'A day in the life of Kevin Donellon', 'Kevin at the crossroads', 'Born survivors', 'Victims of their success'.

83 *World in Action*: 'The coal inquiries', 'Three men and the Board', 'Mr Grimshaw sees it through'.

84 *Macdonald, memo to Forman, 2 August 1973 (bf. 1071), *Fitzwalter, memo to Forman, 'The Official Secrets Act', 16 August 1988 (bf. 1434).

85 *Macdonald, untitled analysis of recent *World in Action* series.

86 *World in Action*: 'The village that quit – well not exactly', 'The village that quit – 21 years on'.

87 *Press briefing for '*World in Action* – 30 years', 1993 (bf. 0692).

88 *World in Action*: 'The Ben Hunter way', 'Wanted: a home of their own', 'Out of mind'; see *The Times*, 13 May 1974, p. 8.

89 *Minutes of Programme Committee meeting, 23 May 1975 (bf. 1061); *The Times*, 13 May 1974, p. 8, 5 June 1974, p. 3, 7 February 1975, p. 3.

90 *Macdonald, untitled analysis of recent *World in Action* series.

91 *Macdonald, untitled analysis of recent *World in Action* series.

92 *Macdonald, untitled analysis of recent *World in Action* series.

93 *Macdonald, untitled analysis of recent *World in Action* series; *D. Crow, paper produced for Harry Watt, 'Granada's documentary track record', 6 February 1976 (bf. 1090).

94 Macdonald, 'A short history of group gropes'. For a discussion of the impact of John Birt and Peter Jay's 'Bias against understanding' articles, see Chapter 4.

95 *Macdonald, untitled analysis of recent *World in Action* series.

96 *Forman, appendix to letter to Sir B. Young, 'Some general notes on *World in Action*', 18 June 1973 (bf. 1071).

97 *Forman, letter to Young, 18 June 1973.

98 *The Times*, 15 November 1973, p. 4.

99 *Forman, 'Some general notes on *World in Action*'.

100 T. Williams, MP, quoted in *The Guardian*, 12 April 1975, p. 1.
101 *'Granada Television programmes on the tea estates', internal paper (bf. 1340); Granada internal telex to Macdonald (no author given), 23 April 1974 (bf. 1070).
102 *Macdonald, untitled analysis of recent *World in Action* series.
103 *The Times*, 21 April 1975, p. 1, 24 April 1975, p. 12; *A. Doig MP, letter to Independent Television Authority [sic], 22 April 1975 (bf. 0721); *Macdonald, letter to M. Gillies (IBA), 8 May 1975 (bf. 0721); A. Jowett, 'A world where making enemies is all in a day's work', *UK Press Gazette*, 2 April 1984: 11.
104 M. Gillard, *A Little Pot of Money: The Story of Reginald Maudling and the Real Estate Fund of America* (London: *Private Eye*/Andre Deutsch, 1974); Fitzwalter, interview with the authors.
105 Fitzwalter, interview with the authors.
106 *Plowright, undated internal paper outlining the implications of the IBA's ban (bf. 1208). See also Fitzwalter and Taylor, *Web of Corruption*; P. Goddard, 'Scandal at the regulator', *Television*, May 2006, pp. 28–9.
107 Interview with the authors.
108 *Fitzwalter, memo to Macdonald, 16 November 1973 (bf. 1071).
109 Fitzwalter, interview with the authors; *Daily Mail*, 7 May 1974, pp. 16–17; see Fitzwalter and Taylor, *Web of Corruption*.
110 Fitzwalter and Taylor, *Web of Corruption*: 246–7.
111 Fitzwalter, interview with the authors.
112 HC 490, 15 July 1977.
113 Interview with the authors.
114 *Plowright, memo to senior Granada executives, 'Maudling', 18 November 1977 (bf. 1209).
115 *The Times*, 23 April 1974, p.1.
116 *'From now till '72'.
117 Interview with the authors.

4

1975–88: the Fitzwalter years

'A misbegotten child of two ill-assorted parents'?

Although the late 1960s represented its most innovative period, 1975 could be argued to represent the peak of *World in Action*'s achievement. After eight years outstripping its rivals in popularity, innovation and, generally, impact, the series had by now amassed a fine track record and reputation, especially in the field of investigation. 'We have made more breakthroughs, with more vigour and courage than any of our competitors', claimed David Plowright.[1] By comparison, *Panorama* was widely thought of as dull, not least by the Annan Commission.[2] But 1975 was a difficult year for *World in Action*, with a virtual mutiny of programme staff (see Chapter 6), the nation's economic problems adversely affecting television profitability and the 'Birt–Jay thesis' calling established current affairs practices into question.

When John Birt and Peter Jay accused television news and current affairs of a 'bias against understanding' – for prioritising stories at the expense of sufficient concern with and explanation of issues and causes, and for falsely assuming that 'the macrocosm is the microcosm writ large' – the television industry responded with a collective shudder.[3] Industry fears were compounded when these criticisms were roundly endorsed by BBC and IBA chairmen and in letters to *The Times*. A public discussion of the role and methods of current affairs journalism was matched within companies themselves. Within Granada there was a robust rejection of much of Birt and Jay's analysis,[4] but the criticisms hit home. It was all too easy to recognise *World in Action*'s approach, with its concentration on 'stories' rather than 'issues' and on personal experience as a means of illustrating national circumstances, within Birt and Jay's critique. That this approach was partly responsible for the popularity and accessibility of *World in Action* (especially in comparison with Birt's *Weekend World* (London Weekend Television, 1972–88)) did nothing to allay Birt and Jay's charges of incoherence or their claims that it would lead to bad policy by engendering a political concentration on symptoms rather than causes. To make matters worse, Birt and Jay laid the blame firmly with programme-makers who saw more mileage in ' "concerned" interviews with victims of the system and "grabbing" interviews with the guilty landlord or council official' than in abstract analysis.[5] The problem, they claimed, was with television journalism itself:

> a misbegotten child of two ill-assorted parents, neither of which is well adapted to the needs of news analysis. One parent is the newspaper office, typically the local paper's newsroom. The other is the film business, more specifically the documentary film.[6]

As a result, they claimed, 'the documentary film ethos comes to contaminate . . . the choice and treatment of stories'.[7]

Jeremy Wallington was charged with Granada's response. He shared some of Birt and Jay's anxieties about television journalism: 'Most of the content of the many hours of journalistic programmes is second-hand'. But *World in Action* was an exception and could provide a way forward. It alone regularly competed with newspapers in broadcasting 'original news of their own discovery'. Wallington condemned 'bias against understanding' as a

> shaky and partisan concept, filled with political dangers for many capable and imaginative television journalists . . . Such phrases are like Triffids. The seed is scattered in the wind of speeches and writings of politicians and others until the television producer is so pinioned he can barely move.[8]

Rather than a way forward, 'bias against understanding' would represent a major setback if it were to be used to stunt the growth of television journalism, he suggested. The appeal of 'the cosy ways of "issue journalism"' was to those more familiar with *The Times* than the *Daily Mirror*, he continued: 'The fact that it does not connect with the great majority of viewers is, to them, of secondary importance.' In contrast, Wallington argued, the 'ingenuity' of *World in Action*'s approach, typified by the device of the back axle shipped to Rhodesia in 'Smith's back door', 'could lead to television being able to transmit, on a regular basis, programmes on the most abstract but elusive issues, while remaining popular'. Ironically, this was a problem that Birt and Jay had acknowledged – that issue journalism 'runs the risk of being boring'[9] – but to which they offered no coherent solution.

Looming over this debate was a gradual national decline in audiences for news and current affairs and a search for ways to revive audience interest.[10] Despite Board level misgivings at Granada about an exercise that was seen as self-serving on the part of Birt, and some introspection amongst the *World in Action* team, Birt and Jay's criticisms had little practical impact on the series.[11] Granada's chosen prescription was the opposite of theirs. In 1976, Denis Forman questioned whether current affairs programmes were made 'with enough art and skill to engage the audience', while suggestions were made that *World in Action*'s subjects were failing adequately to reflect contemporary society as they had in the 1960s and to communicate 'in an interesting fashion' with audiences.[12] This can be interpreted as a proposal for more, rather than less, story journalism and indeed, by 1980, with the Birt–Jay row having blown over, David Boulton's draft for the IBA's annual year book read:

> *World in Action* relies unashamedly on 'story journalism' . . . Good story-telling remains the most vivid, penetrating and, dare-it-be-said, popular technique for explaining and analysing the complex events of the world around us. For *World in Action*, life is a perpetual search for the relevant microcosm.[13]

Lapping and Fitzwalter

But if 1975 represented *World in Action*'s peak, there was no immediate decline. More accurately, the series rested on a plateau a little below this summit for the next five years before a series of programmes and events helped to reinvigorate it at the beginning of the 1980s. Gus Macdonald resumed day-to-day control of the series in September, with Boulton moved to 'Special Projects', but this was always intended as a short-term fix.[14] In July 1976 and for the next two years, *World in Action* passed into the hands of Brian Lapping and Ray Fitzwalter. Lapping's experience with the series was limited but he had a fine track record with Granada's sporadic political documentary strand, *State of the Nation* (1966–88) and his appointment could be expected to bolster *World in Action*'s political coverage. In early 1976, Lapping's *State of the Nation* team had produced a notable 60-minute contribution to *World in Action*, 'Chrysler and the cabinet', reconstructing the British cabinet's tortured decision to give aid to Chrysler to save its British car manufacturing interests. In a novel twist on drama-documentary, each participant was played by a well-informed journalist rather than an actor, using inside knowledge to reflect their standpoints and sometimes to speak their words.[15] As the senior partner, Lapping was given Macdonald's title of Executive Producer. But the appointment of Fitzwalter, then a distinguished journalist but with little production experience, represented a key moment in *World in Action*'s development. As Editor for more than 11 years and then as Executive Producer and Head of Current Affairs until his departure from Granada in 1993,

Fitzwalter's name was to become synonymous with *World in Action* and it with him. At the same time he became one of the most prominent and respected figures in television journalism, described by Forman as 'the arch-investigator of the murky corners of society', by Boulton as 'the longest-serving and best Editor *World in Action* has ever had' and by Patrick Stoddart as 'possibly the last man in British television to let a story get in the way of a good fact'.[16]

With the involvement of the team, Lapping and Fitzwalter set about the kind of re-evaluation of *World in Action*'s strengths and purposes that had become common over the years, sensing that the programme had not entirely recovered from the personnel difficulties of 1975 and was neither as inspirational nor as consistently successful as it had been. Discussions identified the strengths and aspirations of the *World in Action* approach as involving:

- 'journalistic rigour' (subjects and treatments should be worthwhile and 'our rational analysis [should be] put across with emotional impact');
- 'simple stories' (including a microcosmic approach to big issues where appropriate);
- stories that were original or at least told with a new clarity;
- a choice of subjects that reflected popular concerns;
- more stories able to reflect issues of mainstream national concern (a perceived weakness of the series at this point);
- 'instant response' to breaking news (this was to remain an area of acknowledged weakness, more for *World in Action* than its competitors, largely because of the difficulty of marrying journalistic ambition to the series' production routines);
- 'access films' that could let 'the viewer see for himself' (this reflects a faith in an observational approach akin to Macdonald's early 1970s 'narrative vérité' programmes but less prominent since).[17]

Based on such discussions, Lapping and Fitzwalter produced a list of 'the ingredients WIA needs' in March 1977 which is interesting in its reflection of the earlier, similar lists drawn up by Plowright and Macdonald (see Chapter 3) and also as a marker for the Fitzwalter years. It would be fair to say that they reflect an approach that was to change little during Fitzwalter's editorship:

1 New material – high journalistic ambition.
2 'Gropes' – thorough and original digging.
3 Mainstream topics – dealing with the central issues of public affairs that come to concern our viewers, and at the right time.
4 Observational topics – events as they actually happen to which we get real access . . .

5 The voice of the English working man or woman. And we want to add:

6 Sheer bloody surprises: the outstanding example was 'Mick Jagger' . . . We should aim to transmit at least one outrageous and improbable programme each year.[18]

'We have not exactly hit the bullseye in any of these', they went on. 'What it all has to add up to is an increase in our frequency of attaining peaks: programmes which stand out in the memory years after transmission.' *World in Action* continued effectively to fulfil its role and to draw audiences to a wide range of subjects and approaches under Lapping and Fitzwalter, but their partnership produced few programmes that were wholly successful by this measure. In early 1978, team criticism of 'the failure to produce a major breakthrough in programme-making techniques' remained.[19] However, three programmes at least stand out in retrospect as being of particular continuing interest, partly for the controversy they caused. Unusually for the series, the best known was a political interview. In early 1978, beginning the campaign that was to culminate in her 1979 election victory, Margaret Thatcher used *World in Action* as a platform for her notorious and carefully calculated remarks about immigration: 'People are really rather afraid that this country might be rather swamped by people with a different culture'.[20] These sentiments catapulted their speaker and the series to the front pages of the following day's papers, as pundits analysed them for hints of a racist or populist agenda, and set the tone for much of the ensuing campaign. But the controversy was essentially a product of the careful calculation of her campaign team and *World in Action*'s involvement was largely fortuitous.

Perhaps unsurprisingly, the other two programmes were both investigative. 'Made in Hong Kong' involved a return to Hong Kong, this time to reveal the exploitation of child labour in toy factories and the inadequacy and corruption of the Labour Inspectorate. As a *World in Action* team conducted research and preliminary interviews in Hong Kong, a front-page article headed 'Soviet cash for mystery group in Hong Kong' appeared in the Hong Kong *Star*. Its claims, that the 'foreign leftist' film-makers questioning residents were Soviet spies intent on embarrassing the colony, were repeated in other papers. Granada took these allegations very seriously and immediately sued for libel, both to safeguard the reputations of team members and because such smears could easily threaten *World in Action*'s standing and access throughout the world. The smears damaged the programme too – interviewees and suppliers ceased to co-operate, the distraction and the need for this toy-related edition to meet its pre-Christmas slot meant that filming and editing had to be rushed, the time taken forced the crew to abort a proposed Singapore-based programme that had been planned as part of the same trip.[21] But the damage to both programme and reputation seems to have been limited. 'Made in Hong Kong' sold well overseas, including to Hong Kong, and the libel actions were eventually settled in Granada's favour.

'Buying time' was the culmination of a year of investigations involving clandestine filming and extreme secrecy following tip-offs that drugs and guns were being smuggled into prisons in Wakefield and Liverpool by prison officers.[22] The subterfuge involved in proving the allegations required the team to push investigative journalism to it legal and regulatory limits. Nonetheless, as a result of the programme, prison officers were suspended and *World in Action* was confident that the evidence gathered would support charges against them. But, rather than welcoming the evidence, Merseyside Police conducted hostile interviews with the team and implied that it must have been obtained under duress. West Yorkshire Police were less hostile, compiling a report about the Wakefield officer's conspiracy for the Director of Public Prosecutions, who took no action, and prosecuting him for theft.[23] In the course of their investigation, other crimes at Wakefield were solved including a murder. But in 1981, the prison officer was acquitted after the *World in Action* film was deemed inadmissible as evidence and sued Granada for libel. Despite the team's pride in the investigation and gratitude for the support from West Yorkshire Police, this proved to be a frustrating result for the programme-makers. Not only had a year-long investigation providing *prima facie* evidence failed to produce a single conviction, but three years of further work had been needed to support the various legal consequences.

After two years, Lapping chose to return to programme-making. His replacement was Allan Segal, a *World in Action* producer since 1972. Both he and Fitzwalter had the title of Joint Editor but as the more experienced editor it was clear that Fitzwalter was the senior partner. A change of personnel was perhaps to be welcomed. Earlier that year, Granada's Programme Committee had recognised that:

> The programme achieves a high level of competence, but the old flair for
> publicity, wit and showmanship does not seem to be there any more
> ... [A] more regular change at the top should ideally be part of the
> normal procedure.[24]

In the event, Segal's joint editorship lasted until April 1981, at which point the future shape of the series, in particular a perceived need for reinvigoration, and of its management structure became the subject of a series of discussions at senior level, initiated by David Boulton as Executive Producer, Current Affairs. Out of these discussions came a decision that Fitzwalter should become sole editor of *World in Action*, a position he was to occupy until late 1987.

1980: 'a new self-confidence'

Regardless of the management concerns that were to emerge, 1980 was a momentous year for the series, marked by a series of high profile investigative programmes and accompanying controversies. In Boulton's assessment, *World in Action* 'exhibited a new self-confidence' in 1980 and 'above all, it recovered its investigative muscle'.[25] 'Investigative muscle', of course, reflected Fitzwalter's biggest strength. 'The man who bought United' was one such muscular investigation, revealing the involvement of Louis Edwards, major shareholder of Manchester United, in a slush fund and other corrupt financial practices. Some of the evidence for this came in a phone conversation between Edwards and a shareholder, recorded by the team without Edwards' knowledge and played in the programme, raising an interesting ethical dilemma. This practice drew strong criticism from the IBA and from the *Daily Express*.[26] The revelations about Edwards, however, caused a sizeable public splash: police requested a transcript and video and launched an investigation, Manchester MPs asked for a Department of Trade inquiry, a club shareholder sought an Extraordinary General Meeting and Edwards' successors (he died four weeks after transmission) began a libel action.[27] With United a vital part of the culture of Granada's home region, this programme also demonstrated *World in Action*'s independence from local commercial considerations. Later, Fitzwalter noted unapologetically that: 'Granada had a hard time at Manchester United for a long time after our programme on the club'.[28]

Ambitious investigations were also mounted into the supply of armaments to South Africa and into a company exploiting legal and barely-legal schemes to enable its affluent customers to avoid taxation. Both programmes involved a wealth of detailed research and told tales of great complexity. 'South Africa's bombshell' uncovered the trail, involving no fewer than 11 countries, through which South Africa had obtained the means to manufacture nuclear field artillery from leading arms manufacturers in Britain and the USA, contravening the international embargo. It was praised by critics and received first prize at the Monte Carlo Television Festival, but Joan Bakewell, whilst commending the detail in *World in Action*'s account, pointed to the difficulty of telling such a story comprehensibly on television without the opportunity to re-read that could be offered by a newspaper article.[29] 'The Rossminster affair' told of the Inland Revenue's biggest tax fraud investigation, looking at a series of schemes that involved senior MPs and other public figures, bribery allegations and a potential fraud of £500m. The complexity of the case and the difficulty of obtaining pictures led Fitzwalter to reject it three times as a programme idea, but the eventual report was described as 'gripping'.[30]

In the same year, 'The trials of Stanley Adams', the third of four exposés of Hoffman-La Roche, the Swiss pharmaceutical conglomerate, told the classic tale of a whistleblower. In 1975, 'The Roche affair' had revealed that Adams, formerly a Roche product manager, had reported the company's illegal trading practices to the EEC only to be charged himself and imprisoned for industrial espionage following an EEC indiscretion. The following year, after the catastrophic release of dioxins at the company's Seveso plant, *World in Action* mounted a programme ('Living dangerously') looking at the causes and consequences of the disaster. This programme had the dubious distinction of being 'blacked' by the local ACTT shop after it was found that crew filming near Seveso had been unwittingly exposed to dangerous health risks, although the union relented after a Granada apology.[31] 'The trials of Stanley Adams' updated the earlier account of Adams' case, including the tragic suicide of his wife while he was being held incommunicado, and discussed the need for legal protection for whistleblowers and compensation for Adams. In presenting it, *World in Action* reverted to a practice used in earlier investigations such as *The Rise and Fall of John Poulson*, where an in-vision presenter, in this case Boulton, was used to anchor a complex story. It was one of very few *World in Action* programmes to be repeated, after the European Court of Justice upheld Adams' compensation claim in 1985. In 'The trails of Hoffman', in 1983, the series returned to Seveso to examine the legacy of the disaster and Hoffman-La Roche's subsequent actions.

Another investigation deriving from a whistleblower was 'Mr Kane's campaign', in which several earlier *World in Action* themes – Hong Kong, official secrecy and trouble with the IBA – seemed to coincide.[32] Kane, a former radio operator at the British intelligence listening post in Hong Kong, presented allegations of a long-standing and wholly lax policy towards security at the post over many years, with no attempt to keep classified documents secret and thefts, defections and missing documents covered up. The programme's genesis was unusual. Kane first approached the *New Statesman* but asked that a television company should also be involved to give his story the widest circulation. Thus *World in Action* was asked to collaborate on an on-going press story.

Having met Kane and satisfied himself that the story was worthy of pursuit by *World in Action*, Fitzwalter sent a team to corroborate his claims, a difficult task involving smuggled equipment and snatched filming due to the refusal of the Foreign Office and GCHQ to co-operate and to Hong Kong sources' fears of repercussions under the Official Secrets Act.[33] By this time, the *Daily Mirror* was also involved and there was pressure to publish. A transmission date of 12 May was initially agreed, but it was put back for a week for further work. However, the *Mirror* and the *New Statesman* still published in the week of 12 May.[34] At this point, the IBA had not approved the programme for transmission and, when Boulton and Mike Scott were shown it, they felt that it was still not satisfactory. However, the early publication was fortuitous. In the light of the press revelations, David Ennals MP realised that he had been ill-advised about the situation in Hong Kong for which he was the responsible minister, raised the issue in parliament and asked that his contribution to the programme could be re-recorded, giving a new topical hook to it.

With a fresh interview with Ennals included and Boulton now satisfied, Granada sought last-minute IBA approval for transmission on 19 May. The IBA's officers refused; the programme 'could be in breach of the Official Secrets Act in a manner that could be prejudicial to national security', they ruled.[35] IBA officers' ideas of what could have been prejudicial in the programme seem to have largely been based on conjecture although, according to Fitzwalter, Lady Plowden admitted to consulting an unidentified 'outside source'. But this self-censorship was ironic given both the subject of the programme and the IBA's concerns about exterior shots of GCHQ. Despite proving problematic in the 1973 'Secrets' programme, these had been shown on television many times since. 'Far from being a breach of national security', argued Fitzwalter, 'bringing attention to the state of affairs would be an argument for an improvement in national security'.[36] But in making the programme, *World in Action* had ignored the D-Notice Committee on the premise that its 'advice' was unenforceable. Called to give evidence before the Commons Select Committee on Defence on this matter, Boulton explained:

> We chose to ignore the advice of the two D-notices concerned. We chose to ride the fact that we were technically breaching the Official Secrets Act because we felt that there was an overriding public duty to do so.[37]

For the IBA, D-Notices and the Official Secrets Act warranted a more rigorous attitude. In spite of this, the publication of the *New Statesman* and *Daily Mirror* articles had already placed most of the programme's revelations in the public domain. 'Cosmetic changes', including the removal of the GCHQ exteriors, eventually persuaded the Authority to change its position and 'Mr Kane's campaign' was finally shown on 9 June 1980.

'Mr Kane's campaign' illustrated the awkwardness of close collaborations between *World in Action* and the press. Naturally, from time to time, the series would find itself investigating issues that were also of interest to newspapers and, as part of a wider journalistic community, members of the programme team would routinely be in contact with journalists working elsewhere. Granada seldom prevented its journalists from writing occasional features for the press and such features also became an increasingly common way of publicising forthcoming *World in Action* programmes. Rarely, team members worked regularly for the press, the most prominent example being Michael Gillard's long-standing contributions to *Private Eye*'s 'City Slicker' column, although the occasional conflicts of interest that arose from Gillard's dual role embarrassed Granada on more than one occasion. In these ways, relatively informal collaborations between *World in Action* and the press were a regular aspect of the series, although rigid secrecy was always maintained over stories where necessary. Formal collaborations, as with 'Mr Kane's campaign', were much less common and even here information was traded with care and confined to material already known of by the other parties or that the programme could not use, partly to protect the exclusivity of more sensitive information in *World in Action*'s possession.[38] Operational differences between television current affairs programmes and the press exacerbated the difficulties of such collaborations: a daily newspaper can publish at its convenience whereas a current affairs series generally has to meet a single weekly slot; heavier regulation meant that television required a higher standard of corroborative evidence than did the press; when two organisations break a story the later one (generally television) risks the prospect of an injunction issued against it on the basis of the earlier publication. The involvement of the *New Statesman* in 'Mr Kane's campaign' pointed up a further difficulty: the perception of impartiality was vital to *World in Action* both for its standing with the IBA and for its own credibility, so the appearance of material credited to the series in an avowedly left-wing journal caused much disquiet both at Granada and at the IBA, particularly when the *New Statesman* referred to the programme as having been 'suppressed' by the IBA at the behest of MI6.[39]

World in Action only worked so closely with the press on two other occasions. 'When in Rome' revealed systematic payments from Shell and BP to Italian political parties in return for tax concessions involving the corruption of Prime Minister Andreotti.[40] Italian legal documents leaked to a senior *World in Action* researcher provided its source but the volume of information was such that Wallington agreed to share the investigation with distinguished *Sunday Times* journalist Godfrey Hodgson. As a result, Hodgson joined the investigating team, revealing part of the story in his paper with extensive credit to the series before acting as in-vision reporter (and 'detective hero'[41]) in the one-hour *World in Action* report the following day. 'A question for Europe', coinciding with the Italian elections and examining the wider questions about multinationals' relations with governments and the EEC that the Italian case raised, was shown as a follow-up two months later, this time without the involvement of the *Sunday Times*. 'Jonathan of Arabia', the joint *World in Action/Guardian* investigation into cabinet minister Jonathan Aitken's undisclosed links with the Saudi royal family was the other major collaboration. The investigation was initiated by the *Guardian*'s David Pallister following a tip-off to its editor from Mohamed Al-Fayed, but *World in Action* producer David Leigh was closely connected with the newspaper and quickly became intrigued. Eventually, the investigative effort was shared to the extent that Pallister received a programme credit. The clinching evidence with which the Guardian and *World in Action* defeated Aitken's subsequent libel action was found by a *Guardian* journalist and by a solicitor working for *World in Action* – leading, of course, to a follow-up programme.[42] The end credits for 'Jonathan of Arabia – Act two: The dagger of deceit' name not only the *Guardian* and *World in Action* personnel who worked on the investigation but also their legal teams at the libel trial! In one other instance, *World in Action* agreed an unusually co-operative deal with journalists from the BBC's *Man Alive* when each found the other preparing a programme based on the revelations of a civil servant whose exposure of waste and recommendations for cost-savings at the Ministry of Public Buildings and Works had been deliberately suppressed.[43]

Despite the quality and significance of these investigations, the story of *World in Action* in 1980 is dominated by the fallout from a single programme, 'The steel papers'.[44] Against the background of a lengthy strike in Britain's nationalised steel industry, *World in Action* was already preparing a report on the issues involved when, quite unexpectedly, 250 sensitive documents came into the team's possession from a British Steel Corporation source who insisted only that his anonymity be safeguarded. They included BSC minutes and demonstrated that key aspects of the Corporation's case were known to be untrue and that government pressure had brought about the strike – patently revelations of considerable public interest. The Corporation was informed that *World in Action* had the documents, a calculated risk since BSC could have sought an injunction preventing their use, but Sir Charles Villiers, its chairman, was happy to be interviewed for the programme, telling the *Daily Mail* afterwards that BSC had been given 'a pretty fair hearing'.[45] But after 'The steel papers' was transmitted, BSC's attitude hardened and an injunction requiring the return of the documents was granted. When they were returned with identifying marks removed in order to protect the source, a High Court order followed requiring that he be named. Granada appealed but lost at the Appeal Court and again before the Law Lords. Its case had rested on the fact that the source's name was known only to his Granada contact, Laurie Flynn, a *World in Action* researcher. Flynn, an experienced freelance, refused to disclose his source, referring to him only as M. Ole (mole). By now the situation was extremely serious: having exhausted the appeals process, Granada was to pay a fine escalating for each day that the source remained unidentified. Moreover, Forman and Plowright faced the prospect of imprisonment for not revealing a name that even they did not know. Flynn himself was not a party to the proceedings. Granada's executives had no contractual powers to insist that he named his source and no hesitation in supporting the principle that the source should be protected – a remarkable example of a television company protecting its journalistic integrity, and standing by a pledge given by one of its staff, regardless of the financial consequences. Granada's insurers had long since expressed their unwillingness to support the action, so the cost could easily have ruined the company. A further problem facing Forman was: 'enterprising members of staff who, wishing to share in the glory of martyrdom, would tell us darkly that they too had some knowledge of the identity of the mole'.[46] Whether true or not, he and Plowright quickly dismissed such claims. The resolution to this impasse was fortuitous, facilitated by the appointment of a new BSC chairman who judged that continuing to act against Granada would achieve little except damaged public relations. It was rumoured that BSC had identified the source internally. On 16 August, three weeks after the Law Lords' judgement and more than six months since 'The steel papers' had been shown, the threat to Granada was lifted – it was to pay the full costs of the case and undertake never to repeat the programme. After some negotiation, BSC authorised the showing of an uncontroversial extract in a retrospective programme in 1984[47] but to this day copies in the Granada archive are labelled: 'There is an injunction still being held against Granada by British Steel. This production can never be transmitted'. Two months later, a humble Conservative-voting BSC records officer confessed to being the source. Flynn, he said, had been so determined to protect him at all costs that: 'It crossed my mind several times that he wanted to be martyred'.[48]

Besides the legal dramas and the gravity of the penalties faced by Granada, the case can be seen as a landmark in its implications for journalists' relations with their sources. For Lord Denning, who presided over the Appeal Court hearing, it was no less than 'the most controversial case of modern times'.[49] In clarifying the protection given under the law to journalists refusing to disclose their sources, Denning introduced a test of responsibility: Although breach of confidence alone was not sufficient reason to compel disclosure, 'if a newspaper should act irresponsibly then it forfeits its claim to protect its sources of information'.[50] In his judgement, Granada had abused its power in giving insufficient notice to BSC that it had the documents, in not allowing Villiers to see the programme's script before his interview and in allowing Villiers' to be 'cross-examined' by the interviewer, Tony Wilson, whose conduct was 'deplorable'. Moreover, to mutilate documents that were the property of BSC to prevent identification of the source was 'disgraceful . . . as bad as the obstruction of a witness'.[51] In Granada's view, Denning was mistaken on the first three points: BSC had been given as much notice as possible – more than 24 hours – when *World in Action* had decided which documents it could use in the programme; on arrival, the BSC chairman was given a full script to read; his interview, in which Wilson 'was not impolite and only interrupted twice', was shown uncut.[52] In fact, Villiers had been treated more considerately than was common at *World in Action* in such circumstances. Scripts were rarely available to be shown to interviewees and it was normal that interviews were cut to length. The question of the mutilated documents relates to the wider illogicality of Denning's judgement. Hitherto, the public interest had generally been held to justify protection for the identity of sources since, without it, such individuals would be discouraged from divulging secret information where its disclosure was in the public interest. But under Denning's test, the maintenance of anonymity depended upon the 'responsible' behaviour of those to whom the information was disclosed, something that no whistleblower could rely on or control. Here, the mutilation of documents, an act intended to protect the source, became in itself a cause for him to be named. The effect of the ruling was that the private interest of BSC in locating a disloyal employee was held to outweigh the public interest in his disclosures.

Not surprisingly, journalists were robust in their support for Granada's stance and their reaction against Denning's judgement. Immediate criticism came from the Institute of Journalists, the Campaign for Press Freedom and the National Union of Journalists, which called the ruling 'disgraceful'.[53] The *Observer*'s leader was headed 'Why Denning is an ass'. A highly critical *Times* leader brought forth support from Michael Foot and from eight senior figures from BBC Current Affairs, amongst others.[54] The Director-General of the BBC and the Chairman of the Press Council added their voices when the ruling was upheld by the Law Lords, while another *Times* leader called it 'restrictive, reactionary and against the public interest', arguing that it would:

> have the effect of inhibiting journalistic investigation of corruption, malpractice and incompetence . . . Informants will be more wary of providing information to journalists, fearing disclosure of their identity, and reporters . . . may no longer feel themselves confident in making promises of confidentiality. The consequence will be that secrecy will prevail, and that the possibility of a cover-up by institutions with something to hide will become that much easier.[55]

'You have presented the case with great conviction and in a manner that we all admire', responded Forman in a grateful letter to the editor of *The Times*, indicating also that it was Denning's charge of 'irresponsibility', advanced 'by people who have no knowledge of the normal procedures of journalism' and never countered by the Law Lords, that weighed most heavily on Granada's journalists.[56] The judgement also provoked political reaction: some ministers were reportedly uneasy at the verdicts, the Prime Minister said that the issues raised should be considered by the Law Commission and one MP introduced a Private Members Bill to safeguard the protection of sources.[57] Despite defeat and the threat of ruin in the most serious legal battle it had ever faced, Granada's attitude was largely self-congratulatory, at least at *World in Action*. Boulton told the team:

> WIA in 1980 generated more column inches in the news pages than in any year I can remember. It made news and created issues . . . It got talked about, argued about in pubs and buses as well as legal and parliamentary chambers . . . Backed to the hilt by DF [Forman] and the whole board, it took the brunt of a bruising fight for principle and emerged with honour intact. Whatever else it was, it wasn't a dull year; and for these achievements, congratulations all round.[58]

But the steel case had an even wider impact. Following a Labour amendment, a new paragraph, referred to by Lord Goodman as 'the Granada Section', was added to the Contempt of Court Bill then in parliament.[59]

For the first time, journalists were given a qualified statutory right to protect the confidentiality of their sources. And in a strange reversal, Denning claimed in his memoirs that 'on reconsideration' he believed that he should have found for Granada after all.[60]

Into the eighties

As the 1980s continued, *World in Action* continued to occupy its hallowed place at the heart of the ITV schedule and of British public affairs. Outwardly, it appeared to maintain the format, thematic agenda and investigative approach that had made it the pre-eminent current affairs series of the 1970s. In practice, however, it was beginning to face a growing variety of pressures. Nationally the popularity and perceived salience of television current affairs seemed to be in decline, but within Granada there were also budgetary, technological and labour relations pressures and a general perception that the series had lost its innovative edge and risked staleness. As early as 1980, David Boulton was writing that the form of most *World in Action*s had hardly changed since 1968 and that they lacked the arresting visuals and scripting that had characterised the series ten years earlier.[61] Looking back, these pressures seem to mark the first hints of decline for the series, but this cannot have been clear to those involved at the time. In the next chapter we look in detail at the nature of these pressures, steps taken to address them and the much greater pressures faced by the series in the 1990s. But *World in Action* continued to produce programmes of considerable quality and significance, even into its final years. Here we examine some of the more notable editions of the early and mid-1980s.

In one way, changing consumption patterns in news and current affairs could benefit *World in Action*. Writing in 1982, Fitzwalter noted a shift in news and current affairs coverage from the press to broadcasting ('papers no longer provide us with competition') and a move away from 'enquiring journalism' in all media, leaving a 'demand that is simply not met'. 'More often than in the past', he wrote, 'we are being approached from outside – asked to put our journalistic muscle into specific projects'. With *World in Action*'s (and its editor's) existing strengths in this field, Fitzwalter reasoned that: 'the time has come to go for more watchdog television in a more full blooded way'.[62] With television now dominant in breaking news and topical coverage, still an acknowledged weakness for the series, Fitzwalter was advocating a competitive role for *World in Action* in exploiting its distinctiveness: 'Greater exclusivity, the promise that *World in Action* might bring you something different that mattered, should be worth more'. His prescription for the series – 'investigations, foreign stories with an angle, social enquiry' and a redevelopment of 'access and observation'[63] – sums up well its main concerns over the next few years.

Outside approaches never became commonplace but one particular example, 'The set up', stands out.[64] A law centre solicitor contacted *World in Action* producer John Ware claiming that detectives had threatened to frame his client for heroin possession unless he organised an armed robbery that would implicate another man. Persuaded that the allegation was worth pursuing, Ware had only two-and-a-half hours to meet, assess and conceal a tape recorder on the man before his next meeting with the detectives. Hidden still and video cameras were used to capture later meetings. By the time the man went into hiding to avoid the detectives, the team had acquired enough evidence to persuade lawyers and the IBA to clear the programme. It was hastily edited over the following weekend and shown unbilled in place of the planned edition of *World in Action*, a mere 19 days after Ware received the initial phone-call. In a *coup de thèatre*, Scotland Yard's complaints investigation bureau were given details of the programme's evidence 15 minutes before transmission. Plainly, the series was still delivering investigative journalism that accorded with Fitzwalter's perception of demand and remained bold enough to shoulder the associated risks of non-transmission. 'The set up' was shown in the same year as Fitzwalter's oft-quoted speech to the Edinburgh International Television Festival in which he asked 'Can the whistle keep on blowing?' and responded with a sharp burst on a whistle of his own.[65] But this was not a rash attachment to investigation: 'You can't use these techniques indiscriminately', he warned. 'They must be justified.'[66]

Certainly investigative journalism was by now the subject of growing pressures. For one thing its 'victims' had become more litigious. It was in the nature of such programmes that law suits would be threatened and sometimes started, but in 1983 *World in Action* had suffered its first legal defeat for many years. A court awarded £20,000 in libel damages to a plain clothes policeman, seen in shot, unidentified, for two seconds in a 1981 programme about police corruption ('A conflict of evidence').[67] Granada paid twice that amount in 1986 to settle another case brought by a dentist who was the subject of a brief factual reference in 'Drilling for gold', a 1984 programme about dentists' abuse of the NHS payments system.[68] Both libels were unwitting but, in common with similar cases against other programmes, they reflected a growing willingness to sue.

Much more serious, however, was the adoption by large companies of sophisticated tactics to delay or restrain transmission of critical programmes, a practice that emerged out of *World in Action*'s fight with Barratt Homes, the national housebuilder. 'Your home in their hands', part of a two-programme investigation into flawed building techniques in June 1983, was concerned with Barratt's timber frame construction methods and the risks of fire and rot that arose from claims about Barratt's faulty workmanship. Fears at Barratt and in the building industry about its findings prompted the National House Building Council publicly to make a pre-emptive approach to the IBA two days before transmission, claiming that the programme would have a 'wrong perspective' and lack balance. On this occasion, the IBA was unmoved and the programme went ahead.[69] Both Barratt and the NHBC responded by making complaints about the programme to the IBA and then to the newly-established Broadcasting Complaints Commission, Barratt claiming that it had suffered 'treatment which is unjust or unfair' under the 1981 Broadcasting Act, the NHBC claiming a breach of the IBA's own guidelines.[70] Barratt also made very public claims about the damage that the programme had done to its business, blaming it for a slump in profits and the loss of 1,000 house sales.[71]

In January 1984, with more material on Barratt now available, including some prompted by viewers' responses to 'Your home in their hands', *World in Action* began to prepare 'Your starter for life', a follow-up programme looking at Barratt's mass-marketing of starter home packages including furnishings, legal fees and mortgages for first-time buyers.[72] Barratt not only withheld co-operation but embarked on a campaign to obstruct, delay and discredit it. In February, responding to advance notice of the planned programme and a request for an interview, Barratt asked for further information about the programme's aims. By March they were also seeking a preview before agreeing to co-operate. Even if the programme had been complete, it was always *World in Action* policy not to give previews to participants and the request was politely declined. Barratt then sought to thwart the programme on several fronts: a press conference was held with the intention of publicly discrediting research by *World in Action* and the Royal Institute of Chartered Surveyors into first time buyers' satisfaction with starter home packages, Barratt's lawyers wrote to Granada and the IBA expressing concern about the programme's fairness and seeking details of interviewees complaints, Barratt attempted to pressurise other participants – a mortgage lender, the Royal Institute of Chartered Surveyors, aggrieved householders – to withdraw from the programme and make statements against Granada. Such statements as Barratt managed to obtain, and several dossiers of complaints about Granada, were sent successively to the IBA by Barratt's lawyers, who also asked that the IBA require Granada to grant Barratt a preview. This was followed by a request for written assurances that the full Authority would preview the programme before transmission. Barratt and Granada met separately with the IBA at the end of April and with one another on 9 May but Barratt continued to insist that no interview could be granted without a preview. Smelling a rat, *World in Action* still refused: a preview would be 'a breach of fundamental principle'.[73]

By now, IBA officers were becoming rattled and sought legal advice. They had recently lost a court case brought by Mary Whitehouse because *Scum*, the borstal movie which Channel 4 had screened the previous June, had been passed for transmission without a referral to the full Authority.[74] As a result the IBA were extremely sensitive to criticism of their procedures and fearful of a further legal challenge. The *Scum* case probably provided the inspiration for Barratt's tactics. While the IBA's lawyer advised that a preview was necessary, Granada's did not, but Granada now felt that it had no option to agree to one and, after some delay on Barratt's part, this was arranged for 14 June. At the end of the screening, Fitzwalter recalls asking the Barratt team for a convenient interview date:

> And there were three of them, and they said, 'what interview?' And they'd no intention of doing an interview at all. And the IBA were conned. And we rang the IBA and said that they are not only not prepared to do an interview, they never expected to, all they wanted to do was to come and take notes on what was in the programme so that they could attack it before it was transmitted, which is what they did.[75]

The following day the IBA's solicitors received yet another lengthy and detailed request for amendments from Barratt's legal team.[76] When 'Your starter for life' was finally transmitted on 18 June, Barratt called a press conference at 3pm where it used its detailed knowledge of the content to launch a pre-emptive attack on the programme. As Mike Scott put it:

> One consequence of such a situation is that reception of the programme can be coloured by a print journalist's report, not about the programme, nor about its content, but about allegations of a television team's misconduct, which although we know to be untrue, makes a more interesting story. Certainly it seemed to me that the *Times* report on Tuesday morning showed a much greater interest in Barratt's allegations about Granada than in the important things we had to say.[77]

In the event, the programme did contain the long-awaited interview, shown – in accordance with Barratt's demands – uncut at the programme's close. As a result, this edition of *World in Action* ran five minutes longer than usual.

Although the edition went ahead, Barratt's obstructiveness, described by the *Sunday Times* as a 'game of cat and mouse' with Granada, largely succeeded.[78] Fitzwalter complained that 'the programme has been made excessively dull and has been toned down as a result of the pressure applied to it' by the IBA at Barratt's insistence.[79] Other programmes also suffered as a result of scheduling uncertainty caused by the three month delay and the lack of 'due editorial attention' available to them.[80] Negotiations over 'Your starter for life' and the need to prepare submissions for the BCC's investigation into 'Your home in their hands' took enormous amounts of staff time away from the preparation of programmes to the extent that Scott was moved to propose reinforcements to the team.[81] No less worrying were 'the outstanding number of allegations' made publicly against *World in Action*'s reputation, ranging from the trivial to some which, in Fitzwalter's opinion, were 'plainly defamatory'.[82] Nor was this merely the understandable action of a business seeking to preserve its reputation in the face of attack. In a notable legal opinion on the programme for Granada, Richard Rampton QC not only passed it for broadcast but stressed 'the special public interest factor and the need to transmit as early as possible because the affected public had no recourse to any organisation to ventilate their concerns'.[83] Besides gathering enough information to attack its contents publicly, delaying the programme had been Barratt's main objective, as their lawyer acknowledged to Fitzwalter:

> He said, 'I can't stop this programme but I can drive it out of the house-selling season' . . . And what he was aiming at, you see, it should have gone out when most people are starting to buy houses, towards Easter and he got it to late June, and he was trying to drive it into August. And it was really cynical.[84]

More generally, this attack on the practices of current affairs journalism set a grave precedent. Speaking in 1984, Fitzwalter outlined the problem for programme-makers:

> Detectable in all this is a double standard of behaviour. Such complaints properly demand fairness of treatment and they get it in good measure; they watch to see whether a programme-maker coughs or sneezes lest there be an opportunity to allege that he is guilty of some new misdemeanour. But they may act by a different code . . . at every opportunity they may allege bias, using different standards of evidence from those they properly demand of programme-makers.[85]

The success of Barratt's tactics, both in harrying the IBA and in obtaining a preview, gave rise to imitation, most notably involving a programme shown the following month. Part of 'Business in Oman' (its title perhaps a conscious back-reference to 'Business in Gozo', one of the programmes exposing the corruption of John Poulson) involved an investigation into the death in custody of Robin Walsh, the British secretary to the Tender Board at the Omani Ministry of Defence. In late June 1984, solicitors for the Sultanate wrote to the IBA seeking a preview on the grounds that *World in Action* had not accepted help with the programme from the Sultanate (in fact, help had been sought but not given) and consequently that statutory requirements for due impartiality 'may not be complied with'.[86] When a preview was refused, the Sultanate sought an order in the High Court requiring the IBA to fulfil its impartiality obligations, based on unattributed statements that the programme might turn out to be unfair. The Court refused to grant it, but did require the IBA to give an undertaking to ensure that the programme complied with the Act.[87] So the Sultanate had succeeded in securing a preview for the programme before a meeting of the full Authority, where it would be subject to much more stringent scrutiny than was normal. Under pressure, and wary of the resulting publicity, the Authority did order changes. Fitzwalter was furious:

> That put us in great difficulty because it's the last programme in the series. They went to court I think on the Thursday before we transmitted on the following Monday, and then the IBA came on to us on the Friday demanding this and demanding that. And there's no doubt they damaged that programme, they weakened it and we had nothing else to transmit, and the programme – we didn't feel we could save it till the Autumn and it was an outrageous example really of a foreign government being able to push the IBA about.[88]

Like the Barratt case, this appeared to Fitzwalter to be an example of a legal loophole, to be

> exploited against the public interest in favour of someone, usually someone with money and power, often both, who would rather most people did not know . . . No public body is normally ordered to do what it normally does.[89]

Further attempts to apply this doctrine of prior restraint to current affairs journalism so that vested interests could be protected soon arose. One involved the *TV Eye* series (Thames 1979–86); in another British Nuclear Fuels sought a preview of a proposed *World in Action* programme before deciding whether to co-operate. In the latter case, Mike Scott managed to persuade the IBA not to concede a blanket right of preview to those under investigation.[90] Thereafter, to the surprise and relief of current affairs programme-makers, the practice disappeared as quickly as it had arrived.

Beyond the investigative sphere, *World in Action* continued to pursue a wide-ranging and distinctive agenda. This was a period marked by substantial topical stories – urban riots, the Falklands war, the miners' strike. Of course, *World in Action* felt the need to contribute to an understanding of each, even though such stories belonged to the territory in which the series tended to be least successful. For Boulton, 'the basic task of any current affairs series' was 'to illuminate current issues'; for the team, such stories could not be ignored 'if we are to maintain a serious claim to comprehensive current affairs coverage', but in practice coverage had often been 'woefully inadequate'.[91] Besides periodic suggestions, never fully taken up, that *World in Action* form an 'instant response unit' prepared to respond swiftly to breaking stories, one solution occasionally adopted was described as the 'cheated "instant response" (prepared before the event)'.[92] By a remarkable coincidence, a programme on street crime in Toxteth ('A dangerous age') was already due for transmission on the next Monday when rioting broke out there at the weekend, so the series not only appeared authoritative in covering a topical story in Granada's own region but a ready-made set of contacts were available to contribute to a follow-up programme ('Toxteth revisited') that was shown two weeks later.

The response to the Falklands crisis was patchier in outcome but the most extensive in the series' history. In a sequence of seven programmes (5 April to 7 June 1982), five were devoted to the Falklands, all but one abandoning the narration-over-film format for the extra responsiveness of studio presentation. As well as political and military aspects, they examined public perceptions and the war's cost, financially and personally. One programme represented the culmination of 'The Falklands 100', following the 'Granada 500' model, in which a representative studio audience interrogated political and military figures about the war and were polled daily. For this programme, 75 viewers were also able to vote by computer link in an early experiment in interactive television. Denis Forman congratulated the team for 'Britain on the brink', the earliest Falklands programme ('WIA is so seldom a fast-reactor . . .'),[93] but a programme five weeks later, 'Falklands – United Nations talks', on international attempts to broker a deal between Britain and Argentina, provoked 'WIA's own Falklands crisis'.[94] For the only time as *World in Action* Editor, Fitzwalter failed to deliver a programme for transmission and a standby was shown instead. The team identified several causes for this symptom of 'our inability to react with speed and authority to major domestic and international stories': principally a lack of studio expertise and equipment exacerbated by the programme's 'traditional disdain for studios' but also a sense that Fitzwalter's own expertise was better suited to long-running investigations than fast-breaking stories.[95] Taking his responsibilities seriously, Fitzwalter immediately wrote out his resignation. 'Not accepted' is typed baldly on the archived copy.[96] With the immediate conflict resolved, the series was again able to revert to its strengths. 'Britain's other islanders', a film drawing attention to the government's treatment of the people of Diego Garcia in the light of its defence of the Falklands, had been held back to be shown in the week after the ceasefire.[97] There were five further follow-ups over the next four years, examining the circumstances of the conflict (including the British decision to sink the warship *General Belgrano*), British arms sales to Argentina immediately before the war (a subject first covered, with admirable prescience, in March 1981) and one family's loss. Characteristically, although the series' response to the Falklands as a news story was mixed, it was on much firmer territory when it could be treated as an investigative subject. However, the last-mentioned programme, 'A widow's story', revisiting a participant in a programme during the conflict whose husband had subsequently been killed in action, brought forth an exchange that reveals much about the approach of *World in Action* and Granada. On a memo giving information about forthcoming programmes, Forman has scribbled: 'Why do we make such sentimental twaddle into a WIA? ... Is there a twist perhaps? Was he a traitor?' In response, Mike Scott writes: 'Ray Fitzwalter vigorously repudiates that it's sentimental or twaddle. He does, however, acknowledge that it saved a lot of money by using past material'.[98]

In contrast, *World in Action*'s response to the 1984–85 miners' strike was negligible for a series of its calibre, a failing acknowledged by Forman.[99] Six programmes touched on the issue but only three – 'Women on the line', on the empowerment of miners' wives, 'Softly, softly strike force', examining variances in police tactics and 'Father and son', about a family divided in their support for the dispute – offered even limited insight into the circumstances of the strike. Ample coverage was available elsewhere – for twelve months, British television news was dominated by this hugely visible and divisive story – but in retrospect *World in Action*'s failure here seems to illustrate not only the series' ongoing difficulties with topical stories but perhaps a wider marginalisation of traditional current affairs series as key contributors to the public understanding of major events.

In less topical areas, *World in Action* remained both more consistent and more successful. Various programmes helped to maintain its connection with a popular audience. The overall size of this audience was decreasing, but audience research for the 1985–86 season revealed that the demographic profile of viewers contained considerably more unskilled viewers than was the average for ITV, albeit balanced by fewer C2s.[100] The 'stunt' remained an occasional device to explore social and political issues in an accessible and novel manner, as well as to draw publicity for the series. Probably the best-remembered stunt of the 1980s came in response to high unemployment and criticism (often rejected by ministers in the Conservative government) of the low level of welfare benefits. *World in Action* persuaded Matthew Parris, himself a Conservative MP and defender of the policy, to live on social security for a week. Fitzwalter describes 'For the benefit of Mr Parris' as 'a classic ... It transformed dull, boring unemployment into a talking point in every pub and that was enormously pleasing to do'.[101] He suggests that its impact came because it arose not as a profile of Parris but out of the issues involved. Its origins were in 'a pile of boring documents about people on social security and the dole' and in compelling evidence that government arguments that life should be made tougher for the unemployed were false.[102] The team had also become disillusioned with examining economic and social hardships through programmes reflecting factory closures, job losses and industrial decline, so the idea to involve Parris offered a novel twist and an element of challenge, however artificial, to an otherwise hackneyed subject. Not only did the programme elicit 13 million viewers, but it brought Parris to the attention of London Weekend Television who, two years later, persuaded him to abandon his parliamentary career to present political interviews for *Weekend World*.[103] Twenty years on, he repeated the experience of living on the dole for a documentary sequel.[104] *World in Action*'s own sequel, 'The honourable member for the unemployed', in which an unemployed man from Parris's constituency took over Parris's parliamentary duties for a week, had much less impact than the original.

Campaigning programmes offered another means to draw popular attention to the series and to illustrate major events through an accessible microcosm, especially when they produced demonstrable results. Two particularly effective programmes from this period dealt with the effects of immigration laws and the closure of a Scottish shipyard. In 1981, Anwar Ditta, a British citizen living in Rochdale, had spent four years attempting to persuade the Home Office to allow her children to join her from Pakistan. The Home Office claimed that the children were not her own and refused to accept documentary evidence to the contrary. Her case was the subject of a local campaign (which brought it to the attention of Granada's regional news team) and was a *cause célèbre* among socialist groups, but Mrs Ditta had found it impossible to gain support from the national media. 'These are my children' recounted her campaign, showed a *World in Action* team searching for and finding corroborative evidence of the children's parentage in Pakistan and gave the results of blood tests showing conclusively that the children were hers – one of the earliest examples of DNA testing in Britain. Three days later, as a direct result of *World in Action*'s intervention, the Home Office agreed to reverse the decision. Granada was delighted both at the decision and at minor changes in the Nationality Bill that it heralded: it was 'a very specific result from a campaigning programme'.[105] An equally unequivocal result followed a 1984 programme about the Scott Lithgow shipyard on Clydeside. British Shipbuilders, the yard's state-run parent company, blamed the cancellation of a late-running oil rig contract on its workers and announced the yard's closure. The government described the performance of the workforce as 'abysmal' and, despite a local unemployment rate of 25 per cent, refused any financial assistance to save the yard. But *World in Action* obtained evidence that the contract had foundered due to technical and management problems which could have been foreseen. On the day after 'The sinking of Scott Lithgow' was shown, the government had a change of heart, agreeing to provide financial assistance to enable the yard's sale to a private buyer 'with a clean slate'. However successful, programmes such as these could only examine individual examples of a more general malaise. Clydeside shipworkers and the Ditta family may have been jubilant at their results, but it is debatable whether such programmes could have much lasting general impact on public perceptions of, or government policies towards, the decline of British manufacturing or the overall treatment of immigration applications.

The early 1980s also saw the most acclaimed programme in a ten-year investigative strand, also with a populist flavour, in which the series sought out ex-Nazi war criminals. As well as appealing to a thirst for retribution, these programmes were strongly dramatic, generally involving danger, secrecy, the pursuit of a quarry, clandestine filming and a conclusion in which the villain is unmasked. Two programmes filmed on the same trip to Paraguay in 1978 began the strand. The first had been a general account of that country's role in harbouring war criminals and right-wing terrorists ('The last refuge'); the second a 60-minute investigation of the flight from justice of Dr Josef Mengele, the Auschwitz 'angel of death', tracing his settlement in Germany, Argentina and finally Paraguay. In making 'The hunt for Doctor Mengele', producer Mike Beckham was arrested by the Paraguayan authorities, interrogated, threatened and then expelled from the country. The film itself was smuggled out of South America through a network of 'safe houses'. Systematic concealment of the identities of known Nazis in the USA by the FBI, CIA, State Department and Catholic church was the subject of 'Alive and well in the USA', a 1980 investigation which drew lavish praise for its drama, risk-taking and shock value. In *The Times*, Joan Bakewell wrote:

> The hotter the subject, the cooler the treatment. Appalling facts need no fancy phrases. *World in Action* has elevated the anti-techniques of surreptitious reporting into a house style. Packing their cameras away into holdalls and focussing through spyholes, they go hunting their quarry. For some reason the evidence they find is all the more convincing for being out of focus, jump cut or with plenty of camera jolts and knocks ... Intrepid cameraman George Jesse Turner, chased by the killer of Treblinka, simply kept his camera running.[106]

When notified in 1983 by Fitzwalter that *World in Action* intended to return to the subject, Mike Scott was sceptical:

> The hunt for Nazi war criminals seems to be an oft-repeated story. Is your target in Chile really worth the difficulties and expense? I had rather thought that Dr. Mengele was our peak on the subject.[107]

There may have been grounds for a concern that a further quest for an ex-Nazi was motivated as much by the popularity as the currency of such investigations. 'The hunt for Doctor Mengele' had after all won a gold medal at the New York International Film Festival. But 'Colonel Rauff's revenge' was to outdo even this for the drama and danger involved and it was 'Rauff' rather than 'Mengele' that was chosen to illustrate the strand for a retrospective programme on the series in 1991.[108] Walter Rauff, an SS colonel who developed mobile gas chambers responsible for 200,000 deaths, had lived undisturbed in Chile for more than 20 years when *World in Action* found him. The centrepiece of the programme was the longest stake-out in the series' history. In a country known for its protection of criminals and its hostility to external investigation, George Jesse Turner hid for six hours a day in the back of a small van outside Rauff's suburban home filming through a slit in a cardboard Johnnie Walker box. But when Rauff finally emerged after eight days, the team not only filmed him but even managed to obtain an impromptu interview.[109] The programme led to a parliamentary plea for Rauff's extradition.[110] One further ex-Nazi was investigated by *World in Action* and this time much less secrecy was required. In 1988, Kurt Waldheim, newly appointed President of Austria, was the subject of a damning two-part investigation entitled 'The man who lived a lie', showing how his past had been concealed.

Notes

1 *'Statement to WIA meeting in Manchester, 9 October 1975' (bf. 1268).
2 R. Lindley, *Panorama: Fifty Years of Pride and Paranoia* (London: Politicos, 2002), pp. 218–19.
3 The 'Birt–Jay thesis' encompassed four articles in *The Times* – the first ('Can television news break the understanding-barrier' (28 February 1975)) credited to Birt alone, the others ('Television journalism: Without pride of ancestry' (30 September 1975), 'Television journalism: Without hope of posterity' (1 October 1975), 'How television news can hold the mass audience' (2 September 1976)) to Birt and Jay. All are collected in P. Jay, *The Crisis for Western Political Economy and Other Essays* (London: Andre Deutsch, 1984), pp. 191–218.
4 *Minutes of Programme Committee meeting, 10 April 1975 (bf. 1061).
5 Birt and Jay, 'Television journalism: Without pride of ancestry', in Jay, *The Crisis for Western Political Economy*, p. 201.
6 Birt and Jay, 'Television journalism: Without pride of ancestry', in Jay, *The Crisis for Western Political Economy*, pp. 196–7.
7 Birt and Jay, 'Television journalism: Without pride of ancestry', in Jay, *The Crisis for Western Political Economy*, p. 200.
8 Wallington, 'The chance to tell the truth', *The Listener*, 10 April 1975: 462–3.
9 Birt, 'Can television news break the understanding-barrier', in Jay, *The Crisis for Western Political Economy*, p. 194.
10 Birt and Jay, 'How television news can hold the mass audience', in Jay, *The Crisis for Western Political Economy*, p. 207. *World in Action*'s average audience share had declined from 40.6 per cent in the four seasons from 1967–71 to 33.8 per cent for 1972–76, although it was then to rally to 37.9 per cent (1977–81) before a further decline set in.
11 Ray Fitzwalter, telephone interview with the authors.
12 *Minutes of Programme Committee meeting, 13 May 1976 (bf. 1061).
13 *Boulton, 'IBA booklet contribution', 27 August 1980 (bf. 1072). On publication, the opening sentence was modified to read: '*World in Action* relies on what Granada Television term "story journalism"'' (E. Croston (ed.), *Television and Radio 1981* (London: IBA, 1980)).
14 See Chapter 6.
15 B. Lapping and N. Percy, 'Introduction' to Granada Television, *Chrysler and the Cabinet: How the deal was done*, Granada and Political Broadcasting 7 (London: Granada Television, 1976).
16 Forman, *Persona Granada* (London: Andre Deutsch, 1997), p. 134; *Boulton, memo to M. Scott and Plowright, 'The future of WIA', 18 February 1982 (bf. 1054); *Sunday Times*, 1 April 1990: p. E1.
17 *Minutes of *World in Action* team meeting, 23 July 1976 (bf. 1161), (partly summarised with comments added).
18 *Memo to *World in Action* team, 'Some thoughts on our programme', 10 March 1977 (bf. 1161).

19   *Lapping, memo to junior WIA team members, 'Meeting with Forman, Plowright, Scott, 18.1.78', 20 January 1978 (bf. 1161).

20   *World in Action*: 'Margaret Thatcher'.

21   *M. Gillard, memo to Lapping, 'GTV v. the star and others', 29 December 1976 (bf. 1071)

22   This edition is also discussed in Chapter 7. For an account of the IBA's response to it, see P. Goddard, '"Improper liberties": Regulating undercover journalism on ITV, 1967 – 1980', *Journalism*, 7:1 (2006): 56–58.

23   *J. Blake, memo to Fitzwalter, Lapping, I. McBride, M. Short, 'Problem areas re. Prison story', 10 May 1978; *J. Blake, memo to Dickson, 'WIA – "Buying time"', 29 September 1978; *McBride and Short, memo to Lapping and Fitzwalter, 'Merseyside and West Yorkshire police', 16 October 1978; *McBride, memo to Fitzwalter, 'Buying time: Dundas', 12 January 1981 (all from bf. 0681); Fitzwalter, interview with the authors.

24   *Minutes of Programme Committee meeting, 25 January 1978 (bf. 1061).

25   *'WIA: What now? Where next?' (internal discussion paper), 22 September 1980 (bf. 0744).

26   30 January 1980, p. 8.

27   *The Times*, 30 January 1980, p. 10, 27 February 1980, p. 12.

28   In A. Jowett, 'A world where making enemies is all in a day's work', *UK Press Gazette*, 2 April 1984: 11.

29   *The Times*, 21 October 1980, p. 8.

30   Jowett, 'A world where making enemies is all in a day's work'.

31   *T. Brill, memo to A. Quinn, '*World in Action* – Seveso', 22 October 1976 (bf. 0744); *Unattributed Granada letter to L. Lloyd (ACTT Film Shop steward), 27 October 1976 (bf. 1161).

32   Unless otherwise indicated, the following account is drawn from: *Plowright, 'Draft aide memoire – *World in Action*: The Jock Kane story', 8 July 1980; *Forman, letter to Sir B. Young (IBA), 6 June 1980 (both bf. 1071); *Fitzwalter, 'The Official Secrets Act'.

33   *Boulton, memo to ACTT representative, 'Short crew request no. 1: Hong Kong', 9 April 1980 (bf. 0720).

34   *New Statesman*, 16 May 1980: 738–44.

35   *Plowright, 'Draft aide memoire – *World in Action*: The Jock Kane story'.

36   In *The Times*, 10 June 1980, p. 3.

37   Quoted in *The Times*, 9 July 1980, p. 4, 10 July 1980, p. 2.

38   *Mike Beckham, memo to Boulton, 23 May 1980 (bf. 0720).

39   Fitzwalter, interview with the authors; *New Statesman*, 23 May 1980: 774–7.

40   Unless otherwise indicated, the following account is drawn from: *D. Harker, draft letter to W. Deedes (*Daily Telegraph*), 4 May 1976 (bf. 1072); *Sunday Times*, 11 April 1976, pp. 2, 6–7.

41   *The Times*, 13 April 1976, p. 11

42   L. Harding, D. Leigh and D. Pallister, *The Liar: The fall of Jonathan Aitken* (London: Penguin, 1997).

43 *World in Action*: 'In the public interest'; *Sunday Times*, 7 May 1978, p. 53; see L. Chapman, *Your Disobedient Servant* [2nd edn] (London: Penguin, 1979).

44 Unless otherwise indicated, the following account is drawn from: *Forman, 'British Steel Corporation v. Granada Television' (narrative prepared by Boulton for Granada Television board), 28 July 1980 (bf. 1072); Forman, *Persona Granada*, pp. 295–7; A. Goodman, *Tell Them I'm On My Way* (London: Chapmans, 1993), pp. 108–16; M. Bilton and P. Knightley, 'Granada: We do not know who the mole is', *Sunday Times*, 3 August 1980, p. 3; B. Penrose and S. Freeman, 'Why I did it – by the steel mole', *Sunday Times*, 2 November 1980, p. 4.

45 Quoted in Goodman, *Tell Them I'm On My Way*, p. 110.

46 Forman, *Persona Granada*, p. 295.

47 *World in Action – The first 21 years*, tx. 27 December 1984; *Ian Evans (BSC), letter to Boulton, 7 December 1984 (bf. 0692).

48 Penrose and Freeman, 'Why I did it – by the steel mole'.

49 Lord Denning, *What Next for the Law* (London: Butterworth, 1982), p. 246.

50 Quoted in *The Times*, 8 May 1980, p. 19.

51 Quoted in *The Times*, 8 May 1980, p. 1.

52 *Forman, letter to Young (IBA), 22 July 1980 (bf. 1071).

53 *The Times*, 8 May 1980, p. 1.

54 *Observer*, 11 May 1980, p. 10, *The Times*, 8 May 1980, p. 19, 9 May 1980. p. 1, 17 May 1980, p. 8.

55 *The Times*, 31 July 1980, p. 15.

56 *Forman, letter to W. Rees-Mogg (*The Times*), 6 August 1980 (bf. 1072).

57 *The Times*, 9 May 1980, p. 1, 4 July 1980, p. 5, 1 August 1980, p. 3.

58 *Boulton, 'WIA: What now? Where next?'.

59 Boulton, *World in Action: The First Twenty-One Years* (booklet) (Granada Television, 1984), p. 13; *The Times*, 20 May 1981, p. 2.

60 Denning, *What Next for the Law*, p. 251.

61 *Boulton, 'WIA: What now? Where next?'.

62 *Fitzwalter, memo to Scott and Plowright, 2 June 1982 (bf. 1053).

63 *Fitzwalter, memo to Scott and Plowright, 2 June 1982.

64 The following account is drawn from: N. Horne, 'A piece of the action', *Sunday Times*, 25 November 1984, p. 54.

65 Fitzwalter, 'Can the whistle keep on blowing?', speech to Edinburgh International Television Festival, 27 August 1984.

66 Fitzwalter, quoted in Horne, 'A piece of the action'.

67 *Scott, memo to programme-makers, 13 July 1983 (bf. 1056).

68 *R. Watson, memo to Scott, 9 July 1987 (bf. 0742).

69 *Sunday Times*, 26 June 1983, p. 4.

70 *Mutch memo to S. Berthon, P. Greengrass, 'Barratts complaint to the BCC', 18 April 1984 (bf. 1053).

71 *The Times*, 14 March 1984, p. 21.

72 Unless otherwise indicated, the following account is drawn from: Fitzwalter, 'Can the whistle keep on blowing?'; *'Material for press fact sheet' (undated/ unattributed chronology of events concerning 'Your starter for life') (bf. 0772).

73 *'Material for press fact sheet'.

74 The judgement was overturned in 1985 on appeal.

75 Fitzwalter, interview with the authors.

76 *T. Hardy (Slaughter & May), letter to J. Rink (Allen & Overy), 15 June 1984 (bf. 0745).

77 *Scott, memo to Fitzwalter, '*World in Action*: Your starter for life', 21 June 1984 (bf. 1070).

78 *Sunday Times*, 17 June 1984, p. 58.

79 *Fitzwalter, memo to Scott, 'Your starter for life', 14 June 1984 (bf. 1070).

80 *Fitzwalter, memo to Scott, 'Your starter for life', 14 June 1984.

81 *Scott, memo to Fitzwalter, 26 June 1984 (bf. 1053).

82 *Fitzwalter, memo to Scott, 'Your starter for life', 14 June 1984.

83 *Fitzwalter, memo to Scott, 'Your starter for life', 14 June 1984.

84 Fitzwalter, interview with the authors.

85 Fitzwalter, 'Can the whistle keep on blowing?'

86 *Jaques and Lewis, letter to Forman, 26 June 1984 (bf. 1072).

87 *The Times*, 21 July 1984, p. 4; Fitzwalter, 'Can the whistle keep on blowing?'

88 Fitzwalter, interview with the authors.

89 Fitzwalter, 'Can the whistle keep on blowing?'

90 *Scott, memo to Fitzwalter, 'Material preceding live interviews', 24 September 1984 (bf. 1053).

91 *Boulton, 'WIA: What now? Where next?'; *World in Action* team members, discussion paper for Granada Current Affairs meeting, 25 May 1982 (bf. 0744).

92 *Lapping, Minutes of *World in Action* team meeting, 23 July 1976 (bf. 1161). A 'fast response unit' was actually established under Simon Berthon at the end of 1985 but produced very few programmes, hampered partly by *World in Action*'s non-metropolitan base: *Scott, memo to Fitzwalter, 'WIA: The future', July 8 1985; *Berthon, memo to Scott, 'London studio', 15 January 1986 (both bf. 1053).

93 *Forman, memo to *World in Action* team, 7 April 1982 (bf. 1072).

94 *Boulton, memo to Plowright and Scott, 27 May 1982 (bf. 1056).

95 *World in Action* team members, discussion paper for Granada Current Affairs meeting, 25 May 1982 (bf. 0744).

96 *Fitzwalter, letter to Scott, 10 May 1982 (bf. 1053).

97 *Boulton, memo to Plowright, 'WIA – Diego Garcia', 8 June 1982 (bf. 0744).

98 *Fitzwalter, memo to Scott, 'Advance information – *World in Action*', 9 June 1983 (with handwritten annotation by Forman); *Scott, memo to Forman, '*World in Action*', 23 June 1983 (both bf. 1072).

99 Forman, memo to Plowright, Scott, Fitzwalter, 6 December 1984 (bf. 1072).

100 *D. Bidston, memo to Fitzwalter, '*World in Action* 85/86 series', 6 October 1986 (from papers donated to the authors by Steve Boulton). 48 per cent of the audience were DEs compared with 39 per cent for all ITV output. 26 per cent were C2s compared with 36 per cent for all ITV output. Audience size varied between 4 and 8 million and averaged 5.7 million.

101 Fitzwalter, interview with the authors.

102 Fitzwalter, interview with the authors.

103 Authors' correspondence with Matthew Parris.

104 *For the Benefit of Mr Parris, Revisited*, tx. 29 January 2004, ITV1.

105 *D. Boulton, memo to Forman, Plowright, Scott, 19 March 1981 (bf. 1072).

106 25 March 1980, p. 11.

107 *Scott, memo to Fitzwalter, 17 June 1983 (bf. 1053).

108 *World in Action: 30 years.*

109 *B. Blake, memo to Fitzwalter, etc., '*World in Action* – The first 30 years', 9 November 1992 (bf. 0692).

110 *The Times*, 9 August 1983, p. 3.

5

1988–98: current affairs as commodity

Outwardly at least, British television current affairs was still essentially a stable, valuable and highly successful form of programming at the end of the 1980s. Although the popularity of *World in Action* in the 1960s could never be recaptured, current affairs had matured. For nearly three decades, *Panorama*, *This Week/TV Eye* and *World in Action*, the triumvirate of long-running current affairs programmes, had commanded huge respect and contributed substantially to the political health and public knowledge of the British nation, supplemented periodically by other series and single documentaries. They had been responsible for many of the finest, bravest and most significant moments in British television journalism and continued to perform this role to great effect. Programmes relating directly or indirectly to Northern Ireland illustrate this well. Although *Panorama* was in crisis at the time, facing a loss of nerve exemplified by the non-transmission of a 1988 programme about the SAS in Northern Ireland, *This Week* made the courageous 'Death on the rock' and Yorkshire Television's *Shoot to Kill* was a text of comparable importance.[1]

World in Action's contribution to this field was no less distinguished. *Who Bombed Birmingham?*, made by Granada's revived drama-documentary unit, was the successor to three *World in Action* investigations, which had painstakingly uncovered conclusive evidence that the Birmingham Six – convicted for the IRA pub-bombings in Birmingham in 1974 – had been innocent, that their confessions had been extracted under duress and that forensic evidence against them was unreliable. *Who Bombed Birmingham?*[2] retold the story of the investigation with all the drama of a detective movie, but added further revelations from the *World in Action* investigation: that the innocence of the Six had been known to the authorities since the year after their trial, and the names of the real bombers. Significantly, the heroes of the film were not the Six themselves but Ian McBride and Charles Tremayne, the *World in Action* journalists whose investigations had uncovered the story, together with Chris Mullin, the MP with whom they had collaborated. All three were played by well-known actors. Portraying the investigation into the case of the Six in a dramatised form brought an audience of ten million and a much greater impact than *World in Action*'s earlier investigations of the case.[3] Efforts to free the Six had continued almost since their arrest and successive Home Secretaries had rejected, or in two cases granted, appeal hearings, but the fresh evidence uncovered by *World in Action* and the publicity generated by *Who Bombed Birmingham?* were vital elements in their eventual release a year later. In all, between 1985 and 1991, *World in Action* devoted six programmes to the case including 'The Birmingham 6 – their own story', a triumphant special edition containing an exclusive interview with the Six in the week of their release.

Current affairs under pressure

Although the tripartite system of major current affairs programmes worked well on British television until the end of the 1980s, with Channel 4's *Dispatches* gaining a worthy reputation as a valuable fourth strand, for various reasons it no longer operated properly at ITV in the 1990s. *This Week* was cancelled at the end of 1992 and not replaced. *World in Action* continued until the end of 1998, when it was replaced by *Tonight With Trevor Macdonald* – a wholly different programme with more populist journalistic ambitions. Of course, *World in Action* continued to mount significant programmes in the 1990s, involving achievements as substantial as the revelation of cabinet minister Jonathan Aitken's corruption and perjury in the two 'Jonathan of Arabia' programmes. But it began to be subject to new pressures and the character of the series changed in several ways. Essentially, four linked elements precipitated the eventual cancellation of *World in Action* and the first signs of these were already visible in the late 1980s. They were:

1 Increased commercial pressures at ITV, leading to a stronger imperative to maximise profits.
2 The provisions of the 1990 Broadcasting Act.
3 The establishment of the ITV Network Centre as a means for companies to manage scheduling.
4 Changes at Granada Television, including to the departure of David Plowright as Executive Chairman.

We examine each of these elements below before looking more generally at the character of the series in the 1990s:

Increased commercial pressures at ITV

After a financial crisis in the early 1980s, ITV's advertising revenues rose substantially in the latter part of the decade.[4] But a variety of reasons, some specific to individual companies, meant that this period was also marked by growing pressures to increase profitability and cut costs. The launch of Channel 4 in 1982 had several effects on the economics of Independent Television. It increased the availability of television advertising slots, reducing the companies' scope to set prices for in-demand slots almost at will. It also encouraged the rise of independent producers, able to make programmes substantially more cheaply than ITV companies, which was a factor in focusing greater attention on ITV's in-house production costs and initiating a search for economies.[5] The financial relationship between ITV and Channel 4, in which the companies paid a 'subscription' in return for the revenues from selling the new channel's advertising, was also disadvantageous to company profitability. Revenues from Channel 4 failed to offset the cost of the subscription and financial planning was also undermined by frequent changes to the calculation of the Levy – the duty reclaimed by the Treasury from the profits of ITV companies.[6] John Ellis also notes that television production had become increasingly ambitious and sophisticated by the 1980s, with corresponding rises both in audience expectations and typical production costs.[7]

With their history of high profitability, ITV companies had sought to diversify into other sectors and, by the 1980s, were often controlled by groups with a wide variety of other investments. Unusually, Granada Television had itself been an offshoot of a long-standing cinema and theatre business when it was awarded its first ITV licence. The cinema and theatre business declined over the years but Granada Group had been particularly acquisitive, investing its television profits in numerous other enterprises including television equipment rentals, bingo, publishing and motorway catering, together with many foreign broadcasting and leisure interests. Of course, this reduced the significance of the television company within the Group – which, by 1986, was 'essentially a TV rental company with a significant, but in financial terms relatively minor, television franchise operation and a few bits and pieces tacked on'[8] – and made it more vulnerable to downturns in other industries in which the Group had invested. The overall performance of the Group had become disastrous by the mid-1980s and a hostile takeover was only avoided through the intervention of the IBA.[9]

A further challenge to the stability of Independent Television came from satellite and cable television, offering possibilities for a wider range of broadcasters and channels, and new outlets for television advertising.

In the late 1980s, this threat was more notional than actual – cable TV expanded very slowly and even by 1992 was available only to 1.5 million homes, while Sky, the first high-powered satellite broadcaster, was not on air until 1989[10] – but it was to be increasingly damaging to ITV in the 1990s. For Granada, the impact was more immediate: its involvement in the British Satellite Broadcasting consortium that won the first British satellite broadcasting franchise boosted the Group's share-price considerably, but start-up costs were huge and BSB's *de facto* takeover by the still-unprofitable Sky reduced still further Granada's ability to recoup its losses.

As early as 1987, these various commercial pressures were beginning to have demonstrable effects on Granada and *World in Action*. In that year, the IBA was persuaded to increase ad minutage in prime time by 30 seconds per hour.[11] The Authority did not intend this time to be taken from programmes and David Glencross stated specifically that it should not affect the running time of *World in Action*, but the Network Operations Sub-Committee (NOSC) thought differently.[12] The NOSC, in which companies debated the operational details of network scheduling, could be a site for bitter inter-company rivalry and was dominated by Thames, the London contractor. The NOSC decided that the additional time could be found by cutting the standard running times for some programmes, including reducing half-hour documentaries (amongst them *World in Action*) from 26'05" to 25'05". In the face of much resentment from Thames, Ray Fitzwalter, by now *World in Action*'s Executive Producer, refused to accept this. The result, as David Black, Granada's Head of Presentation noted, was that 'every opportunity was taken to snipe at *World in Action* and its running time' at the NOSC meetings.[13]

This sort of attack on the series was symptomatic of a wider antagonism between Thames, maker of *This Week*, and Granada, which felt that Thames used its dominant network position to discriminate against *World in Action*. A memo from Fitzwalter notes that, under Thames' influence, schedulers had 'hammocked' *This Week* efficiently between two popular dramas while *World in Action* was forced to follow a comedy repeat. Furthermore, Thames refused to promote *World in Action* in London although Granada regularly promoted *This Week*. 'Despite all this', he added, '*World in Action* does better on average than *This Week* but we are beginning to wonder why we should keep trying'.[14] In maintaining the programme's running time, Granada won the initial skirmish but rumbles of resentment continued. In 1990, Thames' Tim Riordan sought to force the issue. As NOSC chairman, he officially informed Granada that if *World in Action* did not adhere to the new network standard running time of 25'05", Thames would opt out of the programme's end credits.[15] Fitzwalter was aghast, seeing this as a sign of increasingly troubled times for Independent Television: 'The running time of ITV programmes compared with the BBC are beginning to look ludicrous', he wrote.

> It's no surprise that many viewers feel they get more programme value on the BBC ... It is worth bearing in mind that most of the many pressures on *World in Action*, and we are the most scrutinised programme on ITV, press us to say more rather than less: to represent more points of view; present more evidence; to give more sophisticated explanations.[16]

Although in the television industry end credits were assumed to be sacrosanct, Riordan's threat was no bluff. The first *World in Action* of April 1990, 'Sting and the Indians', examining the failure of the pop star's rainforest charity, overran by 30 seconds except in the London region where its credits were faded abruptly. Granada complained to the IBA but by the end of that month had given in to the pressure and grudgingly accepted the shortened running time.

ITV's new financial realism in the late 1980s had other manifestations and again Thames led the opposition to Granada. *World in Action* had always had sufficient flexibility to vary its running time and the 'Sting and the Indians' overrun was hardly unprecedented. 'We could get an extra thirty seconds, or even at times an extra two minutes', explains Fitzwalter. 'That was rare and we didn't want to do it lightly. But you reached a point where you couldn't do that any more.'[17] Occasional one-hour *World in Action* 'specials' were another tradition of the series, but it became increasingly difficult to obtain slots for them in the schedule. Between 1980 and 1987, most years had seen three such 'specials', but after 1987 there were only two more: 'A force to be reckoned with', showing the extent of corruption at the West Midlands Serious Crime Squad, and 'The Birmingham 6 – their own story'. As a result, longer *World in Action* reports could only be shown in two and occasionally three parts over successive weeks. Despite these developments, at this stage there was little discernible effect on the ethos of the programme.

The 1990 Broadcasting Act
Sharp-eyed readers of *Broadcasting in the 90s*, the government's 1988 White Paper, would have noted the following phrase:

> Each Channel 3 station will be required ... to show high quality news and current affairs dealing with national and international matters, and to include news (*and possibly also current affairs*) in main viewing periods.[18]

The implication of this was clear: current affairs was no longer to be seen as an absolute requirement in prime-time. The 1990 Act which followed removed much of the legislative and regulatory framework that had stimulated the development of current affairs on ITV and safe-guarded its place in the schedule. The IBA was replaced by the Independent Television Commission (ITC) – intended as 'lighter touch' regulator, certainly a less pro-active one. Interventionist content regulation was replaced by a system that was 'more arm's length and more post hoc'.[19] And the regulator no longer had powers to 'mandate' particular programmes, including *World in Action*, within the schedule. Indeed, it no longer had direct authority over scheduling at all, a power that the ITA had been granted in the 1963 Television Act. Instead, scheduling became the responsibility of a body established by the companies. This led to the creation of the ITV Network Centre, set up in mid-1992 and assuming its full powers at the start of 1993.

The ITV Network Centre

As early as February 1991, Granada was already wary of the effects of the changes to ITV's scheduling arrangements heralded in the 1990 Act. Instead of being 'part of the structure of ITV', for which an hour per week of current affairs was 'part of licence commitments',[20] *World in Action* would merely be contracted for a specific period to deliver current affairs to the Network Centre. So, in the opinion of Andrew Quinn, Granada's Managing Director, the series needed to be sold to the network as 'an attractive package which can earn its keep in the schedule whilst contributing to the range and diversity that the ITC seek' and that meant delivering consistently high ratings.[21] At the time, Quinn suggested that audiences of at least four to five million would be necessary but, by July 1992, a much higher hurdle had been set. Paul Jackson, Chief Executive of Carlton Television, warned that the network's main requirement of current affairs programmes would be that they were made to win audiences of ten million, adding acidly: 'not to get people out of prison'.[22] To stay in the prime-time schedule, programmes would have to deliver a consistent audience of eight million. Quinn himself reiterated the eight million threshold in an interview in *The Times* on his appointment as the first ITV Chief Executive in July 1992: 'Any programme is going to have to fight for its place in the schedule. Anybody who thinks they can preserve a genre of programming by moaning that it might vanish will see it vanish', he said.[23] Speaking of his own record, he also dropped a heavy hint about the priorities of the new ITV: 'Not having produced a programme does not matter, he says, "What matters is that I know how programmes are made *and how much they cost*"'.[24]

The signs of the decline of ITV's public service obligations and the removal of the conditions in which companies might see serious journalism as a means to earn 'brownie points' could not have been more starkly demonstrated. Publicly, Quinn's recipe for increasing *World in Action*'s ratings was better marketing and promotion, but there were many critical voices who questioned the sincerity of ITV's continuing commitment to peak-time current affairs. Roger Graef also questioned ITV's rationale, pointing out that advertisers saw the composition of the news and current affairs audience with its high proportion of wealthy ABC1 viewers as much more important than aggregate ratings figures.[25]

Despite fluctuations, *World in Action*'s ratings were gradually growing. Its 1985–86 season had averaged 5.7 million viewers with a range between 3.9 million and 8.1 million.[26] Its 1987/88 season averaged 5.3 million viewers.[27] After his appointment as Editor in August 1989, Nick Hayes managed to increase ratings by 45 per cent, partly through a carefully-planned 'relaunch' in Autumn 1991, and in the opening weeks of the 1991–92 season, the series averaged 7.2 million viewers.[28] By the end of that season, against the background of Jackson and Quinn's demands for popularity, *World in Action* had raised its average to 7.5 million with a peak of over 10 million.[29] So it appeared that the series was capable of sustaining an average viewership that was nearly as large as that demanded by the network and could regularly exceed it. But a liability of current affairs was its inability to deliver a consistent weekly audience in the way that, for example, drama series could. Viewing figures tended to depend heavily on the subjects of individual editions and the appeal of other channels' offerings at the same time. For much of its run, *World in Action* had been fortunate to be scheduled in opposition to *Panorama*, but this arrangement ceased with *Panorama*'s move to 9.25pm in February 1985 and the series was at the mercy of competitive scheduling. Sometimes this worked in its favour, as in Autumn 1988 when *World in Action*'s ratings seemed to benefit from the BBC's decision to show repeats of its unsuccessful sitcom *Clarence*.[30] But increasingly, *World in Action* was coming to be identified as one of the weak points in ITV's schedule. Not surprisingly, this gave to rise to pressure to select subjects with the greatest audience appeal, as we shall see.

Changes at Granada Television

Throughout its history, Granada had carefully nurtured its status as the most public service-oriented ITV contractor and was seen as the company 'that most clearly symbolised quality'.[31] For much of this history, *World in Action* had been its flagship, offering continuing proof of the company's willingness to invest in serious programming offering democratic value. Many of its department heads and executives had worked on the programme and, since the mid-1980s, David Plowright, deviser of the revamped *World in Action* in 1967, had been Granada Television's chairman. Among the first signs that Granada's financial position was beginning to impinge upon these traditions came in an operation to 'downsize' the company in 1989. Those accepting voluntary redundancy included Leslie Woodhead and David Boulton, programme-makers who had held numerous senior positions in the company following stints as *World in Action* editors. Given their contributions to the company's reputation, these departures were a matter of particular regret to Plowright.[32]

For Granada's traditions, though, worse was to come. At the start of February 1992, as the company's new franchise was beginning, Plowright himself became involved in a power struggle with Gerry Robinson, chief executive of Granada Group, and lost. Responding to poor results within the Group as a whole, Robinson demanded that the television arm should seek to increase its profitability by two-and-a-half times in the next financial year. Plowright refused to contemplate a course that, he felt, risked betraying Granada's franchise commitments and eliminating all but its most ratings-driven output.[33] The board backed Robinson, so Plowright was forced to resign. 'The night of the long knives', as it became known, prompted outrage both inside and outside Granada. All one thousand staff signed a letter of protest[34] and many were in tears in scenes not unlike those accompanying Greg Dyke's departure from the BBC in 2004. Sir Paul Fox echoed the sentiments of many in broadcasting in describing Plowright as 'the last of the musketeers', in succession to the Bernsteins and Denis Forman.[35] It seemed that the craft era of ITV was rapidly passing. As Fox put it:

> the people who grew up making programmes are disappearing from the boardrooms. The people now in command are sharp and intelligent and they have learnt their trade elsewhere ... The old and the new do not share a sense of calling.[36]

Over the next year or two, many of the ex-*World in Action* people in senior positions at Granada also left. They were disillusioned with the direction of the company and the actions of the board. Some felt that their own positions had become untenable. Among them was Ray Fitzwalter, by now Granada's Head of Current Affairs.[37] No longer was Granada the 'special' family company that many had always perceived it to be, and *World in Action* was no longer regarded as a 'special' programme. Instead, it was seen as Granada's lowest-rated prime-time series.

World in Action in the 1990s

Budgetary constraints on *World in Action* began to increase through the 1990s as commercial pressures intensified further. By the time of Steve Boulton's editorship (1994–98), the series' budget was subject to continual attacks. Generally, Granada's archives for the decade contain much more about the series' ratings and much less about programme content than in earlier periods. The 1990 Broadcasting Act had introduced quotas for independent production on ITV and this was widely seen as an innovation that could benefit current affairs by providing a source of fresh ideas and expertise. 'The lords of the rings', a two-part investigation into the activities of the International Olympic Committee, was the first independent production for *World in Action*, shown in June 1992. Vyv Simson and Andrew Jennings, its producer and researcher, were experienced former-*World in Action* personnel, however, and the programmes coincided with their book on the same subject, allowing the series to capitalise on existing high profile research with little risk.[38] Further independent productions followed at the rate of about two a year, involving ex-*World in Action* personnel such as Nick Hayes (producing a programme for Ray Fitzwalter Associates) as well as programme-makers new to the series. But a consequence of the attacks on his budget was that Boulton found that, no matter how strong their programming ideas, hiring independents was a luxury that he struggled to afford.[39]

Other network companies were also subjecting *World in Action*'s coveted time slot on Mondays at 8.30pm to increasing pressure. As early as 1988, in parallel with their attempts to reduce its length, Thames in particular had attempted to coerce Granada to move *World in Action* to 8pm or 10.30pm.[40] Granada successfully opposed both options and the series kept its slot, but the general perception of *World in Action* as representing a 'problem' for the network persisted and the issue re-emerged periodically over the next few years. In April 1994, the BBC introduced a third weekly episode of its highly-rated soap opera, *Eastenders,* on Mondays. In the week of its launch, the ITV Network Centre responded by sacrificing *World in Action* in order to schedule a James Bond film as a spoiler. David Plowright commented that it was 'a sign of the television times when *World in Action* is silenced by a soap opera and not by those agents of government and big business who have tried and failed'.[41] Such competitive expediency would not have been possible before the 1990 Broadcasting Act was in force, of course. Until then, the IBA had responsibility for ensuring a 'balanced' schedule and *World in Action*'s place in it was mandated.

Further proposals to move *World in Action* emerged in June 1995 when advertiser pressure in the face of the decline in ITV's ratings led to an emergency meeting of the ITV Council to consider schedule changes.[42] The meeting discussed a proposal to move the series to 10.30pm – out of prime-time altogether, reducing its audience, its tariff (network price) and probably its viability. To prevent this, Granada was forced to accept a compromise proposal to move the series to 8pm from January 1996. But this placed the series in direct competition with *Eastenders*, with which it could never hope to compete for ratings. In this slot, the target of eight million viewers would be impossible to meet. Steve Boulton was unhappy. It had long been recognized that even 8.30pm was too early for the *World in Action* demographic and *Panorama*'s 9.30pm slot was regarded with admiration.[43]

In the 1990s, *World in Action* continued to mount programmes of considerable public value and to have some substantial journalistic successes. Of these, the two 'Jonathan of Arabia' programmes, based on a joint investigation with the *Guardian* newspaper, are the best known and Boulton took huge pride in them. A framed copy of the *Guardian*'s triumphant front page[44] took pride of place on his office wall within days of Aitken's conviction. Another notable focus was the beef trade. In 'Money for nothing' in 1991, *World in Action* investigated the Irish beef industry's systematic abuse of the European subsidy system amid suggestions of Irish government collusion. It was a classic exposé in the best traditions of the series and, characteristically, had a further life in the courts. The allegations were investigated by an Irish High Court Tribunal of Enquiry, becoming a *cause célèbre* in Irish politics where they led to the collapse of the Fianna Fáil/Progressive Democrat coalition and to the 1992 General Election. But Ireland's Official Secrets Act enabled the Irish government to suppress much relevant evidence, with the result that *World in Action* was paramount. Ironically, the only person threatened with punishment over this affair was Susan O'Keeffe, the *World in Action* researcher who had uncovered the story. O'Keeffe was charged with contempt of court for refusing to name her sources and, although the Beef Tribunal vindicated most of her allegations,[45] she only evaded a two-year prison sentence when the Irish state's case against her collapsed in January 1994. For 'upholding a vital journalistic principle', O'Keeffe received an award from the Campaign for Freedom of Information and at Granada her case was likened to that of 'The steel papers' in 1980.[46] A year earlier, *World in Action* had mounted its first programme on BSE (Bovine Spongiform Encephalopathy). In 1995, when the human consequences of the disease began to emerge, Kate Middleton and Isobel Tang were assigned permanently to the story. Between August 1995 and June 1996, four programmes emerged in quick succession revealing fresh scientific evidence, examining the effectiveness of restrictions on infected cattle and illustrating the suffering of victims of nvCJD and their families.

One of *World in Action*'s last major investigations, a two-part enquiry into Marks & Spencer, the high street clothing retailer, turned out to be less successful. The first programme, 'St Michael – has the halo slipped?', used hidden cameras to show the company's suppliers using child labour in Morocco and suggested that some of its clothes were mislabelled as British. Marks & Spencer issued a pre-emptive denial of the child labour claims on the day of transmission and eventually sued for libel. When the case came to court, instead of hearing legal arguments, the judge took the unprecedented step of asking the jury what meaning they felt that the programme conveyed. Granada maintained that it had never suggested that Marks & Spencer knew of or condoned the actions of its suppliers. The jury said that they had. No further arguments were allowed. Granada had no alternative but to pay the damages demanded and the costs of the case – a bill of £1.3 million. 'Journalists tend to believe they can rely on facts, and on their being available for examination in any argument', explained Ian McBride, but this 'libel roulette' put 'another burden and potential hazard in the way of inquiring, challenging, journalism . . .'[47] The case raised another issue about the viability of *World in Action* in the new ITV environment too. It showed that even if the network was prepared to schedule such a low-rated programme in prime time and to give it a suitable tariff, it still required Granada to be prepared to shoulder the costly legal risk that its journalism could bring. Courts found against *World in Action* with exceptional rarity, but the programme could surely no longer expect the kind of backing from Granada that had been enjoyed in 1980 when even Denis Forman had been prepared to go to prison for the programme.[48]

Despite the journalistic ambition of these programmes, the character of the series was changing in ways that had been foreseen by various commentators at the time of the 1990 Broadcasting Act. Following publication of the 1988 White Paper proposals, Richard Lindley had suggested that the American *60 Minutes* model was likely to become the only type of current affairs journalism that could remain viable in the increasingly competitive television culture that was to come. Despite its popularity, Lindley maintained that in *60 Minutes*:

> complex stories must be ruthlessly simplified. Its emphasis on reporters . . . means you sometimes hear more of them and their adventures than you do of their interviewees. And because the emphasis is on people and

human stories, it's difficult for the programme to tackle an issue unless there's an obvious hero or a heroine, a villain or victim.[49]

He went on to quote Jonathan Powell, then Controller of BBC 1, warning that 'the vulnerability of human nature may become the only currency of current affairs'. Others in the industry had similar predictions as the era of the 'new' ITV dawned. Glenwyn Benson, editor of *Panorama*, and Paul Woolwich, the retiring editor of *This Week*, both gave interviews lamenting the likely demise of ITV current affairs from prime-time. Benson suggested that competition from *This Week* and *World in Action* had been crucial to the maintenance of standards at *Panorama*.[50] Woolwich wrote that the network's demand for *World in Action* to appeal to eight million viewers would mean that: 'difficult and demanding subjects, such as Ulster, will be ignored in favour of more obvious "glamour" themes'.[51]

Of course, *World in Action* had always sought to be popular and wanting to maximise audiences was natural. 'If the ratings are bad I feel I have failed. It is like owning a shop where nobody buys the goods', Dianne Nelmes explained on becoming Executive Producer in July 1992.[52] The series had always used imaginative or dramatic devices – 'stunts' – to make complex or dreary subjects more accessible and editors took great pride in transforming a dull subject into a public talking point. But the network pressure that it now faced offered a stark demonstration of the central tension within the concept of television current affairs: *World in Action* found itself caught between contradictory imperatives to cover more populist subjects so as to maximise ratings, and to cover the subjects which were of the greatest public value and worth so as to maintain its authority and reputation. Woolwich described this dichotomy as 'Catch 22'.[53]

Reviewing the range of *World in Action*'s programming in the 1990s, various developments seem to confirm the predictions of Lindley and Woolwich that the series could survive only by devoting less time to 'difficult and demanding subjects' and by prioritising accessible human stories that would appeal to viewers. There were notably fewer programmes involving foreign subjects, for example, and the message of audience research in 1991 was that 'viewers have the biggest resistance to this kind of story'.[54] They tended to cost more than domestic programmes despite often receiving lower ratings, although *World in Action* was also conscious of the need to fulfil its brief 'to cover stories across the world'.[55] There was also a detectable increase in editions featuring or fronted by members of the public. Generally, these 'people like us' describe or re-enact their experiences in confronting challenges involving health, crime, public policy or the service industries. This represented a partial refocusing of the series away from journalistic and 'expert' voices and in favour of 'experiential' programmes or versions of 'consumer populism' involving public or consumer testimony. It also produced programmes that contained less exposition of issues and were closer in form to the tradition of observational documentary. In this, they reflected a more general trend in British television towards the emergence of Reality TV as a distinctive strand of programming. Woolwich was right about the pursuit of 'glamour themes' too: there was also a lot more sex.

Various editions of *World in Action* from the late 1980s onwards exemplify different aspects of these trends. As early as February 1989, two consecutive weeks were devoted to editions reconstructing the search for a runaway teenager, Mandy, which her parents had undertaken over many months. Within Granada these were described as 'access' programmes, suggesting a laudable purpose of offering airtime to non-professional voices.[56] But a *Times* review was more critical, condemning the programmes for their inauthenticity: much staging of scenes and of supposedly spontaneous talk marked them out as 'collusive fiction', in which viewers were encouraged 'to accept the director's set-ups' and 'real people . . . have to be groomed in the art of playing themselves'.[57] Nowadays, of course, these techniques are so commonplace that the reviewer's reaction seems surprising, but the example serves to demonstrate how different the norms of current affairs reporting were in the 1980s. The review concluded with what almost sounds like an echo of Lindley's words: 'In turning its subjects into reporters, the programme has obtained a useful technical device at the expense of clarity of intent'.

Another innovation in 1989 that some took to be an indicator of weakening standards was the employment of a game-show format for *World in Action*. Hosted by Nicholas Parsons, familiar to viewers as presenter of *Sale of the Century* (Anglia Television, 1972–83), 'Spongers' pitted a poor family against a wealthier family in a game to discover how each benefited from welfare subsidies. Two years later, 'Beat the taxman', used the same formula to reveal the different proportions of tax each family would pay and, in a further innovation, became the only edition of the series made to be shown in the afternoon – on Budget Day at 2.50pm.[58] Fitzwalter encouraged the idea as a means to explain relatively abstract aspects of the national economy in a form that was comprehensible and engaging to ordinary viewers: The programmes 'made a very significant point and translated something that was indigestible into something that millions of people could watch. I still wish we could have done more of that.'[59] Plowright, however, was more critical[60] and so was the IBA, which received several viewer complaints. Responding to a complaint about 'Spongers', Lady Littler, Acting Director General, defended the legitimacy of the topic and of the approach but added: 'Its mode of presentation was novel but it offered insufficient scope for analysis of the complex statistical information presented' and was, on balance, not 'a very helpful vehicle'.[61] And although experimenting with the form of current affairs may have been a laudable justification, a more prosaic one was cost. As studio shows, these programmes could be produced much more cheaply than regular *World in Action*s shot wholly on location. 'Beat the taxman' was a response to the need to spread the series budget over a larger number of programmes.[62]

Another innovation was the development of 'experiential' undercover reporting. Although strictly controlled, undercover techniques had been an important part of the armoury of television investigative journalism since the 1960s as means to gain evidence of wrongdoing.[63] But miniature camera technology now made it possible for programmes to be built around a journalist assuming a false identity over a long period and recording the struggles that he or she faced. Such techniques depended greatly on the personality of the reporter and sometimes threatened to focus as much on the process of concealment as on the subject of the enquiry. They were popular, however: *World in Action*'s first such project, the three-part 'No fixed abode', in which Adam Holloway lived rough on London's streets for a month in 1992, drew ten million viewers.[64] Holloway reprised his role on the New York streets in 1995 and programmes depending upon concealed identities became increasingly common after the recruitment of Donal MacIntyre to *World in Action* in that year. Various journalists posed as ordinary consumers to uncover scams or deceitful sales techniques. But MacIntyre was prepared to spend long periods undercover in pursuit of stories, most notably in an 11-month investigation of drug dealing in Nottingham.[65] Having honed his technique in various roles at *World in Action*, often in collaboration with Alex Holmes, MacIntyre left with Holmes for the BBC where their *MacIntyre Undercover* (1999) series became a *tour-de-force* in undercover journalism, inspiring various similar television projects and helping MacIntyre to become a public personality.

The greater emphasis on the undercover reporter was accompanied by an increasing use of surveillance techniques and set-ups as the basis for programmes. In this, developments at *World in Action* were reflecting, perhaps unwittingly, the changes in factual television more widely that led to the growth of Reality TV. Among programmes adopting the candid camera technique of setting traps for unsuspecting people and recording their reactions were 'Many behaving badly' and the two-part 'House of horrors'. The former billed itself as investigating the honesty of the general public and surveillance cameras showed how people reacted to the temptation of money or valuables left at cash machines, in shops or in the street. 'House of horrors' filled a Surrey house with hidden cameras and invited local traders to repair supposed faults with its fabric or with domestic appliances within it, using the video evidence to confront them and expose them as 'cowboys'. Both programmes claimed a public purpose for their activities. Experts, including psychologists and politicians, were invited to comment on the revelations of public dishonesty in 'Many behaving badly', and 'House of horrors' was made in conjunction with the local Trading Standards office. But these programmes also contained a substantial element of voyeurism, offering viewers the 'thrill' of witnessing bad behaviour on the part of people who are unaware of being observed. A similar gratification was available in 'Neighbours from hell', which exposed nuisance neighbours. Again, although the programme featured interviews with affected householders and a range of experts, its evidence came from CCTV and camcorder footage of bad behaviour. Tellingly, both 'Neighbours from hell' and 'House of horrors' were spun-off as Reality TV series in their own right. The 'Neighbours from hell' concept was taken up by Carlton Television and several series were commissioned under that title. Three further editions of *House of Horrors*, now a series in its own right, were shown as a summer replacement for *World in Action* in 1998 and further series followed regularly.

Perhaps the programme most cited as an indication of how the standards of ITV current affairs were declining was from 1992 and coincided with the ITV Network Centre's demands for *World in Action* to appeal to audiences of eight million viewers. 'The sultan of sleaze' was an 'exposé' of the *Sunday Sport* publisher David Sullivan. Its suggestion that his newspaper was mildly pornographic was hardly a novel revelation and the programme risked accusations of hypocrisy by including numerous scenes involving scantily-clad models to demonstrate the point, giving rise to a complaint to the Broadcasting Standards Commission that the programme itself contained 'pornographic content'. The complaint was not upheld. 'Last night's *World in Action* seemed more like a whinge from some moral crusader than a serious investigation by ITV's current affairs flagship', complained *The Times*' critic. 'An investigative programme of *World in Action*'s reputation should direct its artillery at less easy targets.'[66] *Panorama*'s editor suggested that the French referendum on the Maastricht treaty, conducted the previous day, provided an obvious alternative target.[67] Nonetheless, nine-and-a-half million viewers tuned in for 'The sultan of sleaze' and it was hardly surprising that *World in Action* should choose to make occasional programmes of this sort in view of the pressures that it was facing to maximise its ratings.

Even 'Jonathan of Arabia' was not immune to criticisms that it made compromises in order to enhance viewer appeal. Its eventual effect in bringing down a cabinet minister was sensational, and its sense of drama was enhanced by the last-minute inclusion of Aitken's pre-emptive 'sword of truth' speech.[68] But the visual conceits that the programme employed – notably regular, unanchored shots of an Arab riding a camel across a desert – were poorly received by some and criticised for their racial stereotyping. In *The Times*, Simon Jenkins described them as 'simply ludicrous' and was particularly critical of the programme's approach:

> There was sand, camels, actors in wigs and gowns, Rolls-Royces, cushions and much Arab junk. At no point was Mr Aitken accused of any crime, merely of consorting with shadowy figures from an unsavoury regime for his personal profit. So? His worst sin was our old friend, failing to complete the MPs register of interests.[69]

It is true that some of the charges presented were quite flimsy and Aitken may have ridden out the scandal had he not chosen to sue. The success of the *Guardian* and *World in Action* in the subsequent trial was not a result of them having proven the truth of each allegation. Instead, it came about through the fortuitous emergence in the course of the trial of evidence proving that Aitken had perjured himself.[70] And the 'Arab' in the programme was merely a sumptuously-dressed actor riding a hired camel across the chilly sands of Southport.

'Packaging facts like Hollywood packages fiction'

In view of the pressures it was facing – to cover more appealing subjects in more engaging ways so as to maximise audiences, to preserve its 'voice' in an increasingly cluttered television market, to maintain its journalistic ambition and authority – it is perhaps remarkable that *World in Action* in the 1990s remained, for the most part, recognisably the series that it had been for so long. Few in 1992 would have predicted that it could have survived in prime-time for another six years but when the end finally came, it seemed inevitable. Two events in early 1998 helped to precipitate it: the loss of the Marks & Spencer libel action, which focused minds on the financial risks of investigative journalism, and Steve Boulton's decision to depart as editor. The *Guardian* connected Boulton's resignation with further pressure to reduce budgets and to move the series 'down market' in an attempt to attract more viewers. It quoted an unnamed senior *World in Action* source saying:

> The pressure is now to get away from international coverage, away from Northern Ireland and away from the type of stories on poverty and deprivation that make people feel uncomfortable. In will come consumery items. We are run by accountants now.[71]

But ITV had already announced plans to review its current affairs coverage and Steve Anderson, formerly a *World in Action* producer and now ITV's Head of Current Affairs, explained: 'Simply because a programme has been around for a long time does not mean it does not have to modernise'.[72] It was clear that the writing was on the wall.

The prediction made ten years earlier by Richard Lindley proved remarkably prescient. In March 1998, ITV announced that it was seeking bids to mount a new hour-long, multi-item current affairs series, stating quite openly that it was to be modelled on the *60 Minutes* formula. By the middle of the year, there was no longer any pretence that *World in Action* could continue as well: the new programme – 'the biggest development in current affairs broadcasting for a generation' – would be its replacement.[73] Granada itself won the commission for a series that its bid document described as 'the new *World in Action*', promising to:

> focus more on human emotion and drama, develop our story-telling skills, be less sniffy about seeking the journalistic angles on popular stories ... be bolder about selling our product to the viewers ... and 'package our facts like Hollywood packages fiction'.[74]

In some respects, *Tonight with Trevor McDonald*, with the popular newsreader intended to add 'personality' and viewer appeal, was a successor to *World in Action*. Jeff Anderson, Boulton's replacement as editor, moved to become the first editor of *Tonight* and the new programme also inherited many of *World in Action*'s remaining personnel. But there was no mistaking the new, populist orientation of *Tonight*. After a disappointing start, changes of format, including a reversion to a 30-minute, single subject format, helped it to find a long-term place in the ITV schedule and a regular audience of around five million viewers by 2000. But, suffering like its predecessor from the need to compete for a time-slot dominated by *Eastenders*, its viewing average soon declined to a figure closer to three million.

After a little over 1,400 editions, the final edition of *World in Action*, 'Britain on the booze', reporting on the nation's alcohol consumption, was shown on 7 December 1998. Curiously though, the series has found an afterlife of a sort in popular and critical imagination as an icon of ITV achievement and a reminder of its decline. Its cancellation, alongside that of *News at Ten*, is habitually cited as evidence of the disintegration of ITV's 'public service' orientation. But of course the truth is more complex than this. By its end, *World in Action* had declined too and evidence of the populist elements for which some have condemned *Tonight* was already apparent in certain editions. And ITV should perhaps be seen more as the victim of political, economic and statutory changes imposed upon broadcasting than as the architect of its own withdrawal from the public service policy that *World in Action* came so strongly to embody.

Notes

1 See R. Lindley, *Panorama: Fifty Years of Pride and Paranoia* (London: Politicos, 2002), esp. pp. 340–5; P. Holland, *The Angry Buzz: This Week and Current Affairs Television* (London: I. B. Tauris, 2006), pp. 200–4; R. Bolton, *Death on the Rock and Other Stories* (London: W. H. Allen, 1990); P. Bonner with L. Aston, *Independent Television in Britain, Vol. 5: ITV and the IBA, 1981–92: The Old Relationship Changes* (London: Macmillan, 1998), pp. 67–79.

2 Tx. 28 March 1990, starring John Hurt, Martin Shaw and Roger Allam.

3 I. McBride, 'Where are we going, and how and why?', in A. Rosenthal and J. Corner (eds), *New Challenges for Documentary* (Manchester: Manchester University Press, 2nd edn, 2005), pp. 489–90.

4 Bonner with Aston, *Independent Television in Britain, Vol. 5*, pp. 267–8.

5 Bonner with Aston, *Independent Television in Britain, Vol. 5*, pp. 167–70; R. Allen, 'London Weekend Television in the 1980s: programmes, public service obligations, financial incentives', in C. Johnson and R. Turnock, *ITV Cultures: Independent Television Over Fifty Years* (Maidenhead, Berkshire: Open University Press, 2005), pp. 108–19.

6 Bonner with Aston, *Independent Television in Britain, Vol. 5*, pp. 24–6, 317–21.

7 J. Ellis, 'Importance, significance, cost and value: Is an ITV canon possible?', in Johnson and Turnock, *ITV Cultures*, pp. 51–3.

8 Article in *Management Today*, August 1986, quoted in Bonner with Aston, *Independent Television in Britain, Vol. 5*, p. 302.

9 See Bonner with Aston, *Independent Television in Britain, Vol. 5*, pp. 302–3.

10 P. Bonner with L. Aston, *Independent Television in Britain, Vol. 6: New Developments in Independent Television, 1981–92: Channel 4, TV-am,*

Cable and Satellite (Basingstoke: Palgrave Macmillan, 2003), pp. 426, 432.

11 See Bonner with Aston, *Independent Television in Britain, Vol. 5*, pp. 265–6.

12 *R. Fitzwalter, memo to D. Black, 'Your memo – Monday night's schedule tightness', 14 October 1988 (bf. 1412).

13 *Black, memos to senior Granada executives, 'Monday night's schedule tightness', 'Monday night's schedule tightness – situation update', 12 and 13 October 1988 respectively (bf. 1412).

14 *Fitzwalter, memo to Black, etc., 24 October 1988 (bf. 1412).

15 *J. Howells, memo to S. Morrison, '*World in Action* R/T', 1 February 1990 (bf. 1412).

16 *Fitzwalter, memo to Howells, '*World in Action* R/T – your memo', 5 February 1990 (bf. 1412).

17 Fitzwalter, interview with the authors.

18 *Broadcasting in the 90s: Competition, Choice and Quality* (London: HMSO, Cm 517, 1988) emphasis added.

19 Bonner with Aston, *Independent Television in Britain, Vol. 5*, p. 382.

20 Fitzwalter, interview with the authors.

21 *A. Quinn, memo to Plowright, '*World in Action*', 13 February 1991 (bf. 1412).

22 *The Times*, 6 May 1992, p. 5, 4 August 1992, p. LT7.

23 *The Times*, 4 August 1992, p. LT7, and see also 31 July 1992, p. 5.

24 *The Times*, 4 August 1992, p. LT7 (emphasis added).

25 In *The Times*, 29 September 1992, p. LT6.

26 *Fitzwalter, memo to World in Action Team containing audience research report, 8 October 1986 (from papers donated to the authors by Steve Boulton).

27 *D. Bidston, memo to Quinn, 'Research input to Board meeting of 11 May 1988', 5 May 1988 (bf. 1412).

28 *The Times*, 22 July 1992, p. LT5; *N. Hayes, 'Relaunch', memo to S. Morrison, 20 February 1991 (from papers donated to the authors by Steve Boulton); *T. Patterson, Granada internal fax to Quinn, 31 January 1991 (bf. 1411).

29 *The Times*, 4 August 1992, p. LT7, 22 July 1992, p. LT5.

30 *J. Lamaison, memo to Quinn, '*World in Action*', 21 February 1989 (bf. 1412).

31 R. Graef, in *The Times*, September 15 1992, p. LT7.

32 *Plowright, memo to Quinn, 6 September 1989 (bf. 1384).

33 R. Graef, in *The Times*, September 15 1992, p. LT7.

34 *The Times*, 4 February 1992, p. 4.

35 In *The Times*, 5 February 1992, p. LT6.

36 *The Times*, 5 February 1992, p. LT6.

37 See M. Darlow, *Independents Struggle* (London: Quartet, 2004), p. 533. Darlow also quotes Fitzwalter recalling a Granada management meeting in which Robinson warned: 'Anybody in the new Granada who doesn't put profits first, second and third has no place.'

38 V. Simson and A. Jennings, *The Lords Of The Rings: Power, Money &* *Drugs in the Modern Olympics* (London: Simon & Schuster, 1992).

39 Ray Fitzwalter, interview with the authors.

40 *Bidston, memo to Quinn, 23 November 1988 (bf. 1412).

41 Letter to *The Times*, 9 April 1994, p. 19.

42 *The Times*, 26 June 1995, p. 10.

43 *Hayes, 'Relaunch'; Steve Boulton, comments to the authors.

44 'He lied and lied and lied', *Guardian*, 21 June 1997, p. 1.

45 Beef Tribunal, *Report of the Tribunal of Inquiry into the Beef Processing Industry* (Dublin: Stationery Office, 1994).

46 Campaign for Freedom of Information, 1994 Freedom of Information Awards press release: http://www.cfoi.org.uk/awards94pr.html; *Press release, '*World in Action*: 30 Years', January 1993 (bf. 0692); 'The steel papers' is discussed in detail in Chapter 4.

47 In the *Guardian*, 4 March 1998, p. 16.

48 Over the case of 'The steel papers'.

49 R. Lindley, 'The bit between the brackets', *Airwaves*, 17, Winter 1988/89, pp. 6–7.

50 In *The Times*, 29 September 1992, p. LT6.

51 In *The Times*, 6 October 1992, p. LT7.

52 In *The Times*, 22 July 1992, p. LT5.

53 In *The Times*, 6 October 1992, p. LT7.

54 *Hayes, 'Relaunch'. We have identified 25 of the 161 editions shown in the years 1972–75 as having a theme of 'Foreign nations or governments'. Comparable figures for 1982–85 were 21 of 157 editions and 13 of 150 for 1992–95. The trend indicated here is clear cut but, of course, there were many more editions than these which featured overseas locations in whole or part.

55 *Hayes, 'Relaunch'.

56 *'*World in Action* advance information sheet', 13 February 1989 (bf. 1412).

57 *The Times*, 28 February 1989, p. 20.

58 'Beat the taxman' is also discussed in Chapter 7.

59 Ray Fitzwalter, interview with the authors.

60 *Plowright, memo to Quinn and Morrison, 16 May 1989 (bf. 1384).

61 *Lady Littler, letter to M. Grenfell, copied to Quinn, 27 June 1989 (bf. 1411).

62 *Lavin, memo to Ferguson, 'WIA series 28 – 1990/1991, 16 July 1991 (bf. 0742).

63 See P. Goddard, '"Improper liberties": Regulating undercover journalism on ITV, 1967–1980', *Journalism*, Vol. 7:1 (2006): 43–63.

64 D. Nelmes in *The Times*, 22 July 1992, p. LT5. Note that BBC's *Nationwide* had made a very similar series in 1981 – see T. Wilkinson, *Down and Out* (London: Quartet, 1981).

65 *World in Action*: 'The untouchables' and 'Wayne's world'.
66 *The Times*, 22 November 1992, p. LT2.
67 G. Benson, in *The Times*, 29 November 1992, p. LT7.
68 At a press conference on 10 April 1995, shortly before 'Jonathan of Arabia' was transmitted, Aitken declared: 'If it falls to me to start a fight to cut out the cancer of bent and twisted journalism in our country with the simple sword of truth and the trusty shield of fair play, so be it.' Such remarks seemed particularly imprudent after his conviction for perjury on 8 June 1999.
69 *The Times*, 12 April 1995, p. 16.
70 L. Harding, D. Leigh and D. Pallister, *The Liar: The fall of Jonathan Aitken* (London: Penguin, 1997).
71 *Guardian*, 4 March 1998, p. 3.
72 *Guardian*, 4 March 1998, p. 3.
73 See *Media Guardian*, 6 July 1998, pp. 2–3, for example.
74 Quoted in *Media Guardian*, 18 January 1999, pp. 6–7.

6

Organisation and culture of production

In one sense, *World in Action* was like a factory; in another, like a newspaper office. Over 35 years, it was involved in the almost permanent production of documentary journalism, but each item that it manufactured was distinct, specific and the product both of individual skill and teamwork. In this chapter, we look out how this level of production was achieved and sustained. Later we look in detail at some aspects of the production process and at the support that the series gained from its unique status within Granada Television. Initially, however, we concentrate on the *World in Action* team – a continually-evolving and, arguably, privileged group – and how it operated.

The rise of the 'fast poets'

The idea of the team is the core concept of the long-running current affairs television series. In becoming fixtures at the heart of British television over many years, *Panorama*, *This Week* and *World in Action* were built around teams of programme-makers who could offer experience, flexibility and continuity. Particularly at *World in Action*, individuals could sometimes spend months researching or uncovering a story or be deployed instantly to cover breaking news. The idea of the team also incorporated a right to fail. Occasionally programme ideas would come to nothing or research would lead nowhere, but failures of this sort could be absorbed within the wider structure of the series because other, successful editions were always in various stages of completion. Nowadays, *Panorama* remains the only major current affairs series still benefiting from this team production ethic. Individual commissions, either for stand-alone programmes or as part of a strand such as Channel 4's *Dispatches* series, are now a more common form of production. The financial pressures that this can generate, especially for small, independent production companies, threaten to replace the 'right to fail' with the 'need-to-succeed-at-any-cost', even creating incentives for programme-makers to make ethical compromises or perhaps to engage in wholesale fakery.[1]

Dozens of people were involved in making *World in Action* at any given time. The press release announcing its revival in 1967 speaks of 'a production and technical team of fifty'.[2] These included technicians, sometimes attached to the series but more often drawn from a pool of Granada technicians or hired in (as with the Samuelsons crews in the early years of the programme, discussed in Chapter 2), production assistants, cost accountants, secretaries and so on. But most discussions of the team refer principally to the group of researchers and producers who planned, researched and fashioned each edition. At *World in Action*'s inception, Tim Hewat's intention was to have six permanent 'editors' (i.e. producers) and up to five researchers, supplemented by a full-time scriptwriter and up to four 'contributing editors'.[3] The latter were intended to be experienced journalists on a retainer who would attend weekly meetings with the team, 'lend an outsider's view to the affairs of the programme'[4] and, Hewat hoped, occasionally undertake specific assignments. The purpose of these 'editorial consultants' – Michael Shanks of the *Financial Times* and David Floyd of the *Daily Telegraph* – was 'to input into us anything they thought which might be relevant to having a programme, or to simply answer questions', recalls Peter Heinze.[5] In the event, no specific assignments were undertaken by Shanks or Floyd and, as the series grew in confidence, the idea of 'contributing editors' was dropped. Hewat's set-up was unusual, too, in involving producers drawn from a film-making background as well television-trained journalists. Later it became quite uncommon for *World in Action* producers to operate the camera themselves unless working in special circumstances, but several 1963 editions were shot *and* produced by Stephen Peet or Louis Wolfers.

Despite some staff turnover, the *World in Action* team expanded little between 1963 and 1965. The series began with six producers and four researchers; in April 1965 it employed four producers, two 'researcher/producers', and five researchers.[6] The 'contributing editors' had gone and producer/cameramen were no longer a regular element of the team. The 'researcher-producers' were researchers on the series who had been identified as potential producers and offered traineeships, illustrating what was to become a common means of progression. Many later *World in Action* producers began as researchers on the series before being identified as suitable candidates for training and promotion. In part this reflects the much greater responsibility given to researchers at *World in Action* than at *This Week* or *Panorama*. The nexus of programme-making at *Panorama* tended to be the producer and reporter, with the latter undertaking the principal journalistic role.[7] *Panorama*'s researchers had a much lowlier function, doing what Ray Fitzwalter describes as 'sweep-up jobs for the whole *Panorama* team'.[8] The role of researcher at *This Week* was similarly 'a supportive one' and certainly not a stepping stone to an appointment as a producer or director.[9] Not only were *World in Action*'s researchers generally much more experienced, some 'as experienced as anybody in Fleet Street', but they were assigned to individual programmes for which they would provide much of the groundwork: 'Usually a researcher would get it going and break the back of all the initial enquiries, potential interviewees and things like that, and then be joined by the producer/director part way through'.[10] Sometimes the researcher's role encompassed most of the effort on the programme and 'a senior producer came in as a kind of bus driver for the last three weeks to actually get it to the screen'.[11] Guidelines given to new recruits to the series state this explicitly:

> Researchers have as important a role as producers especially if the former has either initiated the idea or has a specialist knowledge of the material. Generally speaking, the researcher has virtually the same function as the producer, save that he/she cannot direct the film.[12]

So, while the *World in Action* team began as a collection of television producers, film-makers and journalists, its members could soon be characterised simply as 'programme-makers' offering a range of crucial skills in varying combination. Responding to a viewer in 1969, Leslie Woodhead wrote: 'Our program[me] makers have a variety of backgrounds, some journalistic, some film documentary, but for them all our favourite description is "fast poets" . . .'.[13]

Another distinction between *World in Action* and its competitors lay in the opportunities offered to women. Writing about *This Week*, Patricia Holland criticises the virtual exclusion of women from authoritative roles on the series, where they were generally restricted either to the lowly rank of researcher or to the provision of on-screen 'glamour' at least until the late 1970s.[14] In his chapters discussing *Panorama*'s reporters, producers and presenters, Richard Lindley mentions only one woman programme-maker who made a significant impact on the series before the 1980s.[15] Women seemed more prominent at Granada in the 1960s than in most British television organisations and, while the numbers of men and women were hardly equal, *World in Action* was rarely without women producers and researchers in the team. Four women worked as researchers in the first year of the series, three of them full-time, including Jenny Isard, who quickly became a producer. Nor were they confined to 'softer' subjects as was commonly the case elsewhere. In the years to 1980, *World in Action* made use of a variety of strong women producers and researchers, among them Ingrid Floering, Vanya Kewley, Claudia Milne, Eva Kolouchova, Linda McDougall, Norma Percy and Sue Woodford. Only as series editors did women fail to make their mark. Grace Wyndham Goldie and Caryl Doncaster were colossally important in establishing *Panorama* and *This Week* but, in its 35-year run, *World in Action*'s only female editor was Dianne Nelmes, who occupied the position for 6 months in 1992.

The revived *World in Action* of 1967 was altogether a bigger operation than that under Hewat, partly because it incorporated a dedicated 'Investigations Bureau'. In planning it, David Plowright envisaged a team of 16 – a deputy editor, 6 producers and 9 researchers – which had increased to 17 – involving 9 producers and 7 researchers – by its launch date.[16] Proportions of producers to researchers continued to vary according to circumstances and editors' preferences in subsequent years, and it was not uncommon for staff to be put to service on other Granada projects periodically, so the team never had a rigid composition. No fewer than 13 producers contributed to the series in 1969, 12 of them contracted to Granada at the time, although only 4 worked exclusively for *World in Action*.[17] From the 1970s onwards, the standard team amounted to roughly 22 people, normally comprising more researchers than producers (a ratio of 13:9 had come to be thought of as ideal by 1980).[18] With researchers undertaking so much programme preparation, Fitzwalter feels that this was sensible:

> Particularly with a programme that had some depth to it there would be more research, and some would be discarded, than there would be weeks of production. So it was a sensible thing to have slightly fewer of one and slightly more of the other. And, to be blunt, producer/directors were more expensive, so you tried to use them more economically.[19]

But, he adds, '*World in Action* had a great strength in its flexibility of people'. Sometimes more than one researcher was used for a single programme or different parts were made by different researcher/producer teams.

From time to time, the team was supplemented by a reporter as well, although the number of shows lending themselves to in-vision presentation was always small. Mike Walsh, for example, was recruited from Thames' *TV Eye* series at the end of 1980 and featured in a number of programmes as studio presenter or field reporter. For Fitzwalter, however, this was no more than a useful sideline and his chief benefit to the team was that he was 'very good and highly inventive as a journalist'.[20] In the 1990s, reporter-presenters became slightly more common – a role taken sometimes by members of the team, by members of the public or by outside journalists recruited for the purpose. Producers from outside the team, and sometimes from outside Granada itself, also made periodic contributions. Denis Mitchell, who contributed seven editions to the series between 1968 and 1976, held a free-floating brief at Granada commensurate with his reputation for impressionistic observational film-making. Also working at Granada at the time was Michael Grigsby, two of whose films, characteristically 'giving a voice' to those whose struggles are generally hidden, were shown as editions of *World in Action*: agricultural workers in 'Working the land'; illiteracy in 'A well kept secret'. Other producers joined the team briefly to take on specific commissions as freelances, often to relieve short term staff shortages. Similarly, outside journalists were also involved on occasions. Introduced as 'the *Daily Mirror*'s special correspondent', John Pilger made three programmes for the series in 1970–71 including the controversial 'The quiet mutiny' about American soldiers in Vietnam, but struggled to work within the stricter regulatory requirements of television. Pilger soon found that he no longer had confidence in senior Granada personnel, whom he felt were conniving in 'inserting lies' into his films in response to ITA pressure; Jeremy Wallington recognised that 'to be successful, [John] will still need to opinionate to a degree which we do not allow our own producers', a situation that the company found increasingly too troublesome to tolerate.[21] Another outside contributor was Godfrey Hodgson, then with the *Sunday Times*, who was involved with three editions between 1970 and 1976. The first two, including 'How to steal a party', Leslie Woodhead's much-praised observational film of the Democratic Convention, drew heavily on his expertise as a commentator on American politics. 'When in Rome', the third, was a fine piece of collaborative investigation uncovering political corruption in Italy.

London and Manchester

In 1963, *World in Action* was established in a long, narrow open-plan office at Granada's Golden Square headquarters in London, physically separated from the main areas of the building.[22] As Granada held the Northern ITV contract, the series was understandably keen to incorporate northern locations and stories where possible and Granada's Quay Street studio complex in Manchester was used as a base for some editions. Nonetheless, *World in Action* remained firmly a London-based programme, with Hewat and the team valuing their location on a single site close to the metropolitan centre. Replacing *World in Action* in the summer of 1965, *The World Tonight* took over these arrangements and London became the hub of its international operation. Significantly, however, staff who would not be required for the new series were offered, and in some cases declined, work with Granada in Manchester.[23] But Hewat's attachment to a London base was not shared by David Plowright. Plowright and his *World Tomorrow* team had transferred much of their effort to Manchester by the time he came to plan for Granada's new current affairs series in early 1967, with the result that Manchester became the main operations centre when the revived *World in Action* was launched. This coincided with a shift within Granada Television away from the glittering, cosmopolitan world of Sidney Bernstein towards the more serious commitment of Denis Forman. Whereas Bernstein continued to base himself in the Group's London headquarters despite the rise of Granada Television in Manchester, Forman gradually assumed more of his duties and saw the need to establish Manchester as 'a sovereign state'. By the late 1960s, London had been relegated to 'an outstation' of Granada Television.[24]

For the remainder of its run, *World in Action* was divided between London and Manchester. Editing and post-production were generally handled in Manchester, with personnel travelling from London to attend where necessary. But the Investigations Bureau was based in London because it was thought sensible to conduct in-depth research at a location close to national newspapers, corporate headquarters and major libraries. Jeremy Wallington, the Bureau's first head, had worked on investigations for the *Sunday Times* and the *Daily Mail*, so it was natural for him to establish a *modus operandi* based on his experience in running Fleet Street investigation teams. With Plowright heading the series in Manchester and Wallington running investigations in London, a culture of split leadership grew up. So when Plowright became Head of Current Affairs in 1968, he was replaced at *World in Action* by joint editors – Wallington in London and Woodhead in Manchester. A succession of joint editorships followed, even after the Investigations Bureau ceased to have a formal identity or dedicated personnel in the mid-1970s.[25] One consequence of this was that when he and Brian Lapping were appointed as Joint Editors in 1976, Fitzwalter found himself forced to relocate himself and his family to Manchester so as to maintain an editorial presence in each city.[26] Only when Fitzwalter became sole Editor, in 1981, did the series revert to being wholly led from Manchester. Even then, the London arm of *World in Action* remained significant and necessary.

Operating across two locations provided some advantages for the series. For Ray Fitzwalter, it gave *World in Action* a different attitude – 'northern, independent, feisty' – compared to its London-based competitors:

> Unlike other current affairs programmes, which often had originated as Westminster-bound and intimately tied with immediate news, there were the resources to stand back and to probe but to do so to a certain extent from this northern stance which was perhaps more questioning. And it did in the fullness of time give it a more distinct and clear character, for example, than *This Week* and particularly *Panorama*.[27]

He also believed that having two bases conferred an advantage in obtaining stories: 'We were far more likely than *This Week* to pick up things that related to the North of England or Scotland' and 'to see things through the eyes of ordinary people, which we did far more, rather than lecturing to them as *Panorama* would have'.[28]

But there were disadvantages to this arrangement as well. For one thing, it was more expensive. This was a growing problem as financial pressures mounted in the 1980s and ITV became more concerned about costs. Granada froze many of its programme budgets for the 1985–86 season, forcing Fitzwalter to plead for an increase because of the programme's 'inescapable "erratic" costs', partly arising out of its split operation.[29] The lack of a London studio was a further constraint, magnified with the introduction of Simon Berthon's 'fast response unit' in 1985 whose aim was to make topical programmes. 'In a crisis, important people are not going to come to Manchester', explained Berthon, commenting on a live programme shown shortly after Michael Heseltine's resignation from the government. 'We made Monday night's programme with one-and-three-quarter arms tied behind our back.'[30] The 'Heseltine' programme had had to rely on down-the-line interviews conducted from Manchester, obviating the possibility of discussion and necessitating the use of a journalist in Manchester as a discussant, since 'all the MPs are in London' and because 'the London line might have gone down'. Finally, London-based journalists disliked the idea of working even part of the week in Manchester. A map on the wall of the London office was annotated with a cross marking Manchester and a picture of Beau Brummell saying to his general: 'But sir, you promised me I'd never be sent abroad'.[31] On occasions, the Manchester connection led to problems in recruiting high-profile London-based staff. For example, an attempt to recruit Lorraine Heggessey to *World in Action* in 1986, described as a 'dynamic, experienced, 29 year old, action on screen, woman producer/director with flair and executive potential', was thwarted largely by Granada's inability to base her in London despite her willingness to join the team.[32] Heggessey joined *This Week* instead.

A happy ship?

A hallmark of *World in Action*'s working methods under Tim Hewat was the weekly team meeting, an inclusive forum in which the most recent programme would be discussed and criticised, new ideas proposed and the team ethic reinforced. It was an all-encompassing way of life in which it was normal for evenings to be spent either at work or in the pub, where Hewat and the team would continue to discuss programme ideas and set the world to rights. In the early 1960s, a culture of drinking was routine amongst newspaper journalists – a culture that Hewat felt part of. A consequence of this was a very tightly-knit team with a strong sense of camaraderie – 'a private army within Granada', as Forman describes them.[33] A common story of the time, probably apocryphal, has Sidney Bernstein making an internal call to the programme's Golden Square office: '*World in Action* here', says a voice. 'Oh, Granada here', replies Sidney. Such close relations among the team were no longer possible after *World in Action* split into London and Manchester operations under Plowright and the weekly team meeting was abandoned. In the 1970s the team met roughly twice yearly although at one point, between 1976 and 1978, meetings were held monthly for all of those who could attend and regular minutes produced.[34] These were less self-congratulatory affairs than in the 1960s, however, and concentrated largely on strategies to improve the series' work methods, quality and scope. Nor did Fitzwalter find them particularly valuable:

> We used to get the team together, usually all together, about twice a year, but that's all that was possible because you had London and Manchester and everybody was always travelling and some people were always away, and it was very difficult and expensive, and relatively unproductive.[35]

Nevertheless, team members provided considerable support to one another and the sense that the team were special, a group apart, was partially maintained. Of course, the regular production of current affairs programming is necessarily a collaborative practice and a successful relationship between researchers and producers – sometimes between several of each on the same programme – was a crucial requirement. Arguably, the key to maintaining morale was that team members felt involved, informed and trusted by their Editor and by others with a current affairs responsibility. The 1970s team meetings were just one of various practices that helped to engender this: regular team memos circulated programme ideas and noted progress on particular stories and investigations; staff were periodically asked to produce papers outlining their ideas for the future of current affairs; there was open feedback about recent programmes not only amongst the team but throughout Granada' current affairs department. For example, a lengthy exchange over one 1980 programme, the subject of various critical memos from Brian Lapping, was ended by a telling response from David Boulton, the department's Head, criticising 'solemn exchanges of point-scoring memos' as 'ludicrous and pompous', preferring criticism by way of 'argy-bargy over a pint'.[36] Although Hewat's drinking culture had long since departed, 'argy-bargy over a pint' remained the normal method of bonding and settling differences amongst members of the team. One particularly tangible symbol of the series between 1967 and 1975 was provided by the boards displayed on the wall of the Manchester office, to which the title, subject, date, audience rating and names of producers and researchers who worked on it were added for each *World in Action* programme as it was broadcast. By the time they were taken down, these boards occupied a substantial proportion of the wall and contained the details of roughly 350 programmes. Woodhead even took to describing the role of editor as 'keeper of the *World in Action* boards'.[37] Photographs of them were kept for posterity.[38]

Another common bond between team members was a shared distrust of authority and power. Perhaps because it was less metropolitan, *World in Action* was perceived as offering a greater challenge to the Establishment than *This Week* and particularly *Panorama*. 'It was often radical', explains Fitzwalter:

> radical with a small r in the sense of being challenging – challenging to authority, to governments, to corporations and above all in that sense independent. And therefore it often did come up against governments or heavy corporations and seek quite often to get at something that they didn't want to report.[39]

On the other hand, he stresses, whatever individual beliefs team members held: 'they had to behave in a professional and journalistic fashion'. Despite this, a strong perception that *World in Action* was unacceptably left-wing prevailed at the Independent Television Authority for many years (see Chapter 8) as well as in mainstream press criticism, exemplified by Julian Critchley's characterisation of the team as 'Granada's Guevarists'.[40] Part of the reason for this, of course, lies in the nature of journalistic enquiry itself, especially in television current affairs. By nature, such programmes come to be made by 'the kind of people who are interested in investigating society, in challenging subjects, in asking is the status quo acceptable', as David Elstein put it in 1980.[41] Soon afterwards, Anna Coote was suggesting that the assumptions of current affairs programme-makers, their choices of suitable subject matter and styles of reporting are almost always likely to be left-of-centre, however much care is taken to make the programmes themselves 'balanced':

> One mode favoured by current affairs television is the investigation, which thrives on finding out facts that embarrass powerful people. Another is the examination of social problems. Both tend to favour the anti-Establishment liberal-left. I find this neither surprising nor undesirable.[42]

So it can be argued that the very act of enquiring into the workings of society, government or business is politically charged. In one important respect, however, *World in Action* really was more radical than its counterparts. When *This Week* or *Panorama* were radical, they were often so in spite of the ethos of the institutions which produced them. But at Granada, the desire to be independent-minded, to challenge authority and to upset the status quo came from the top, embodied successively in the attitudes of Sidney Bernstein, Denis Forman and David Plowright. Bernstein's response, at Granada's formal franchise renewal interview in 1967, to the Authority's claim that its file of complaints against the company was larger than the files for all the other ITV companies put together, was characteristic: 'We consider that a compliment', he said.[43]

The team's sense of its uniqueness, of its common purpose and of participating in a unified enterprise within Granada meant that morale was normally high. Of course, the 1990s saw an increasing consciousness among team members that their work risked being undermined by the effects of mounting commercial pressures and of the removal of unquestioning boardroom support, but even then 'the process of programme-making was only dented and not destroyed'.[44] Earlier, the impression of a generally happy team is confirmed by Fitzwalter: 'I never thought there was really any unified discontent'.[45] Under Hewat, of course, the feeling of 'specialness' and of 'internal, self-generated excitement' was a powerful motivator.[46] This air of relative contentment was in marked contrast to *Panorama*, nicknamed 'Paranoia' by its staff, where: '[a]t times in its history you would have had to be very unlucky indeed to find a more poisonous place to work'.[47]

Even at *World in Action*, however, there were sources of friction. Most common among these were the ambitions of individual team members. In a hierarchical structure, only a small number of people can rise to the top, so senior producers on the series, for example, could become frustrated at their inability to rise further. The issue of finding new roles for such people to guard against staleness and disaffection recurs in archived memos about the series. A related problem lay in union restrictions on appropriate programme credits. Since television had grown out of the film industry, programme-makers in television current affairs belonged to the Association of Cinematograph and Television Technicians (ACTT), so could not properly be described as 'journalists' – a designation reserved for members of the National Union of Journalists. Instead, they could be called only 'producers' or 'researchers'. This caused much dissatisfaction, as a 1976 memo explains:

> We employ, in effect, four categories of people on *World in Action*: 1. Producers, 2. Directors, 3. Senior Journalists, 4. Researchers, but we restrict them to two titles and pay scales. This arrangement leads to unnecessary hurt feelings, depression and contrariness – and consequently hours of therapy sessions – mostly for the people in Category 3. This arises particularly when they have taken the major responsibility for concept and content of a programme, only to have the main credit – and all newspaper mentions – given to the Producer/Director ... This is particularly true when such people are involved in specialist long term programmes, making their opportunities to win a credit infrequent. They consequently feel that their market value is kept down.[48]

In partial amelioration of this problem, programmes were sometimes subtitled 'an investigation by . . .' to give further credit to the researcher, but this was only available for programmes that were investigative, of course. As a title, 'researcher' could also seem to imply too lowly a status to those approached in the course of planning a programme. Fitzwalter recalls:

> Sometimes, [researchers] would be ringing important politicians or whatever it was, and people would say, well I'd rather talk to your producer, whereas had that person, as they could equally well have done, rung from a Fleet Street newspaper they would have talked to them without any problem.[49]

Mutiny at Golden Square

On the whole, however, these were relatively minor issues. Only once, in 1974, did *World in Action* suffer a wholesale rupture in team confidence and morale. Here a complex chain of events led to what was effectively a mutiny, described by a worried David Plowright as 'a situation in which programme-makers appear to be separating themselves from the Programme Management'.[50] The situation had its source in various grievances felt by the team. Among these was a resentment of Granada's employment arrangements. At this stage, almost all of the team were on one-year rolling contracts rather than in staff positions. Generally, such contracts were renewed without question, but the impression of insecurity that these arrangements engendered among programme-makers is not surprising. In consequence, they also felt peculiarly vulnerable to the whims of management. A further problem lay in *World in Action*'s split location. By 1974, the centre of gravity of the series had shifted towards London where the majority of the team was now based, making it particularly remote from senior management. There were also unusual pressures on the programme's journalism. In addition to the normal range of programme subjects, which still included lengthy investigations, the recurring national story was of Britain's economic crisis, involving raging oil price inflation, the three-day week, striking miners, power rationing and so on. Covering the crisis led to a larger focus on the economy than usual and to several hurriedly-made, collaborative programmes responding to economic events. Notable among these were 'The morning after', in which the series heralded New Year 1974 by interviewing ordinary Britons about the effects of the crisis – a programme involving no fewer than five crews – and its 1975 sequel 'The morning after the year before'.

Unfortunately, these various pressures and concerns were exacerbated by erratic management. Gus Macdonald had been serving as Executive Producer of *World in Action* with David Boulton, as the programme's Editor, effectively his deputy. Boulton is one of the most significant figures in any account of *World in Action* – an unpaid consultant on 'Atomic arms race', the very first edition of the series (he was editor of *Sanity*, the CND newspaper, at the time); producer of or contributor to no fewer than 50 *World in Action* editions from 1969 onwards, as well as many other significant Granada programmes; later an effective Head of Current Affairs for the company. But when Macdonald was given wider responsibilities that included Granada's regional output, withdrawing from day-to-day involvement with the series and especially from close contact with the London office, members of the team became increasingly concerned and dissatisfied with Boulton's judgement and leadership.[51] A factor in this was the assignment of work – some staff seemed perpetually to be overloaded by Boulton while others felt that they were overlooked – and resentment grew as Boulton seemed unwilling to communicate effectively with the team or explain the rationale behind such decisions. The catalyst for action was the treatment of Simon Albury, who had joined the series on a rolling contract at the end of 1973. With six months of his contract to run, Albury received a memo warning him that it would not be renewed unless his performance improved. Albury consulted with David Hart, a fellow *World in Action* producer and head of the ACTT Granada London shop, who agreed that the chief cause of any under-performance on Albury's part had been Boulton's unwillingness to assign any work to him. Replying to Boulton, Albury reiterated his willingness to work on any project that might be offered to him, but little had changed when, three months later, he was informed that his contract would indeed be terminated. Under Hart, and with the unanimous support of the whole London shop (including those unconnected with the series), the ACTT now attempted to institute a formal dispute with Granada over Albury's treatment. Fearing adverse publicity, and unwilling to undermine the authority of its editor, Granada offered an internal enquiry instead. In solidarity with Albury, and to demonstrate that his treatment by Boulton was not an isolated case, the union gathered grievances from almost every member of the team. Some were petty, others serious, but the enquiry examined each of them painstakingly in a series of meetings between union representatives, individual team members and management. Meanwhile, the team made management aware that they were investigating their entitlement to time off in lieu of the additional hours that were routinely worked in preparing programmes – an entitlement that hitherto had rarely been taken up.

At least once a month for over a year, Plowright chaired meetings between staff and management, represented by Macdonald, Boulton and Julian Amyes, working gradually through a list of over 20 grievances. It was 'a most extraordinary, time-consuming and mechanistic procedure'.[52] Fitzwalter recalls that 'they looked at these complaints and they tried to very cleverly bounce them all off or talk them down or say: "it's your word against his word"', but in crucial cases documents could be produced to support team members' claims. Eventually, it became clear to Granada's management that decisive action was necessary to restore the team's faith in the programme's management. At this point, Forman stepped in, writing a document that Fitzwalter describes as 'a masterly attempt to bring [the process] to a conclusion'. It also demonstrates Granada's shock at finding its much-prized belief in its own evenhandedness and support for creativity to be under threat. 'I cannot recall any problem in a programme team that has caused so much concern as the recent trouble in *World in Action*, both within the team itself and to the management', wrote Forman:

> Granada's style of management has been typified over the years, as I believe, by a friendliness between creative people, by a mutual respect between programme-makers, whatever their station, who have traditionally treated each other as equals on the job.[53]

He went on to acknowledge that the management of the programme had 'from time to time fallen out of line with Granada traditions, Granada practices and Granada beliefs', that there had been 'a lack of candour' in Boulton's communications with the team and that threats of dismissal 'as a method of obtaining acquiescence in a decision' were 'quite foreign to the way we normally work'. He also acknowledged the insecurity arising from the London office's separation from Manchester – '[g]rievances can more easily grow when the person or persons they are directed against is generally absent' – although he criticised the 'mild hysteria' of the team's response and the fact that they had failed to take their complaints to a more senior level earlier. In future, grievances should quickly be referred upwards 'until you finish up with me'. More importantly, notice periods were extended, limited assurances given as to the continuation of London employment with the company and Albury's contract was renewed. And Forman was decisive in saying: '[t]he style and structure of *World in Action* management will change', with Boulton and Macdonald having accepted their responsibility in prompting the team's grievances and in failing to deal adequately with them. For all its magisterial qualities, Forman's document was essentially an admission of the defeat of Granada's strategy for handling the dispute and a victory for the complainants. Hart even suggests that he was asked directly what the team's demands were. As a consequence, all were offered staff positions and pension entitlements.

Forman announced that Boulton would take responsibility for a group of programmes mostly concerning the USA, with Macdonald returning to run *World in Action* as Executive Producer. But in the longer term, it was essential for the series to be edited by a person who could both lead the team and maintain its trust. As Forman's statement had put it:

> You must be able to accept the word of your Editor, even in the smallest matter, and he must be able to accept yours . . . I profoundly believe that unless you can carry a team along with your decisions you cannot, for any length of time, be an effective team leader.[54]

Having stood solidly together for over a year, taken on management and won, the morale and cohesion of the *World in Action* team was now huge. In a remarkable example of workplace democracy, reflecting both the politics of the group and the spirit of the times, they decided to elect their own leader. After Granada's management had invited applications for the editorship, the *World in Action* team conducted their own formal interviews with the candidates in London – Manchester members travelled down specially – and put forward the names of four individuals in whom they had confidence. Candidates were then interviewed at a Granada board. Although Granada's management were careful to present it as their own decision, all of the team's selections were interviewed and one of them, Ray Fitzwalter, was appointed as Joint Editor. Brian Lapping, intermittently involved with the series but not a member of the team, was to accompany him. It was 'a clever conclusion' – a return to a system of joint editors based notionally in Manchester and London, one proposed by the team and the other by management, but neither – as Fitzwalter puts it – willing to be the prisoner of either side.

Keeper of the boards

The role of editor (or Executive Producer of *World in Action*, the title sometimes carried by more senior editors of the series) was never a straightforward one, as this story demonstrates. Editors had to manage budgets, to liaise with line managers and keep Granada's senior management informed about programmes in production, to respond to complaints from the public, regulators and powerful people, to clear legal hurdles for many programmes, to provide leadership in both Manchester and London (the latter 'always ... a potential trouble-spot'), to wrest adequate performances from Granada's 'sometimes second-rate' technical departments, to 'prop' weaker producers through moments of crisis and generally to 'keep the show rolling' while 'dealing with the backwash from previous programmes'.[55] Furthermore, of course, there was the need to keep the series fresh and invigorated in relation both to the news agenda and its competitors, and to provide leadership and inspiration to a team of experienced but individualistic specialists, part of the 'first division' of the profession and sometimes with egos to match.

In the early 1980s, as management began to envisage the departure of Allan Segal from his joint editorship of *World in Action*, a series of memos discussed whether it was even feasible for a single editor (Fitzwalter) to perform all of these tasks effectively and, if so, what sort of management support he should receive. Eventually, Plowright concluded that the relationship between the editor and his superior was the key aspect in determining an editor's success. In evaluating different approaches, he criticises the idea that a Head of Current Affairs should take an assertive role as 'Editor in Chief'. Rather, 'the system requires the boss to delegate to nominated editors and leave them with the impression that whatever successes are achieved are their responsibility'.[56] He continues:

I have always believed that *World in Action* functions best under one boss. He could be called an Editor, an Executive Producer or a Head of Department. He could have working under him a bureau, an economics unit, a department of silly ideas, but he is in charge and he is keeper of the boards. He is sensible enough to recognise that around him are people who like to interfere like his Head of Department, his Programme Controller, one or other of the Joint Managing Directors.

In other words, Plowright recognised that the near-impossible job of editor required a freedom to manage and clear lines of responsibility, allowing him to refer upwards when required but to reject interference when it was unhelpful or unwarranted. Here we can see the main difficulties that had led to the crisis of the mid-1970s, embodied in the ambiguous working relationships and division of responsibility between Macdonald and Boulton, and between them and those in positions above and below them. Above all, the requirement is for trust – between team and editor and between editor and head of department – and that too had been lacking in 1974–75. Of course, Plowright's prescription is an ideal and Fitzwalter's period as sole editor was by no means straightforward. Again, breaking news – notably the Falklands War, inner city riots and the miners' strike – threatened on occasions to overwhelm the editorial process and in May 1982 the team was even moved to write a memo about Fitzwalter's relationship with his Head of Department who, by this time, was David Boulton:

> [W]e do not believe that the Editor edits the programme – his decisions are never final, or even largely final. We have had to work on the assumption that any decision he makes is subject to major revision, even reversal, by David often within hours of transmission.[57]

Despite the echoes of 1975 that are apparent here, and with them a reminder of how volatile a mismanaged team might become, these issues were quickly resolved and the team pacified. There were to be no further calls to mutiny.

Making *World in Action*

Identifying a programme subject was the first step towards producing an edition of *World in Action*. Subjects could come from numerous sources – letters from the public (lengthy files of these remain in the archives), tip-offs from people who get wind of a scandal (as in 'The set up'),[58] even off-the-cuff remarks from MPs ('The sailor's jail', inspired by David Owen MP's admission at a party that Portsmouth naval prison – for which he had had ministerial responsibility – was the 'nearest thing I've seen to hell on earth').[59] But the team was both the best and the most common source for programme ideas because programme-makers had the requisite experience. As Fitzwalter says:

> Somebody's got to have a feel for the length and the weight, possibly what's been done before, what's been done in other current affairs programmes, what catches the mood of the times, and all of those things. And what's going to succeed as a programme and what are your underlying criteria ... Most best ideas came ... out of small discussions between often two or three people, sometimes then realising that somebody else had some expertise and you'd go to them. Sometimes it was people on the team with a bright idea, but it would nearly always need working up.[60]

The ability to predict the news agenda was a particular motivator is selecting programme subjects too. *World in Action* was never very effective in responding rapidly to breaking stories, but regularly attempted to give the appearance of doing so by making 'anticipatory' programmes based on ideas that would shortly become topical. Fitzwalter notes how difficult it was to do this effectively,[61] but it was a technique that Hewat used too:

> The trick, which struck me as magic at the time, was to look at long-standing situations and actually have that sort of instinct which, I suppose, newsmen of that quality have, that they know what's boiling all around the world ... But what it was was being really, really well-informed over a very long period of time about everything, and just having that sort of instinctual flair and enough luck.[62]

As time went by, the type of subject that was thought to be appropriate for the series changed. With the growth of BBC2, increases in news coverage and greater competition in current affairs, subjects that had seemed appropriate to Hewat's team – the overseas 'situation report', Paris fashion week, venereal disease – seemed too thin for *World in Action* in the 1970s. By the 1990s, subjects with a markedly popular angle came to seem especially appealing because of their potential to attract more viewers.

Of course, making programmes for *World in Action* involved many different types of assignment in numerous locations with varying degrees of urgency, but documents giving guidelines to programme-makers lay down some ground rules and offer an interesting insight into elements of the production process. Granada had a reputation for financial rigour and *World in Action* always had its own production manager charged with cost control. Except in emergencies, advance budget meetings would be held before shooting began and prior approval was needed before the agreed budget for an edition could be exceeded. Budgets were even given for 'serious research projects'. At some periods it was normal for a post-production meeting to be held following the transmission of each programme, reviewing any financial or logistical problems that may have arisen. There was a policy not to pay for news or get involved in chequebook journalism, although reasonable expenses could be paid to the subjects of programmes. 'Unless gun barrel to temple don't pay in cash', the guidelines add.[63] The programme's strict policy that participants were not allowed to see rushes, scripts or film before transmission is reinforced, although this could be waived in rare cases. Budgetary efficiency seems to have been a matter of professional pride for *World in Action* editors and the majority of producers: 'I was careful with money ... and I'm quite proud of that because I always regarded it as a discipline and you needed disciplines', says Fitzwalter. 'It was pleasing to shoot something on a modest ratio and succeed in making a better programme than somebody who'd shot twice as much', he adds, emphasising the importance of effective research and 'good creative planning' before shooting. 'We know we were better run than *This Week*.'[64]

The editing process under Tim Hewat, in which he wrote every word of the script himself while the Chief Editor assembled visuals to complement it, is described in Chapter 2. Hewat would work throughout the weekend, generally late at night ('Tim wouldn't start writing until eleven'),[65] and often on the day of transmission itself, in an adrenaline-fuelled process greatly influenced by his background in print journalism. After its reinstatement in 1967, *World in Action* no longer possessed this 'newsroom urgency', nor could scripts only be written concurrently with the edit. But the practice of 'crash edits' over the weekend before transmission remained normal. A 1970 document instructs that, on quick programmes at least: 'The tradition of three days without sleep will be maintained'.[66] By 1975, weekend editing was hardly less common, but its cost was becoming more of a concern to the company, as Plowright noted in saying: 'If ... the longer term planning now apparent manages to bring the number of "crash edits" down to anywhere near the target of 50%, a record will have been created and a good deal of money saved for programmes'.[67] Little had been achieved by 1982, however, when Fitzwalter was writing: 'We could aim to abandon the Monday finish as a regular thing and make it occasional when it's essential ... Much "immediacy" is often spurious and matters only to those involved rather than those watching'.[68] The aim here was to have 'a programme in hand' but this was not always easy to achieve, as a 1985 Fitzwalter memo explained:

[O]ver a year or two, we have had periods when we have been a programme ahead and we have comfortably avoided [working] unnecessary weekends (as opposed to essential ones for news urgency reasons) . . . It has been the case since January that we have hit weekend working with virtually every programme.[69]

He advances various reasons for this – understaffing, excessive producer workloads in dealing with programmes referred to the Broadcasting Complaints Commission, the working practices of individual producers – but technical problems represented the largest cause.

The foremost technical problem facing the series in the early 1980s involved graphics, described as 'a constant and ongoing sore'.[70] Countless surviving memos recount breakdowns or errors in shooting graphics, often involving costly re-shoots and severe delays in finishing programmes. Granada's persistent under-investment in equipment and experienced staff in its graphics department was blamed. While other companies were using character generators or computers, Granada was still using letraset in 1983 and booking the single functioning rostrum camera was sometimes impossible.[71] For Boulton, the result was that '*World in Action* looks incredibly tatty week after week . . . *Panorama* looks bright, snappy 1980s and *World in Action* looks 1960s because it is still on incredibly ancient technology'.[72] A good indicator of the effects of such technical problems on the series can be found in a plaintive memo from Fitzwalter about two 1983 programmes: for 'People without a land', on Israel's colonisation of the West Bank, 'an administrative error in the graphics department' meant that 'no graphics man was available at all'. As a result, a vital day was lost and 'a rash of rostrum camera mistakes', including 'two maps shot together in error', meant that the programme could not be finished in time for its Monday slot. When it was shown, the entire programme was transmitted out of sync. In completing 'Too cold to live', which investigated whether elderly deaths from hypothermia were a consequence of changed government policy, *World in Action* was greatly overcharged by a freelance graphics artist hired by the graphics department. But in the absence of any paperwork or financial control mechanism within the graphics department, it proved impossible for the series to recover its loss. Fitzwalter notes that these cases are 'nothing unusual' and repeated almost on a weekly basis, as numerous similar surviving memos demonstrate.[73] Although there was a gradual improvement as the decade progressed, and fewer technical problems caused weekend overtime or delayed programmes altogether, the look of *World in Action* still lagged behind its competitors. In 1982, the team described themselves as 'stone age warriors in a world of satellites, Quantel [and] caption generators',[74] but in 1987 Bill Boyes was still describing Granada' in-house facilities as 'jurassic compared with what the competition in the future has access to', adding: 'Why do we have to fight tooth and nail for every facility we need?'[75] As late as 1991, Nick Hayes was calling for 'much greater attention to the best of post-production video facilities' and especially a 'dedicated graphics/post-production designer ... to improve the look of the programme'.[76]

The desire to curb weekend editing was driven by more than administrative convenience or concern for the look of *World in Action*. As Plowright's 1975 memo suggests, from the mid-1970s the cost of it began to rise astronomically as broadcasting unions became increasingly powerful in dictating the terms under which programmes could be made. A strike took ITV off the air altogether for 11 weeks between August and October 1979 and for the next few years union pressure had a significant effect on the production of the series. The *World in Action* local editing agreement laid out basic working hours and the requirement for a ten-hour break at the end of a working day. Extending the working day or reducing the length of the break incurred incremental and punitive overtime rates, so that a poorly-managed weekend 'crash edit' could easily generate overtime at seven times the normal hourly rate.[77] Moreover, Fitzwalter suggests that technical staff frequently attempted to exploit the situation in order to earn more money – by coaxing producers into 'breaking the break' and by wangling lucrative assignments: 'I used to have trade unionists coming to me saying "I've got an enormous electricity bill this week. Can you put me on that programme?"', he recalls.[78] Union influence had a significant effect on the series in other areas too. Much time was expended poring over any library film that was used in order to demonstrate that no member of the electricians' union could have lit it, for example, and threats were made to 'black' programmes using any form of interior lighting, even if they had been shot under hazardous circumstances or in the midst of war zones.[79]

When embarking on programmes in such places, it became necessary to negotiate on a case-by-case business for a 'short crew' arrangement, involving 'the most unbelievably arcane disagreements with the trade unions'.[80] By agreement, short crews could be used for 'inherently hostile environments' where units needed to be as flexible as possible and the number of staff put at risk kept to a minimum, for 'covert conditions' where filming depended on secrecy or concealment, and for other circumstances where normal crews could not travel due to remoteness, political restrictions or sensitivity of subjects. In each instance, a detailed case had to be made to the ACTT and specially increased rates were payable.[81] Numerous short crew requests for whole or part-programmes survive from the period 1978–82, each carefully explained and involving sequences shot in Paraguay, South Africa, Namibia, Australia, Poland, Cambodia, Uganda, Angola, Guatemala, El Salvador, Spain, Lebanon and, most controversially, Northern Ireland.[82] In some of these cases, the need for short crewing was contested, either before or after the fact, and there was an air of continual suspicion that short crews were sought out of expediency rather than necessity. From time to time, it seems that programme subjects were dropped because of the difficulty of reaching a deal. And as a trade-off for the short crew agreement, *World in Action* was forced to employ production assistants on normal shoots, a practice it had never used routinely nor been required to. The situation exasperated Fitzwalter:

> We'd never used PAs and we'd never needed them and we had no role for them, and we'd run the programme for whatever it was, best part of 20 years ... And they said this was outrageous, that this was a role on WIA that somebody else was doing that a PA ought to be doing, it was PA's work that was being stolen. [They said that] the PA would do a shot list, and we said, we don't use shot lists, and they said they would do them anyway and that was a PA's job to do and the shot list would be provided and very often it was provided – at a point at which it was too late to use it anyway.[83]

It seemed ironic to many *World in Action* personnel, themselves union members, that trade unions, which had traditionally protected the rights of broadcasting staff (not least in the 'mutiny' of 1974) had begun adversely to affect the production and quality of programmes. But this rise in union power was ultimately self-defeating, attracting the hostility of employers and the government of Margaret Thatcher and, eventually, restrictive legislation.

The issue of short-crewing does draw attention to the dangers periodically faced by *World in Action* programme-makers filming in hostile territories. In the course of the series, there were numerous detentions and deportations – the first when Chris Menges and Michael Parkinson were arrested at gunpoint filming for 'The thin red line' in Zanzibar[84] – and in some instances film had to be smuggled out of countries as a result – from South Africa in 'The discarded people' and from Paraguay in 'The hunt for Doctor Mengele', for example. Surviving papers offer tantalising insights into more complex dangers.[85] Setting off to film evidence of torture in Chile (for 'Chile: The reckoning'), Mike Beckham wrote to Gus Macdonald giving not only his itinerary but also a complex code to be used in phone-calls and cables on the assumption that lines were tapped.[86] Vanya Kewley made similar arrangements in attempting to set up an interview with General Ojukwu, erstwhile leader of the breakaway Biafran state, partly so as not to alert the President of Ivory Coast, where he was living in exile (for 'The man who made Biafra').[87] By the end of the 1980s, it had become necessary to take out special insurance against kidnapping when setting out to film in the Middle East (for example in 'The agony of Lebanon', where a team of four were sent 'under the protection of the Lebanese army').[88] The protection of the Philippines navy was obtained for 'Pirates', a film about the rise of armed gangs boarding ships, murdering crew and stealing cargo in the South China Sea, but this did not prevent Andrew Quinn from expressing his concerns:

> Clandestine filming at sea among armed pirates seems to me to carry a very high probability of putting our employees' lives at risk. From the little I have already read in the papers about this problem, I understand they are not above dumping people over the side.[89]

Fortunately, *World in Action*'s crews returned from all of these encounters without injury.

An obvious impetus behind weekend editing, and behind concerns about the delays caused by technical problems, was the relentless pressure to produce a fresh programme every Monday, and Fitzwalter's 1985 intention to have 'a programme in hand' offered the prospect of a standby programme to cover any instance of non-completion. Differing policies towards the production of standby programmes for *World in Action* existed at different times. In the early phase of the series, Tim Hewat instituted a policy that an intentionally non-topical edition would occasionally be made for use as a standby. So 'Sundays', finally shown in December 1964, was a re-edited version of a programme based on material showing how Sunday was observed in Britain and abroad that had originally been assembled two years earlier, before the series began.[90] In this instance, the publication of a report on Sunday trading offered a topical hook to justify showing a programme that had hitherto been kept for emergencies. After the series' reinstatement in 1967, a film about Georgian peasants claiming to be 140 years old offered a similar example. It had been made only because Soviet authorities had prevented Russell Spurr from making another programme. Already in the Soviet Union, he accepted their invitation to shoot this subject instead rather than return empty-handed.[91] Made at the end of 1967, 'Death is afraid of us' sat on the shelf as a standby for three-and-a-half years before it was finally transmitted. Effectively, such programmes had to be timeless, however, and *World in Action* editors were uncomfortable about making non-topical material, preferring the 'programme in hand' solution where possible. Often there was another consideration too. In negotiations with the ITA over the acceptability of programmes, editors found that the non-availability of a standby offered a powerful argument in favour of showing the planned edition. Hewat's attitude was: 'well, if there's no standby show there's got to be this one'.[92] The lack of an alternative was a key factor in the transmission of 'The quiet mutiny', which greatly upset the Authority in revealing the widespread disaffection of American troops in Vietnam (see Chapter 8). Forman was pressed by the ITA in 1969 to ensure that standby programmes were available 'to avoid argument taking place with the Authority under the strain of an imminent air date' and again in 1970, this time in return for an ITA promise of swifter consultation.[93] In the event, there was little change in the policy of either party and by 1973 the IBA was again criticising the absence of a standby programme. 'I feel you would agree that this kind of all or nothing position is not one which leads to the best discussion of the merits of a particular programme', wrote Bernard Sendall. But Forman's reply put *World in Action*'s view clearly: '[W]e have been working on the basis that rather than keep some timeless bromide on the shelf, it is better to have reserves amongst the number of current programmes which are in the making at any one time.'[94] But a contrasting viewpoint comes in a particularly angry memo from Jeremy Wallington and gives a flavour of attitudes at *World in Action* towards the Authority in the early 1970s:

> I accept your order to make a standby programme ... Having said that I would like to register the point that I am doing so under protest. I did not agree with the standby policy when it first arrived and I still don't. There was a time (which I cherish) when, in the event of the ITA expressing anxiety about a programme, we insisted they catch a train to Manchester during the weekend and usually at a most inconvenient hour. Comparing that somewhat arrogant position with the relationship we now have with the Authority, something seems to have been lost ... I am the editor of a programme not the minder of a sausage machine ... Any misunderstandings with the Authority can be avoided by simply telling them precisely what our problems are.[95]

Later, under Fitzwalter, it was accepted that the IBA required a standby programme but the practice of 'covering one programme with another', rather than commissioning 'timeless' programmes, was followed.[96]

World in Action was involved in film production. With rare studio-based exceptions, each edition was shot and edited on film. Internally, when individual editions were not referred to as 'shows' (a term with clear roots in television) they were called 'films' and, at times, were motivated by ideas of a film aesthetic (or 'anti-aesthetic' in the earliest days, as we suggest in Chapter 2). As a film production unit, *World in Action* was highly skilled: '[O]ver the years', explained Chris Malone:

> we have perfected an efficient production system that maximises the turn around time. For example, we can cut a film in two days, finish in the early hours of Monday morning and still have a full neg cut, track laid and dubbed, final print available for transmission that evening. We know the system so well that we can predict to within minutes how long a neg cut will take.[97]

So the movement to shooting on video-tape which took place in 1991 can be seen as a fundamental shift both in the aesthetics of the series and in the production process itself. The possibility of making full-length *World in Action* programmes on tape was first raised in 1982 with Granada's purchase of Electronic News-Gathering equipment, although it could not be deployed at the time due to the absence of a union agreement.[98] When the suggestion re-emerged in 1989, financial pressures on ITV were increasing and thoughts of cost-cutting were the main motivation (*This Week* and *Panorama* had already moved to video-tape). As an experiment, three programmes were made on different tape formats towards the end of that year, but inexperience and poor equipment almost caused one to be abandoned altogether when it took thirty hours to dub a programme that, on film, would have taken eight.[99] Expectations of substantial savings continued but Fitzwalter was more cautious and produced a document weighing up the effects:

> Aesthetic: Film gives *World in Action* a 'documentary feel'; it makes it more exciting to look at, with more shots, faster cut and with an overall more crafted look to the finished product. This gives it an edge over ... *This Week* and *Panorama* whose editing style tends to be more ponderous and flat and have more of a news look.

> Editorial: Tape is less well-suited to post-production of a 30 minute documentary than ... most other programme areas. The editing and re-editing of a *World in Action* is exceptionally intensive. The whole process on tape takes longer and needs to be completed earlier. *Panorama* has to complete its edit two days earlier than *World in Action*, a substantial disadvantage.

> Operational: [Video] cameras are more liable to break down and more difficult to mend than film cameras ... You need more equipment for tape on the road ... In post-production, sound dubbing presents major problems ... BUT you can satellite tape which can be useful for *World in Action*. AND tape is instantly accessible, has a greater range of effects, better cutting and fading and it is much more compatible with modern graphics.

Financial: [Any capacity for savings would come only after substantial investment in equipment, training and recruitment.] The experience of *This Week* is that the move to tape produces a considerable increase in shooting ratios despite attempts to keep it under control. Thames have told us that *This Week* made no savings after changing two years ago.'[100]

Looking back, Fitzwalter is proud to have counselled caution: 'I stopped us rushing and buying equipment that would have not done as good a job for us'.[101] By the following year, greater experience and a new generation of video-tape equipment were beginning to overcome many of the editing problems he had identified.[102] Drawing on the guidance offered by *This Week*'s experience, producers could be warned from the outset of the risk of over-shooting in response to the cheapness and availability of tape compared to film. In September 1991, *World in Action* turned one of its cutting rooms over to tape operation, developing and assessing tape editing on some editions while others remained on film.[103] The experiment succeeded and the other room was also converted at the end of the year. So from the start of 1992, *World in Action* was no longer involved in film production but in making efficient, up-to-date-looking current affairs programmes on video-tape.

A Granada Television production

Throughout this book, we have repeatedly drawn attention to how Granada stood out from other ITV companies – in its fondness for challenging authority and orthodoxy, in its faith in programme-makers and preparedness to promote them, and in its belief in public service broadcasting as a virtue rather than a tiresome regulatory requirement. Until Sidney Bernstein's retirement in 1979, Granada was essentially a family firm run by a Labour-voting entrepreneur who, initially at least, was apt to be condemned by the press as a dangerous socialist. Bernstein gathered able lieutenants around himself, most significantly Denis Forman – a visionary in the development of Independent Television and, in roles from producer to chairman, responsible at least as much as his employer for the record and reputation of Granada Television. To a young *World in Action* researcher in 1963, Bernstein and Forman were 'like Medician princes ... They had that style. And I'm not sure that the other managements were quite that ... clever'.[104] Bernstein was the maker of myths, not least about himself, while Forman was the enactor of them. A flavour of Forman's management of the company emerges in a 1973 memo about a *World in Action* edition subtitled 'Money, money, money', in which he writes:

[I]t is not our sole job as Joint Managing Directors to support *World in Action* in the way she should go, though that is a very important one. Indeed, in certain other companies I could name, there is an absurd notion abroad that the Managing Director's only job, really, is to ensure that his company makes a sufficiency of the aforesaid money, money, money.[105]

Equally significant in the development of Granada was David Plowright, recruited as a journalist in 1959, who provided the vision behind *World in Action*'s 1967 reinvention and ascended to inherit from Forman not only the leadership of the company but his role as its moral compass. As Forman explains, Plowright:

took on *World in Action* as his principal charge and stuck with it, first as producer, then as executive producer and then continuing as its internal inquisitor and public protagonist and finally as its *eminence grise* until his chairmanship ended in 1992.[106]

Overall, the rise of former *World in Action* people, all of them programme-makers rather than administrators, to senior positions within the company was remarkable. The Programme Committee, at the heart of Granada's management operations, was dominated by current affairs personnel (with one exception, 'every member with a creative role ... had had an involvement with current affairs at some stage', notes a 1976 record).[107] Macdonald describes the Programme Committee as 'Granada's Politbureau':

a group of a dozen or so executives and programme-makers who meet monthly in Manchester with a few board members and senior management ... [T]he tone is informal, funny, disrespectful, and on rare occasions passionate to the point of things being thrown.[108]

Certainly, the atmosphere at Granada was generally congenial. Forman writes of the absence of hierarchies, of management by a team of 'like-minded individuals' and of a 'system of growing programmes out of the individuals who were going to make them'.[109] For these people, *World in Action* represented Granada's 'family silver'[110] and, at least until Plowright's departure, it enjoyed unstinting support within the company even when it was the subject of threats. Forman attributes an important part of the programme's success to the determination of Bernstein, Plowright and himself to resist the 'moral blackmail through which the British Establishment seeks to smother any story that could cause them embarrassment'.[111]

As we have noted, trust was the basic element in such a management style, coupled with an understanding of when intervention was required and when it was not. Peter Heinze talks of the 'amazing trust' that

Bernstein and Forman showed in Tim Hewat between 1963 and 1965, but a very short chain of command meant that both were prepared to be involved immediately if a major disruption, such as the banning of 'Down the drain', occurred: 'It was felt there was the *World in Action* unit and from there you went to God – I mean, that was either Bernstein or Forman'.[112] Later, despite shifting management structures, the feeling was the same:

> Basically in Granada it always led, when the heat was on, back to the board ... Granada was always a good company because it had people who made programmes on the board ... and so they had a knowledge and an affinity.[113]

Fitzwalter contrasts this with other broadcasters, especially the BBC, where management 'collapses' under pressure. Despite their seniority, he singles out Forman and Plowright as the most valuable sources of support in his time with the series and had no compunction about consulting them, whether to defend a programme under attack or simply to seek a second opinion. Of course, this close involvement had occasional drawbacks too. A critical memo from David Boulton in 1980 expresses his concern 'at the frequency and degree of higher management intervention in *World in Action* scripts and rough cuts', suggesting that this is 'provoking a real crisis of confidence in the team, and a debilitating doubt in the programme leadership'.[114] Fitzwalter, too, refers to moments when their seemed to be 'too many cooks': 'there are occasions when too many people were offering a view on the wording of a script or whatever it was.' But he recognises that this was an essential counterpart to a degree of management support that brought 'an enormous net gain'.[115] And in response to Boulton's memo, Plowright dismisses the suggestion that such management intervention was a normal state of affairs, noting that it arose from particular problems over the completion and content of three recent editions and immediately suggesting a meeting to discuss how such pressures could be overcome in future.[116]

While it was not uncommon for Granada management to advise on or suggest changes to *World in Action* programmes, it was certainly not their normal role to prevent transmission altogether. As we show in Chapter 8, on the occasions when the ITA or IBA did so, management support was swift, vigorous and robust. But two peculiar instances in the early years of the series, both involving Sidney Bernstein, can be read as instances of management censorship. The first is mentioned only in the recollections of Mike Hodges, a producer with the series between 1963 and 1965, and concerns a programme about John Bloom.

In the early 1960s, Bloom was a popular entrepreneur who had made his name in washing machines and on the society pages. Hodges heard that Bloom was in financial trouble and began to prepare a programme about him, but claims that Bernstein urged that it be abandoned, perhaps fearing that it would appear anti-semitic.[117] Not long afterwards, when Bloom's empire collapsed, a programme describing his fall from grace was made ('John Bloom') but this time without Hodges' involvement. The second case is more widely recorded, including Forman's own detailed account,[118] and concerns a 1965 investigation into freemasonry, again involving Hodges. Forman suggests that the Masons had long been identified as a potential 'target' for *World in Action* and the programme had his and Sidney's wholehearted support. A fortuitous find of Masonic regalia and a book of rituals enabled Hodges to reconstruct an authentic lodge in a friend's flat and to describe Masonic influence with authority.[119] But Cecil Bernstein, himself a Mason, was extremely uncomfortable. He organised a private screening of the rough cut for a group of leading Masons and then confronted Sidney, putting into writing his intention to resign from the company if the programme were to be transmitted. Sidney was deeply upset, caught between conscience and family loyalty. At an emotional meeting, described by Forman, he could explain his position only by saying: 'Denis, I love my brother'.[120] Sidney phoned Alex Valentine, *World in Action*'s editor, taking the unusual step of keeping a transcript of the conversation. In it, his confusion and remorse are clear:

> I can't explain to you in detail but we cannot do the Masonic programme … I am embarrassed. You and I will discuss with Hodges on Monday … It is not censorship. I am opposed to censorship … Hodges and you should stop all work and don't say anything about it … I can't say anything more for the moment.[121]

At the meeting on Monday, Hodges recalls that Bernstein was in tears.[122] Meanwhile, Forman, feeling betrayed and hurt – '[n]othing could hurt more than that the show should be blocked by the very power it was designed to challenge'[123] – contemplated his own resignation. He didn't return to work for nearly a week. When he did, he records, he and Sidney never mentioned the programme again.

A 1973 inventory from Granada's film department contains a list of completed but untransmitted *World in Action* programmes 'taking up valuable space'.[124] It includes ten *World in Action* editions with annotations about each. Among them are 'Masons' and 'South of the border', banned by the ITA in 1971.[125] None of the others had been censored, however. For these, the reasons given for their withdrawal are more prosaic, ranging from 'David Frost', John Birt's attempted exposé of the star interviewer and London Weekend Television executive which revealed little but its producer's inexperience[126] (the annotation reads: 'Gus Macdonald says it's no use for transmission'), to '88 bus route', a programme that sought to do nothing more than record the sights and sounds of an ordinary bus journey. Here, the annotation simply reads: 'Boring'.

Notes

1 See, for example, B. Winston, *Lies, Damn Lies and Documentary* (London: British Film Institute, 2000), esp. pp. 32–3.

2 *'Granada Programme News: *World in Action*', launch press release (no date) (bf. 1209).

3 *Hewat, 'An outline of Granada Reports', 24 July 1962 (bf. 1154).

4 D. Crow, *World in Action '63* (London: Consul, 1963), p. 11.

5 From an interview with the authors.

6 *B. Heads, memo to D. Forman, Hewat, D. Plowright and others, '*World in Action*', 15 April 1965 (bf. 1416).

7 R. Lindley, *Panorama: Fifty Years of Pride and Paranoia* (London: Politicos, 2002), pp. 119–29.

8 Interview with the authors.

9 P. Holland, *The Angry Buzz: This Week and Current Affairs Television* (London: I. B. Tauris, 2006), pp. 40–1).

10 Fitzwalter, interview with the authors.

11 Fitzwalter, interview with the authors.

12 *Fitzwalter and A. Segal, 'Guide for new World in Actioners', 8 January 1980 (from papers donated to the authors by Steve Boulton).

13 *Letter to Mr Borrows, 1 May 1969 (bf. 0751).

14 Holland, *The Angry Buzz*, pp. 18–20, 41–2, 78–82.

15 She was Angela Pope; Lindley, *Panorama*, pp. 52–190.

16 *T. Gill, budget for '*World Tomorrow* (series 3)', 10 April 1967; *undated and unattributed page headed 'TBA – Staff' (both bf. 1497).

17 *J. Wallington (?), memo for Granada senior executives, 'Producers and director assignments 1969', 22 January 1970 (bf. 1356).

18 *M. Scott, memo to Fitzwalter, '*World in Action* staffing', 4 November 1980 (bf. 0744).

19 Interview with the authors.

20 Fitzwalter, interview with the authors.

21 *Pilger, letter to D. Swift (Tempest Films), 6 June 1971; *Wallington, letter to Swift, 5 July 1971 (both bf. 1268).

22 This *World in Action* office and its working arrangements are described in Crow, *World in Action '63*, pp. 10–11.

23 *Heads, '*World in Action*', 15 April 1965.

24 D. Forman, *Persona Granada* (London: Andre Deutsch, 1997), pp. 212–13.

25 At times, joint editors both held the title of Editor; at others, the senior editor was given the title of Executive Producer of the series.

26 Fitzwalter, interview with the authors.

27 Interview with the authors.

28 Interview with the authors.

29 *Fitzwalter, memo to Scott, 'Budget 1985/86', 14 June 1985 (bf. 1053).

30 *Berthon, memo to Scott, 'London studio', 15 January 1986 (bf. 1053).

31 Fitzwalter, interview with the authors.

32 *Fitzwalter, memo to Plowright, 16 September 1986; *Fitzwalter, memo to Scott, 'Producers', 31 October 1986 (both bf. 1053). In 2000, Heggessey became the first woman Controller of BBC1.

33 *Persona Granada*, p. 134.

34 *Archived at bf. 1161.

35 Fitzwalter, interview with the authors.

36 *Boulton, memo to Lapping and others, 'Benn – *World in Action*', 17 January 1980 (bf. 0720).

37 *Plowright, 'Statement to WIA meeting in Manchester, 9 October 1975' (bf. 1268).

38 *Archived in bf. 0767.

39 Interview with the authors.

40 *The Times*, 17 August 1968, p. 17.

41 Quoted in A. Rosenthal, *The Documentary Conscience: A Casebook in Film Making* (Berkeley: University of California Press, 1980), p. 122.

42 A. Coote, 'Right on', in J. Wyver (ed.), Festival Programme, Edinburgh International Television Festival, 1984, p. 69.

43 Quoted in Forman, *Persona Granada*, pp. 239–40.

44 Nick Davies, in an e-mail to the authors.

45 Interview with the authors.

46 *B. Heads, quoted in N. Chanan, 'Granada Television – The Early Years', ch. 9 (unpublished ms., 1977) (bf. 1438). See Chapter 2.

47 J. Paxman, 'Foreword' to Lindley, *Panorama*, p. vii.

48 *Lapping and Fitzwalter, memo to Wallington, 'Status and titles', 14 September 1976 (bf. 1349).

49 Fitzwalter, interview with the authors.

50 *Plowright, 'Statement to WIA meeting in Manchester, 9 October 1975'. Besides documentary sources, the following account draws on the recollections of David Hart, Simon Albury and Brian Lapping, in telephone conversations with the authors, and of Ray Fitzwalter, in an interview with the authors.

51 'I knew how to make good programmes, but not how to manage good programme-makers', Boulton later wrote (in J. Finch (ed.), *Granada Television: The first generation* (Manchester: Manchester University Press, 2003), p. 189).

52 *Forman, statement to *World in Action* team, 8 July 1975 (bf. 1340).

53 *Forman, statement to *World in Action* team, 8 July 1975.

54 *Forman, statement to *World in Action* team, 8 July 1975.

55 In part, this list draws on: *Fitzwalter, untitled memo to Boulton, Scott, 2 January 1981 (bf. 1054).

56 *Plowright, memo to Scott, 'WIA reorganisation – Boulton's memo 15. 1. 81', 6 February 1981 (Bf. 1054).

57 *Untitled memo headed 'To: Current Affairs meeting, From: Team members', 25 May 1982 (bf. 0744).

58 See Chapter 4.

59 *B. Cox, memo to Wallington, 'Portsmouth naval gaol', 23 July 1970 (bf. 0721). 'The sailor's jail' is discussed in Chapter 8.

60 Interview with the authors.

61 Interview with the authors.

62 Brian Winston, interview with the authors.

63 At least three versions of *World in Action*'s production guidelines survive, containing virtually identical text. The most recent is from Ray Fitzwalter in 1986 (*bf. 1412), the earliest from Gus Macdonald in 1975 (*bf. 1268). It is clear that the 1975 version is also derived largely from an earlier document.

64 Fitzwalter, interview with the authors.

65 Winston, interview with the authors.

66 Cited in *Fitzwalter, memo to Plowright, 'Overtime – your note', 5 July 1985 (bf. 1053).

67 *Plowright, 'Statement to WIA meeting in Manchester, 9 October 1975'.

68 *Fitzwalter, untitled paper for Scott and Plowright, 2 June 1982 (bf. 1053).

69 *Fitzwalter, untitled memo to Scott, 13 March 1985 (bf. 1053).

70 *Segal, memo to Boulton, 'Crews, editing and equipment for *World in Action*', 15 December 1980 (bf. 1054).

71 *Fitzwalter, memo to Scott, 4 January 1983 (bf. 1053).

72 *Boulton, question to T. Brill from transcript of Granada seminar 'Production capacity in the '80s', Mottram Hall Hotel, 11 and 12 March 1982 (bf. 1209).

73 *Fitzwalter, memo to Scott, 14 March 1983 (bf. 1053).

74 *'To: Current Affairs meeting, From: Team members', 25 May 1982.

75 *Boyes, memo to WIA team, 'Thoughts for development in the future', 23 July 1987 (from papers donated to the authors by Steve Boulton).

76 *N. Hayes, 'Relaunch', memo to S. Morrison, 20 February 1991 (from papers donated to the authors by Steve Boulton).

77 *Document giving information about production costs (no author given), headed: 'To *World in Action* producers/researchers, Feb 1980' (bf. 0744).

78 Interview with the authors.

79 In one memo, Boulton has to assure the electricians' union that a bedside lamp shown in shot in a Vietnamese hospital had not been switched on by the producer: *Memo to EETPU shop steward, '*World in Action*: Vietnam', 4 March 1980 (bf. 0744).

80 Fitzwalter, interview with the authors.

81 *'A local agreement between Granada Television Limited and ACTT on short crewing in *World in Action*' (undated, *c.* March 1980) (bf. 0720).

82 Predominantly in *bf. 0720.

83 Interview with the author.

84 D. Crow, *World in Action* (London: Mayflower, 1965), p. 70.

85 And see V. Kewley, 'The story – no excuses', in Finch (ed.), *Granada Television: The first generation*, pp. 199–202.

86 *Beckham, memo to Macdonald, 'Chile', 31 October 1973 (bf. 0701).

87 *Wallington, memo to T. Gill, M. Southan, 11 September 1970 (bf. 1268).

88 *S. Prebble, memo to A. Quinn, 7 July 1989 (bf. 1411).

89 *Quinn, memo to Fitzwalter, '*World in Action* filming', 7 May 1991; *Fitzwalter, memo to Quinn, '*World in Action* – Piracy programme', 10 May 1991 (both bf. 1411).

90 *Hewat, '*World in Action* or *Horizon*: Revised story list', undated but prior to January 1963 (bf. 1244).

91 Fitzwalter, interview with the authors.

92 Peter Heinze, interview with the authors.

93 *Unattributed 'note for the record' of meeting between senior ITA and Granada personnel to discuss *World in Action*, 28 October 1969; *B. Sendall (ITA), letter to Forman, 30 November 1970 (both bf. 1090).

94 *Sendall, letter to Forman, 16 November 1973; *Forman, letter to Sendall, 3 December 1973 (both bf. 1072).

95 *Memo to Forman, 30 November 1971 (bf. 1072).

96 Interview with the authors.

97 *Malone, memo to R. Pickles, 'Audio dubbing', 26 October 1989 (bf. 0742).

98 *Brill, from transcript of speech at Granada seminar 'Production capacity in the '80s', Mottram Hall Hotel, 11 and 12 March 1982 (bf. 1209).

99 *Malone, 'Audio dubbing'.

100 *Fitzwalter, memo to B. Smith, '*World in Action* – tape v. film', 28 September 1990 (bf. 1412).

101 Interview with the authors.

102 *R. Pickles, memo to Quinn, Brill, '*World in Action* – move to tape', 30 July 1991 (bf. 1412).

103 *Pickles, '*World in Action* – move to tape'.

104 Brian Winston, interview with the authors.

105 *Forman, memo to Macdonald, 7 March 1973 (bf. 1072). This edition was transmitted as 'The get rich quick guide'.

106 Forman, *Persona Granada*, p. 169.

107 *Minutes of Programme Committee meeting (3/76) held on 13 May 1976 (bf. 1061).

108 In E. Buscombe (ed.), *BFI Dossier 9: Granada – The First 25 Years* (London: British Film Institute, 1981), p. 130.

109 Forman, *Persona Granada*, p. 185.

110 *Prebble, memo to Fitzwalter, '*World in Action* – relaunch', 10 October 1988 (bf. 1411).

111 Forman, *Persona Granada*, p. 169.
112 Interview with the authors. 'Down the drain' is discussed in Chapter 8.
113 Fitzwalter, interview with the authors.
114 *Memo to Scott, Plowright, Forman, 2 December 1980 (bf. 0744).
115 Interview with the authors.
116 *Plowright, memo to Boulton, '*World in Action*', 3 December 1980 (bf. 0744).
117 Mike Hodges, interview with Rodney Geisler, 3 March 1998, for BECTU History Project.
118 In *Persona Granada*, pp. 179–82.
119 Hodges, interview with Geisler.
120 *Persona Granada*, p. 180.
121 Forman reproduces the entire transcript in *Persona Granada*, pp. 180–1.
122 Interview with Geisler.
123 *Persona Granada*, p. 182.
124 *Cuff, 'List of films sitting in M/C vaults taking up valuable space', 4 April 1973.
125 The 'South of the border' case is discussed in Chapter 8.
126 See J. Birt (2002), *The Harder Path* (London: Time Warner), pp. 106–8.

7

Documentary journalism and television form

As we hope to have demonstrated throughout this book, the longitudinal examination of a single series provides an excellent opportunity to explore not only how a specific television project developed and re-thought itself across its different defining contexts but, more broadly, the nature of changing 'current affairs' culture in Britain.[1] This culture is an aspect both of the television industry itself, drawing on the aspirations and commitments of those who work to produce its factual programmes, and of the framing conditions of politics and culture. What should be shown and said? Within what regulatory framework and to an audience with what expectations and prior interests? More directly, how should the programme look and sound? How might it combine its own force and originality of expression with recognition of what else is happening in the schedules? At times, of course, it might define itself precisely against what has become 'conventional'.

This chapter will explore *World in Action*'s history in developing particular formal and stylistic approaches.[2] It will look at the varying purposes of those approaches in addressing and appealing to viewers' sense of the world, a sense that programmes might want simply to extend and deepen but one that they might sometimes wish to challenge and shock. Of particular interest here are the double imperatives of popularity and of seriousness, imperatives which have continued to carry a potentially contradictory dynamic throughout the history of journalism and which require imaginative and tough terms of mutual engagement in order to achieve a properly complementary relationship rather than a nervous, unstable compromise.

To refer to the 'approach' of any series is to use a term which goes beyond formal concerns in the narrowest sense, for it suggests an interest not only in the arrangements of word and image used to present ideas (e.g. library stills and film footage; observational material; reporter presentations to camera; interviews; sounds and images obtained by clandestine recording; commentary), but also in the different categories of information which are to be collated (statistical; historical; ethnographic; personal testimony), as well as the different broad modes of presentation to be deployed in the use of these categories and their combinations (e.g. storytelling; analysis; revelation of previously hidden realities).

This granted, it is impossible to generalise freely about the 'approach' of *World in Action*. Such a limitation in the terms of comment is not just due to the many changes of approach, programme design, personnel and technology that we have documented in previous chapters as they have occurred over the series' long presence on British television screens. It is also because *World in Action*, at every point in its history, has worked with a considerable degree of flexibility, allowing it to approach different subjects in very distinctive ways, to pursue sometimes widely different kinds of journalistic enquiry, and to present the products of these in audio-visual formats that maximised impact and resonance. In the words of one former editor (associated with the programme during the late 1960s and early 1970s):

> What quickly became evident was that instead of all the words that you use in printed journalism you had to find a different way in television of doing it and you had to focus on a microcosm; you had to boil down the major, major issue into a small thing that everybody: the audience, the producer, the director, could actually focus on. And it had to be something visual.[3]

Nevertheless, despite the sheer range of the routes taken to producing 'microcosms' and getting 'something visual' (and also something verbal) into the programme, it is possible to identify six relatively distinct 'projects', for classification purposes: *analyses, exposés, depth narratives, discussions, ethnographic studies* and *biographies*. The value of this broad schema is that it allows scope to approach specific editions of the programme with a useful sense of how their way of coming at a topic, their communicative design and their use of image and sound might relate to other editions, past, concurrent or in future years. It sharpens a sense of connections but also a sense of differences and yet it is loose enough, and obvious enough in the distinctions it signals, not to create problems of cramping the output in too tight a typological system. However, it does involve construing *World in Action* as a single body of work over a 35-year period. We think there are enough similarities in approach across the corpus to justify this 'grand' overview, although, as we have observed in earlier chapters, it should be borne in mind that the distinctive presentational and journalistic ethos of the 1963–65 period was not wholly replicated on the series' resumption in 1967 and there have been many points of disjunction, alongside the continuities, since. For instance, there was a strong orientation towards 'observationalist' modes in the late 1960s, a periodic (and contrasting) emphasis on programmes in which verbal exposition and exchange in studio-based formats were primary, occasional experiments with presenters and, from the late 1980s on, an increasing use of stylistic borrowings from other kinds of popular programming (including the emerging forms of Reality TV and lifestyle/consumer series) in the attempt to sustain audience figures.

We examine these 'project' categories in Section One of this chapter. The basis of the typology has to do with the *communicative purpose and design* of editions, rather than with the particular techniques and strategies used in the realisation of those purposes. Although the categories have implications for the specific discursive elements put to work in a programme, these elements are given more direct attention in Section Two. We should note, too, that the typology is not directly concerned with the kinds and levels of research required as the groundwork for particular editions. The term 'investigative journalism' is often associated with *World in Action*, and quite rightly – but investigative journalism is also strongly linked to the world of print journalism (in Britain, for example, the work of the *Sunday Times* 'Insight' team).[4] It does not represent either a particular type of communicative project, since 'investigative' research could be required by more than one project type, or any specific formal expression on the screen or soundtrack. Section Three of this chapter reintegrates the communicative projects of *World in Action* with the techniques and strategies of realisation via a number of case studies devoted to particular editions, and the chapter concludes with some remarks about formal innovation with specific reference to the challenge of reconciling journalistic quality (a social and political as well as professional value) with popular appeal. In all three sections we discuss material sometimes treated elsewhere in the book with another analytic emphasis, for instance organisational or regulatory. In our use of it here, we have chosen to repeat certain descriptive details in order to increase the coherence of the chapter and lessen the need for readers to move backwards and forwards across the book in order fully to comprehend the account and the analytic significance derived from it.

Section one: the communicative projects of *World in Action*

Of our six 'project types', characterising the range of work with which *World in Action* has been associated over the years, three – analysis, exposé and depth narrative – have been much more common than the others – discussion, ethnographic study and biography. Topically speaking, as interventions in 'current affairs', all of these projects have in common the elaboration of detail around some event or person currently or recently in the public eye, or, in the editor's judgment, belonging there. Thus there is often a strong link, demonstrable in programme discourse, between any given edition and the recent news agenda. But 'recency' is a rather elastic concept. Some editions, for example, were timed to coincide with relevant news events: 'The great train robbery' (1964), 'The Angry Brigade' (1972), and 'Jonathan of Arabia – Act two: The dagger of deceit' (1997) were made for transmission on the concluding day of the trials whose legal business formed at least part of their story. Others had to remind viewers of critical events going back weeks or years: 'Typhoid – Aberdeen' was broadcast within five weeks of the outbreak of the 1964 typhoid epidemic it examines; 'An accident at sea' examines the causes of a sinking two years earlier. Other 'current affairs' – such as poverty or unemployment, the Vietnam war, Northern Ireland, official secrets, BSE – were more long-term, problematic, background dimensions of the social world, to which *World in Action* would return at periodic intervals without the need for any specific news trigger.

Analysis

A *World in Action* project of analysis has as its primary communicative purpose that of elaborating the complex conditions surrounding some event or situation with current/recent news relevance. Analysis is an *aspectual* discourse: that is to say, it seeks to organise different kinds and levels of relevant information into a coherent whole, working out, for each edition on its own terms, the best running order of the aspects that it covers, and the appropriate linkage between them. The first ever edition of *World in Action*, 'Atomic arms race', had an analytic character, and was structured thus:

1	HOOK	The future for infants born in January 1963
2	QUESTION	What is Britain's likely future role as a nuclear power?
3	EXPOSITION	a) The devastation of Hiroshima
		b) Nuclear capability in 1945 vs. 1963
		c) America vs. Russia
		d) The possibility of a nuclear accident
		e) America's defence posture
		f) America and its allies with particular reference to Britain
		g) Other nuclear powers: France and China
		h) The superpower arms race
4	CODA	James Thurber's 1940s thoughts on world destruction, in cartoon form

In this edition, the hook and the coda (where moral reflections are articulated) are independent of the main analysis. The question provides a transition between hook and exposition. The aspectual elements of the exposition are given a loosely chronological ordering, so that the 'backward-looking' segment (Segment a) precedes those dealing mainly with the present (Segments c, d, e, f and g – segment b is transitional) with the final segment more 'forward-looking'. Since chronology does not account for the ordering of segments c, d, e, f and g, it is across this block that the freedom of aspectual structuring is most in evidence. Programmes constructed as analytic projects can work with a logic of exposition developed largely in relation to broad areas of knowledge rather than to specific events, circumstances or people. Their organisation can seem more 'academic' as a result, bringing benefits in terms of a synoptic review of difficult issues best seen in their interconnectedness, but also placing some limitations on popular appeal and accessibility. Whatever the particular principles employed in choosing a certain ordering of materials rather than another, however, the application of a primarily analytic approach will show a wide range of variation in relation to the topic. Among determining factors here will be the extant literature (academic and journalistic) on the area receiving attention and, perhaps, the existing patterns of emphasis in this literature, although of course it is quite possible for an analytic programme to project itself as 'correcting' established treatments in this respect.

Exposé

Exposé has as its communicative project the revelation of information with some shock value; there is often a moral dimension to the shock, inasmuch as the information revealed concerns corruption and malpractice in high places, previously unknown or incompletely explored via the news agenda. Programmes with a project of exposé are common throughout the archive and we have noted some of them in earlier chapters. From the 1960s we can cite 'Ward F13', about the treatment of patients in mental hospitals; from the 1970s, *The Rise and Fall of John Poulson*, about the disgraced architect; from the 1980s, 'Your home in their hands', about practices in the building trade with specific reference to Barratt Homes; and from the 1990s, 'Jonathan of Arabia', about Jonathan Aitken's abuse of his powers as a government minister in support of his close business and personal ties with the ruling family of Saudi Arabia.

Depth narrative

There is a type of production in which the primary purpose is to tell the 'story-behind-the-story': that is, to open up for examination a story which has emerged as such via the news agenda, and to do so by offering an account along largely chronological lines. Storytelling also readily leads to dramatisation, to the articulation of narrative crises and denouements, to the use of expressive elements and other devices to hold an audience's attention. The account may variously project itself as retrospectively significant in relation to the more recent or even 'current' newsworthy event that has been established as a departure point for the programme's own storytelling. Some editions of *World in Action* are primarily constructed along narrative lines because the story itself is illuminating of broader and perhaps controversial issues. The 'heroes' of such narratives may be well known, but they need not be. One example is 'The trials of Stanley Adams' (1983), recounting the tragic treatment meted out to the man who exposed the corrupt trading practices of Swiss pharmaceutical giant Hoffman La Roche. 'The Williams family' (1964), discussed in more detail below, is another – the story of a would-be immigrant from South Africa and his family. In both these programmes, a particular history offers insight into a more general 'problem' facing society, respectively the lack of legal protection available to 'whistleblowers' and the effects of British immigration laws.

Discussion

The discussion mode is a studio-based form of production. Film inserts may or may not form part of the edition, as may questions and contributions from a studio audience, but whatever the variations, the emphasis is upon the exchange of information and opinion between participants with different forms of involvement in the topic under examination. Studio-based production formed no part of *World in Action*'s enterprise in the early years but it became significant later on. The most common, though by no means the only, topics for studio discussion are political, involving a balanced panel of MPs and/or experts chaired by a neutral presenter. 'The breadline' (1969) is one such, in which a cabinet minister and union leaders discuss low pay. A more sophisticated example is 'The BOSS file' (1976), an investigation and discussion of the illegal activities of the South African secret police, chaired live by the *World in Action* presenter Mike Scott, and involving discussants in the studio, interviewed 'down the line' and accessed via film inserts.

Ethnographic study

The ethnographic aim, as understood here, is that of conveying the character of everyday experience for a particular social group, of exploring its behaviours and values through close observation and listening to people's talk.[5] Programmes in this mode typically have a relaxed, expansive character, pulling in circumstantial detail without the urgency to make a point or outline an argument that other programmes might have. 'Sundays' (1964), for example, is an early illustration of work of this kind, concerned with how people in Britain and Europe use their time on this distinctive day of the week. 'A trip round acid house' (1988), following a group of enthusiasts attending underground 'acid house' parties, is a later example. *World in Action*'s most famous ethnographic contribution was '7 up' (1964), about the experiences and attitudes of a number of seven-year-olds from widely different social backgrounds. Here, the intention to make engaging television was combined with a depth and originality of approach that gave the programme (and its successors) a strong sociological impact.

Biography

Biographies (profiles of individuals in the public eye) formed a significant part of the output in the early years (1963–65) of *World in Action*: Lyndon Johnson, Harold Wilson, Stanley Matthews, Charles de Gaulle and Malcolm X were among the individuals whose lives were recounted for the benefit of viewers, often quite uncritically. Later production of this kind is both rarer and less celebratory. In the 1980s, for example, eight programmes were mainly biographical.[6] 'The disarmament man', a 1981 profile of E. P. Thompson, is arguably the 'softest' of these, but even it seeks out Thompson's critics and gives voice to their views:

> He has a distorted view of the realities of the world. He is a threat to peace and freedom.[7]

More commonly, a biographical element is subordinated to other goals, as in the exposé 'Jonathan of Arabia'.

Section two: techniques and strategies

What follows complements the foregoing discussion of overall communicative purpose and design with a focus upon specific techniques and strategies of audiovisual presentation at the level of textual elements. The same technique may prove useful in more than one of the generic forms we have identified, and any given edition will draw upon many of these devices, without necessarily using all of them. Forms of visual illustration, showing events, circumstances and people as they appeared before the camera on location (perhaps for a single shot, perhaps for a more sustained sequence), are inevitably a significant, recurring feature of programmes made according to a variety of designs and recipes.

One edition, 'The merchants of war' (1968), investigating the illegal supply of arms to the Biafran side in their war of independence against the Nigerian state, will provide us with a useful illustration for many of the devices, with supplementary citations where appropriate.

Commentary

The 'voice of God' has become a traditional way of referring to voiceover speech from a narrator who does not appear on screen at any point. In early cinema documentary, such a commentary was often anonymous but also often projected as authoritative beyond any questioning (hence the slang phrase). In more recent documentary work, commentary has been performed by broadcasters, often those involved in the production, or by actors.[8] In the most common cases the narrated discourse provides the overall coherence of the edition, explaining, where necessary, what the images depict, giving descriptions, linking segments of interview, presenting explanations and offering possible judgements. In outlining his initial views about how *World in Action* should look and sound, Tim Hewat had indicated the advantages of clarity, urgency and shape which strong commentary could give to television documentary journalism.[9] In part, this was a reassertion of some of the values of newsreel style after a period of television that had seen an elaboration of studio anchor formats and to-camera presentation.[10] 'Voice of God' narration to the exclusion of any guiding discourse from a visible reporter remained a standard form of *World in Action* presentation but was only a defining feature in the series' earliest period; later periods saw more flexibility, with named reporters sometimes taking a role in providing voiceover, as well as speaking to camera on location, in a studio or both. 'The merchants of war' mixes 'voice of God' narration with sequences in which the reporter, a young Gus Macdonald (here named as 'Angus'), speaks to camera from key locations. In one such sequence Macdonald, concealed in his car, draws attention to the 'luxury villa' in the Lisbon suburbs, which serves as the Biafran headquarters in Europe. 'A question of intelligence', a 1973 edition about the use of police/army intelligence in the Northern Ireland troubles, has David Boulton and Sue Woodford as studio anchors, talking direct to camera with illustrative film inserts as required. There are also rare forays into forms of production allowing filmed footage to 'speak for itself' without voiceover explication. 'The demonstration' uses voiceover narration to provide context and continuity between segments, but the soundtrack for the central, observational section focused on the March 1968 Grosvenor Square riot contains nothing but the sounds of the crowd.[11]

Clandestine observation

World in Action is not the only current affairs series to have discovered
that some kinds of footage can only be obtained if the subjects do not
know that they are on camera. Such footage can constitute 'primary
evidence' in the exposure of wrong-doing in recording events that would
not have happened, or where behaviour would have been modified, if
witnessed overtly. The practice of clandestine filming (sometimes
involving faked identities) has a long history, and so too does ethical
and political debate, and regulation, about its use.[12] 'Smith's back
door' (1967) is an early example, concerned with the export of
proscribed machinery to Rhodesia during the Smith regime; in more
recent times, the award-winning 'Profit before principle' (1997), obtained
footage in this way to demonstrate the pride that a British company
took in its ability to overcome official Labour as well as Conservative
government restrictions in exporting armaments to Indonesia. For
obvious reasons, clandestine filming is most characteristic of programmes
in exposé mode, though it is not unknown in other programme types
and combinations. It is certainly an important element in 'The merchants
of war', in which two *World in Action* reporters pose as owners of
warships, and gain the trust of an arms dealer in the Biafran trade. In
the 'hook' sequence, this edition begins by showing a meeting between
the reporters and the dealer. As they move from a hotel building to a
waiting cab, the narrator explains:

> A cold rendezvous in Geneva, Switzerland. Four people heading for a
> twelve pound lunch. A pretty girl, a Frenchman in a camelhair coat, and
> two men trying to sell him three warships. The two men selling the
> warships are rather nervous. That's understandable: they don't have
> them. They are in fact *World in Action* reporters.

Besides its evidential significance, the capacity of clandestine filming to
deliver the thrills of spying, and the pleasures of successfully deceiving
the 'crooked', give it strong televisual value. The above quotation
indicates how this entertainment value can be cued in the turns of phrase
of the commentary as well as in the filmed action, alongside the serious
reportage. The development of micro-cameras in the 1980s, able to be
hidden on the person, greatly increased the range of possible applications
of clandestine footage within television journalism.

Explanatory graphics and contrivances

The production of conceptual frameworks may call for a degree of
visual abstraction from primary referentiality, an attempt to offer the
viewer diagrams to express relationships between elements of the verbal

explanation. *The Rise and Fall of John Poulson* (1973) requires explanatory graphics to express Poulson's corruption as a factor in his business relationships at local, district, regional and national levels of political life: this geography constitutes the structural basis of the edition, and is realised visually as a series of blocks displayed to form a triangle, with national politics at the apex.

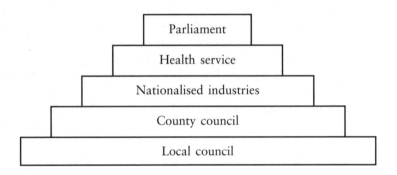

In 'Atomic arms race' (1963) the explanatory abstraction does not take a graphic form: that is, it does not involve a reduction to two-dimensional representation with lines, dots and text. But there is a contrivance on the part of the programme makers which performs an equivalent function, a device used to articulate for the viewer the relative size and composition of the superpower arsenals. Two actors sit in a wholly featureless and dark space, under low key lighting giving strong light/shade contrasts. They face one another from either end of a long table. The darkness obscures their faces to some degree, and this is useful because they are posing, respectively, as Presidents Khrushchev and Kennedy. They look, not at one another but down across the top of the table. Upon this table is a two-dimensional and highly schematic map of the world. For all the detail in it, this sequence of studio television could as well have been a diagram. The bodies never speak, and they barely move. There is no location sound, only commentary. The camera itself moves, and there are edits to give us different angles – to represent Kennedy or Khrushchev's point of view as appropriate.

On our first view of this scene the map is all that is on the table. But we return repeatedly to this 'war room' to see parts of each arsenal, positioned upon this or that country, as the commentary explains what kind of missiles they are, what megatonnage they deploy and what parts of enemy territory they can hit if called upon to do so. This approach to 'staging' a diagram gives the clarity of more conventional graphics whilst nevertheless generating a degree of dramatic power, linking better with other parts of the programme and sustaining a higher level of 'watchability' throughout.[13]

Maps and plans

Maps and plans are spatially contextualising visual elements required in expositions where it is important for viewers to have a sense of action-in-space – for example, to show the involvement of many different countries in the covert, sanctions-busting processes by which South Africa obtained armaments for its war in Angola (in 'South Africa's bombshell' (1980)). 'The merchants of war' uses a simple map to show the route taken by planes delivering arms from Portugal to the Biafrans.

Interventions

Interventions are somewhat different from the techniques/strategies considered so far, inasmuch as they represent work done by the *World in Action* team in order to produce a narrative about its own actions, rather than solely the actions of subjects considered as agents independent of the film-making. These actions are mostly in the service of generating core evidence for the camera or microphone about the topic under investigation – supplying observable events that would not easily manifest themselves spontaneously to the cameras, so as to illustrate a more generalised or abstracted account. 'Smith's back door' intervenes in its subject matter by itself attempting to take a motor axle into Rhodesia in contravention of sanctions legislation. The programme portrays its successes in overcoming the obstacles along the way, with a strong, core scene at the border checkpoint. 'The merchants of war' is similar, in its pretence at selling warships for use in the Biafran war though, as the episode makes clear, the warships don't exist and the transaction is not finalised. On occasions, however, whole programmes have been given over to a form of social experiment generated by a *World in Action* intervention. One such is 'The village that quit' (1971), in which *World in Action* persuaded the population of Longnor, Staffordshire, to give up smoking for a week and filmed the results.

Demonstrations

Demonstrations, like interventions, require *World in Action* to construct as well as to record filmed scenes (at other points in this book, we have referred to the more graphic or showy interventions and demonstrations as 'stunts'). In 'Supermarkets' (1963), for example, a comparison is made between supermarkets and traditional high street shops, by requiring two housewives to collect the same items from the two different

types of retailers. More characteristically, a demonstration takes place
in a studio rather than in a 'real' place. A clear example of a strong
studio demonstration can be taken from 'Guns', an edition of the
associated series *The World Tonight*, where a studio set and a human
subject are used to show the effects of tear gas delivered into the face
of a victim.[14] Another instance of a location setting for demonstrative
business comes from 'The merchants of war'. An early sequence attempts
to demonstrate the extent and the potential cost of the armaments
procured for the Biafrans. Having come across a Biafran 'shopping list'
of requirements, they invite an 'independent expert, who has sold arms
all over the world' to price the list, which he does on-screen, in the presence of a reporter, holding up particular weapons to the viewer's gaze:

> This is a standard heavy machine gun. Its extremely lethal, it's American.
> It's not available in England, not available from new manufacture. It's
> like all these things, it's only available from surplus. Cost? ... I should
> say these things are worth about £200 each.

Performed talk: interviews and discussion
The contribution of interviews to provide testimony from participants,
experts and so on is pervasive in the archive, and as already noted in
Chapter 2, the early years of *World in Action* involved a distinctive
form of interview speech, allowing interviewees to speak direct to
camera. Some interviews put speakers 'on the spot' with confrontational
questioning. In 'Ward F13' (1968), an interview with the manager of
the mental hospital becomes a display of the inadequacy of the inter-
viewee's answers to questions about the inhumane treatment of
patients. Sometimes, subjects are allowed to conceal their identities.
Voices are distorted and faces kept out of sight – as in 'Claimant,
scrounger, snooper, spy' (1980), about ways of detecting social security
benefit fraud. Although the principal actors in 'The merchants of war'
must not know they are being filmed, there are also interview sequences,
including the one with the arms expert mentioned above. Major Wicks,
a supporter of the Biafran side and arms supplier, also proves willing
to talk to the reporter to justify his activities:

> Does your involvement with Biafra go beyond mere cash?
> *Yes, I feel strongly they have a right to their independence.*
> Surely you're inflaming an already bad situation?
> *I don't think so. I don't see it that way anyway.*

Reconstruction
The term 'reconstruction' is most appropriate when, for a few minutes
during an edition, the account is given over to performances by actors

of past events that form part of the subject of exposition and analysis. When entire editions call for such performances, we are in the world of drama-documentary.[15] The viewing effect of partial reconstruction and full-blown dramatization is comparable – the viewer is put in the situation of a witness to unfolding events in the historical world, enacted with a degree of local detail not available to descriptive and analytic discourses. Events are 'shown' not 'told'. The impact is often imaginatively stimulating and strong when compared to other modes of account, which of course programmes using partial reconstruction may also employ.

An early edition deploying reconstruction is 'Typhoid – Aberdeen' (1964). Reconstruction here involves a minimal level of invented dialogue, along the lines of: 'Would you like a cup of tea?' to support the presentation of some dramatic vignettes from the very first typhoid cases occurring in the city – obviously, those before the arrival of the *World in Action* team. In 'The killing of Enrico Sidoli' (1977), the swimming pool murder of a London schoolboy is reconstructed in the hope that witnesses will respond.

Drama-documentary has also been important in the history of *World in Action*. It was pioneered in 'The great train robbery', a programme-length reconstruction of the 1963 crime that fought shy of inventing any dialogue at all and worked entirely through commentary across physical performance. The development of drama-documentary as a relatively common technique at Granada, often associated with Leslie Woodhead and commonly involving painstaking reconstructions of events in the Soviet bloc, began with *The Man Who Wouldn't Keep Quiet* in 1970. Although made in conjunction with *World in Action*, this drama-documentary development involved longer programmes normally shown separately from the main body of *World in Action* work and under their own titles. As late as the 1990s, *World in Action* was involved in drama-documentary production as a means to document events that might otherwise have been the subject of standard *World in Action* editions, including *Who Bombed Birmingham?* (discussed in Chapter 5), a dramatization of the series' investigation into the wrongful imprisonment of the Birmingham Six. *World in Action* also had some background involvement in *Hillsborough* (1996), in which the Hillsborough football stadium disaster of 1989 and its aftermath were reconstructed. In their scope and scheduling, however, such full-length drama-documentaries fall outside the main corpus of *World in Action* programming under consideration here.[16]

Rhetorical elaboration

As well as the kinds of devices which generate exposition (see 'intervention' and 'demonstration' above) there is a further kind of technique of word/image arrangement which we can call 'rhetorical', inasmuch as its contribution to the text lies in its 'imaging forth' of a significant or expressive association, metaphor or other element which is incidental rather than integral to the exposition. Often, rhetorically engaging devices feature at the very beginning of programmes, as an attempt to 'hook' viewers and get their commitment to continued viewing.

'Bronchitis' (1965) begins in a narrow street of terraced houses. Moving slowly towards the camera we see a funeral procession: not a single coffin but four or five of them borne along at shoulder height whilst from doors on either side of the street more and more mourners emerge to swell the procession, and from the side streets further coffins emerge and merge with those already there. The purpose of this display is to emphasise the shockingly high incidence of bronchitis deaths, and the soundtrack for this sequence consists of a slowly striking church bell along with explanatory voiceover. In 'Jonathan of Arabia' (1995), it suited the programme to thematise and strengthen Jonathan Aitken's Arabian connections via the periodic use of the image of a camel, walking across desert sands and ridden by someone in characteristic Arabic clothing. No verbal attempt is made to refer to this figure or to suggest that it somehow represents the MP himself, but the Lawrentian theme of the title is effectively sustained by the image, giving a humorous and deprecating inflection to the account.

Section three: case studies

In the space available here it is not possible to discuss more than a few editions. Nevertheless, it is useful to introduce a little more detail and context into this overview. As we noted earlier, some of the material discussed is also referred to elsewhere in the book but for the sake of coherence of analysis here we repeat some of the descriptive detail to be found in other chapters.

'South Vietnam: A question of torture' (1973)

Generally, domestic topics have a better chance of maximising the audience than topics concerning foreign countries without immediate domestic relevance. Nevertheless, *World in Action* had an honourable record in following important international stories, and throughout the 1970s it regularly returned both to Vietnam and to the theme of torture.[17] The two topics come together in this edition, which is primarily an exposé of the torture practiced by the anti-communist South Vietnamese upon their political prisoners.

The edition has an 'angle' with which to capture the attention of its viewers, and footage to solicit their concern. Both elements are deployed as early as possible. The angle is the shock value of the fact that it is the *anti*-communists, not the Viet Cong, who are to be exposed as torturers: the footage is film of the torture victims. To the accompaniment of recent news film, the commentary begins:

> These communist prisoners of war were released last month in Saigon. Twenty seven thousand communist soldiers were sent back to North Vietnam in exchange for the six hundred American prisoners released by Hanoi. The communist prisoners were not allowed to talk to the press, and the exchange of prisoners of war was almost overshadowed by allegations that many Americans had been tortured in captivity by the North Vietnamese.

Then the shock begins – perhaps the Americans were tortured, but here, before our eyes, is the evidence that communist prisoners most certainly were:

> But America's South Vietnamese allies are now being accused of torturing their political prisoners. These men have just been brought in police trucks from their South Vietnamese prison. This is the first day of their freedom. They've been kept in cages so small that they've not been able to stand upright for five years.

The film demonstrates the effects of this incarceration. The liberated prisoners shuffle along on their bottoms, and the narrator explains that they are unable to move their legs because their muscles have atrophied. Later in the programme we will learn more about these people and how *World in Action* came to film them.

The overall construction of the edition is as follows:

HOOK – visible evidence of effects of torture.
EXPOSITION:
  1 CONTEXT
  a) Claims and counter-claims on numbers of political prisoners held by both sides
  b) South Vietnamese political and military strength
  c) Offences against democracy in South Vietnam
  2 TORTURE
  a) The political opposition: testimony from a dissident judge
  b) The Buddhists: testimony from a victim's mother
  c) Operation Phoenix: testimony of former US intelligence officer
  d) Quang Nai prison: observing prisoners, testimony of American physiotherapists

e) The successor to Operation Phoenix – F6. Recent arrests
f) Con Son prison, the use of tiger cages and lime. Testimony of former prisoner
g) Tiger cage victims
  i. Old folks home in village near Saigon: Testimony of former US Air Force doctor treating victims
  ii. The Buddhist centre 70 miles from Saigon: The case histories of seven men
3 STATISTICS
Estimated numbers of prisoners still in custody
CODA: Some moral reflections.

Whilst considerable power in this edition comes from the strength of the visible evidence – not, indeed, of torture in practice but of its effects upon human bodies, paralysed, crippled, emaciated, expressionless – much impact too is derived from the testimony of interviewees. Some interviewees are themselves victims; some are relatives of victims; some are medical practitioners; some derive their credibility from their own former involvement with the US/Vietnamese military machine. Vietnamese interview testimony is heard as translated voiceover. The medical witnesses cite cases of prisoners tortured to death. The variations here – source of information, place in the country, sex of victim, status of victim, and so on – help to sustain dramatic engagement through an edition which, as the structural description shows, is a relentless catalogue of crime against humanity. Here is some of the victim testimony, relatively mild, delivered in part over footage of Mrs Shau as she is now: blind and emaciated but otherwise recovered:

> NARRATOR: [Mrs Bah Shau] was blinded after lime was thrown in her face. We discovered that she has now been released, after nine months in the tiger cages.

> MRS SHAU: We did not have enough food. We could not bear any longer shrimp paste and salted dry fish. We asked for vegetables. We were told there were no vegetables. Women in the tiger cages were upset and shouted in protest. The warden then threw lime powder on us and beat us. For fifty three days we were not allowed to wash ourselves. Our clothes were rotten. Our hair fell out. Our skin was decayed.

'Buying time' (1978)

'Buying time' is an exposé of the involvement of prison officers in smuggling drugs, money and guns into English prisons, one of many in the *World in Action* archive making use of clandestine filming.[18] Exposés tend to have a forensic character, and there is considerable emphasis on visual and aural components of the production as evidence for the case being made. It is a major objective of the edition to present viewers with the following: identifying shots of individual participants in the narrative, especially the 'villains'; shots of objects involved in the smuggling process (specifically, guns); action footage of crimes in performance; eyewitness/participant testimony; other items of evidential value such as letters from prison inmates and newspaper reports of gun discoveries.

The opening sequence of this edition attempts to point viewers in the direction of the programme's main concerns. The screen is split horizontally; then the top half is split vertically. A still image (captured from film) appears in each of the upper quadrants. The voiceover begins:

> This man has regularly smuggled drugs into a high security prison. This man has regularly carried drugs to prisoners at another jail. Both men are prison officers. Drugs worth an estimated £2,800 on the prison black market have been smuggled into one jail each week. This traffic alone challenges prison security. But there is further cause for public concern. Guns have been smuggled into prisons and these men have played parts in that too.

The main hook for the edition, however, lies in what immediately follows this introduction: an ex-prisoner and former beneficiary of the smuggled drugs is introduced, and the top-left and bottom-right sections of the split screen begin to tantalise viewers with a first taste of the 'secret meetings', which we will see more of later on:

> Terry Woods is a small time criminal from Liverpool. Since 1966 he's been in and out of jail nine times. In secret meetings filmed by *World in Action* he shows how he was involved with both of these officers in prison corruption and how both have taken part in gun plots.

The villain turns 'grass' for *World in Action*'s benefit, and helps to carry out a 'sting' which is not (since it would be illegal and unethical to do so) carried through to full completion. Film (requiring considerable explanation by the narrator) is shown of negotiations between Woods and a corrupt prison officer. Because the filming is clandestine, the sound track is less clear than it might be and we get a written interpretation on the screen:

> WOODS: I've fired them [the guns] to make sure ... They can't trace them back to anyone. They're brand new anyway.

The testimony of Woods, and others (some of whom are allowed to conceal their identities) is also important to the forensic case:

> WOODS: I asked him, would he bring a gun in. We spoke about it, I asked him, would he bring a gun in, and he said yeah.

There is no reconstruction, as such, in this edition. But there is one, small, effort to enter into, rather than just observe, the performance of actions of interest to the account. Early in the edition, an attempt is made to explain the logistics of a drugs delivery from the outside world to the prison via the agency of prison officers and trustees acting as go-betweens. A hand-held camera tracks the route taken on such trips as the commentary observes:

> The route used to drop off the contraband runs along the railway track which passes the jail. Drug couriers walked along this path to the prison car park. This is the route they followed. Consignments of drugs were dropped at this spot, which is hidden from the TV cameras scanning the prison.

The revelatory nature of the information is well enough served by the visual track, though it requires considerable efforts of explanation by the narrator since the involvement of the *World in Action* team is quite complex in character. One of the reporters poses, for the prison officer's benefit, as a 'friend' of Woods and this allows viewers to eavesdrop upon revealing telephone conversations in addition to watching the footage of Woods and the officer together.

'The Williams family' (1964)

This edition tells the story of a family's attempt to move from South Africa to Britain.[19] Inasmuch as there is any general, social issue behind this story, it concerns immigration policy as it affected British passport holders from outside Britain itself. But the facts regarding immigration policy are barely mentioned in this edition, let alone the political, social and ethical dimensions of such policies. Instead the focus is particularistic, concentrating upon the misfortunes of John Williams and his family, caught out by the bureaucratic complexities that surround migration in the post-war world. General points (e.g., that potential immigrants need work permits) are subordinated to narrative continuity: even the status of the Williams as a 'coloured' family from apartheid South Africa is made relevant only by implication, in suggesting that the sons of the family would fare better away from that regime.

The news story, which provoked the interest of *World in Action*, had come to public attention at the point where the family were denied entry to Britain and were obliged to return to South Africa, as they had arrived, by ship. *World in Action* dramatises this moment as the 'hook' for the edition and the pivot of the narrative exegesis:

> And this was the view of England which the Williams family had sailed halfway across the world to see.

It was their only view. Their stay in England lasted precisely twelve minutes. By the time the twelve minutes were up, the Williams family had been taken under escort and put aboard a ship that was to sail back to South Africa that night. John Samuel Williams hadn't understood the rules.

As the narrator speaks, the camera's view centres upon a bright sunlit opening at the end of a covered gangway, the gangway walls offering lines of perspective drawing the eye to that point. Unsteadily, and at walking speed, the camera moves towards the same point, to the sounds of trailing baggage. Viewers are thus offered a perspective congruent with that of the participants, invited to see what they saw, to hear what they heard, before the transition to a more detached observational position.

The storytelling continues, initially via flashback to the origins of the abortive migration attempt. Then, once the narrative has brought the Williams family as far as their moment of crisis, it moves onwards to their activities, and those of their supporters in Britain, in trying to ensure that a *second* attempt would prove successful.

In terms of techniques and strategies, the programme makes use of many of the elements indicated in Section Two. There is no presenter, only the commentary of the alternating narrators (Derek Cooper and Wilfrid Thomas). Audiovisual observation gives us both ethnographic 'scenes in the life of' the protagonists – shopping, playing football, picnicking, and also images depicting specific events in the narrative, for example, the 'British' end of a telephone conversation between one of Williams' supporters and the man himself. Illustrative images are plentiful, as are interviews (with Mrs Williams; with two of the MPs who supported them; with a family friend resident in Britain who tried to help on the day of the crisis; with one of the workers in the charity organisation which provided support). Reconstruction – without dialogue – is used to show some moments in the events leading up to the first migration attempt.

There is rhetorical elaboration too. Expressive use is made of the family piano. The very first image of the edition, preceding the *World in Action* title sequence, is an image of a pair of hands playing the piano. The shot changes; eventually we see the pianist and others surrounding the piano, singing. This is the Williams family: united, simple, of good character. The piano expresses that unity. Later, it comes to express their desire for a new life in Britain; there is talk of it being shipped as cargo on the family's first voyage north, and a long shot of a crane loading on board a large crated item. The piano is even the key to their treatment on arrival. It appears that its presence convinced the authorities that the family had indeed planned to stay more than the allowed three months. Towards the end of the edition, Mrs Williams is asked about the significance of the piano, 'which caused all the trouble in the first place'.

The story also has a moral: at the end of the edition the 'good news' is that the bureaucratic obstacles have been overcome, and the Williams family are on their way back:

> Every day newcomers arrive in Britain from halfway or more across the world. Often the promised land seems grey and drab. Settling in is a difficult and sometimes disillusioning business, and always there's the small print, the complicated rules and regulations about money, and work permits, and the immigration laws. But it's still important that Britain should seem to have a welcome on the mat. When she fails it's nice to know that there are people about who'll remind her that for mother countries, hospitality is a duty. In 48 hours [from the edition's transmission date on 28th July] the Williams family will be arriving in Great Britain. *World in Action* says welcome back.[20]

Although there are elements of ethnographic study (of 'immigrants' as well as of 'coloured South Africans') in this edition, and elements of John Williams' biography, there is no doubting the primary narrative character of this edition, enhanced for popular consumption through such devices as the flashback structure, the 'shock' visualisation of the crisis moment of being turned back on the first attempt, and the expressive use of the piano.

The following three examples stand out because of their departure from the typical and representative.

'Jeremy Thorpe, you're on your own' (1968)

To ring the changes on established styles of political interview, *World in Action* chooses to confront a politician with interviewers whom he could hear but not see. Nor do the voices introduce themselves as particular individuals. They merely give oral expression to questions and criticisms directed at the MP's leadership of his party, the Liberals. He sits under spotlights in a cavernous, darkened studio, empty but for his own chair and a coffee table for his water carafe and glass. Cameras move between different angles and focal lengths to ensure variation (including tight close up). In addition, there is a large screen on one wall of the studio, behind and to one side of the MP. This screen is not always in shot: when it is, usually it depicts the view from one of the studio cameras, a close-up on Thorpe, much larger than the life-sized portrayal shown in the main shot. The opening voiceover explains:

> *World in Action* tonight presents a new kind of political interview. Only one man will appear, this man: the MP for North Devon and the much-criticised leader of the Liberal Party. Jeremy Thorpe, you're on your own.

At points, the voices get Thorpe to swivel his chair and watch, on this same screen, replays from broadcasts by his colleagues within the party, in order to set Thorpe up for questions about party splits.

The approach taken in this edition allows Thorpe's gaze to engage the camera, and thus the viewer, as in the interviewing style preferred by *World in Action* in the years before 1965. However, the visual variations, the audibility of the questioning voice, together with the theatrical, 'Big Brother is watching' *mise-en-scène*, give this particular interview a very different flavour. The format requires the complicity of its subject and was not attempted again. Perhaps it could only have been attempted, as here, when there was a previously established and accepted focus on personal qualities of political leadership rather than on policy issues.

'Beat the taxman' (1991)

This edition gives an unashamedly populist spin to a familiar device in certain kinds of economic news, usually as part of a Budget report: the comparison between typical families at different points in the social spectrum.[21] However, it is more ambitious. It compares an invented working class family with an invented middle class family, in respect of how much money, proportionate to their income, goes in taxation, but it also compares their relative positions now, in 1991, with what they would have been in 1979 before the Conservative governments of Margaret Thatcher introduced major tax reforms. There is an academic report, the work of John Hills at the LSE, which underpins the claims made in the programme.

The edition works out the comparisons through an ironic use of the 'game show' format, fully realised with a studio, scoreboard, celebrity host (Nicholas Parsons, familiar from *Sale of the Century*) and attractive hostess. 'The taxman' sits in a separate studio, at an office desk with a laptop computer at his elbow to perform his calculations, and is introduced to explain different types of taxation. The LSE expert appears as himself, speaking from his own office via film inserts, though he does so within the framework of the 'game', to explain why, after each round, it is the working class and not the middle class family which loses the greater proportion of income in taxation.

The game rewards the families (represented in the studio by the husband and wife) according to how low the 'tax take' is as a percentage of their income, allowing for differential tax breaks, differences in saving and spending habits, and all the different kinds of taxation from income tax through to the local 'community charge' (poll tax). The sting is that the working-class family, though paying out less money than their middle-class counterparts, are having to give a much greater *share* of their income to the taxman. This would not have been the relative position in 1979. The game show device allows Parsons to congratulate the 'winners' with what passes for enthusiasm and sincerity within the format, and the show derives further humour from occasional moments of badinage and a rueful appreciation of their misfortune on the part of the working class couple. At points, 'surprises' are indicated with a presentational flourish, ironically trading on this routine feature of game-show structure. A more conventional approach would have started from the 'shock' of the ways that Thatcherism had increased the tax burden on the less well off and then used the rest of the programme time to justify its claims.

'Profit before principle' (1997)

By the 1990s it had become even more important to engage and retain the interest of the audience in an era of increased competition. Although neither technique is new, this edition offers a 1990s 'twist' with its use of a celebrity in the role of undercover reporter. At the level of formal organisation, the programme makes use of a pre-title 'hook' sequence, now very familiar in drama as well as current affairs, and provides an account with a strong narrative drive, generating moments of revelatory excitement for the viewer. 'Profit before principle' looks at the continuation of a British export trade in military hardware to countries in violation of human rights. It focuses on the figure of Jose Ramos-Horta, winner of the 1996 Nobel Peace Prize and a campaigner for the people of East Timor against the Indonesian dictatorship (and subsequently Prime Minister of that country when it later gained independence). Here we focus on the way the programme opens and establishes its topic, always a strategic phase in *World in Action's* approach to form. The pre-title sequence is shown on the facing page.

After the *World in Action* title sequence, which immediately follows this, the programme re-opens in a more relaxed mode. Ramos-Horta is having his hair styled and coloured. We are given close-ups of the hairdresser at work, and of Ramos-Horta's face, in a mode that inclines towards the observational as we watch this 'everyday' business. The

Image	Soundtrack
Library footage of Ramos-Horta receiving the Nobel Prize, starting with a close-up of the Nobel certificate	Voiceover: Tonight, the current holder of the Nobel Peace Prize goes undercover with *World in Action* to investigate British businessmen who supply arms and equipment to the Indonesian dictatorship
Someone points to military vehicles in a garage. The shot has the appearance of hidden camera footage	Voiceover: The defence salesman, whose company sells guns to the Indonesian army
A man in shirtsleeves stands outside an office block	Voiceover: And the British Territorial Army Captain who claims influence in Downing Street
The same man speaks from behind a desk. This too seems like hidden camera footage	Speaker: 'We are very, very heavily involved in Indonesia'

commentary tells us that this stylist works for Vidal Sassoon and that his previous clients have included 'supermodels and the Spice Girls'. However:

> Today's client is Jose Ramos-Horta, the current holder of the Nobel Peace Prize. He's being disguised because he's agreed to join *World in Action* in an undercover investigation into Britain's support for Indonesia's brutal military occupation of his homeland, East Timor.

So the business is far from 'everyday'. It is the preparation of disguise. We are watching someone being prepared for espionage. We are being taken from the celebrity worlds of 'supermodels' to the realm of international politics, signalling the start of a potentially exciting story as well as of a report. The report's national relevance is then articulated over archive pictures of Tony and Cherie Blair, on the day of Labour's 1997 election victory. The voiceover says:

> Tonight, *World in Action* asks if under the new Labour government, Britain will continue to put profit before principle.

From this beginning, the programme spends some time making the case for Indonesia's continuing abuse of human rights, before moving on to its own 'project': the undercover mission to prove that British companies are indeed supplying the regime with arms. This enquiry allows the viewer to follow Ramos-Horta on his travels in pursuit of audiovisual evidence against the target company. Towards the beginning of this adventure, the disguised Ramos-Horta, accompanied by *World in Action* reporters, gets into a limousine:

> We set up a second meeting with Procurement Services International. Ramos-Horta was to pose as the head of a *World in Action* front company. We phoned before we arrived.

An intriguing story, involving an international celebrity, has been set in train, and it is within the 'spaces' opened up in its narrative flow that a broader journalistic exposition is developed.

Journalistic value and popular resonance

Throughout the history of the series, the various *World in Action* teams have struggled to find forms that will engage the audience as well as doing justice to the topic under scrutiny. This chapter has drawn attention to significant aspects of the struggle, looking at the different project types that can be discerned across the range of programmes and at the techniques and strategies of depiction. It has noted the regular employment of 'hook' sequences and the particular rhetorical form taken by some of these ways of getting the audience firmly engaged. The selected case-studies have indicated in closer detail the local organisation of programme material in some of the more representative and also the more distinctive editions.

Across all of our examples, we see a willingness to innovate, to introduce new elements in what might otherwise lapse into formulaic predictability. The threat of the predictable became stronger, of course, as the conventions of factual television broadcasting started to settle down, and *World in Action* itself became a firmly established point of reference in the schedules.

Perhaps the basic recipe for *World in Action* success lay in its ways of making connections between, on the one hand, the televisual values of action, narrative and people and, on the other, attention to accuracy, investigative drive and expositional clarity. The programme was always on the lookout for new ways of getting this combination right. Among other things, it involved setting up a dynamic between the particular and the general, the concrete and the abstract. *World in Action* teams understood the benefits of condensing a general truth in a brief, illustrative scene or in a sentence or two of spoken commentary or interview remark. They valued the skills of connecting testimony to pictures to commentary in order to be both cogent and accessible. At their best, across the very different political and cultural contexts into which the series played across its run, they found the forms to make it satisfying to watch television as a questioning citizen.

Notes

1 We have noted earlier the recent contribution to an understanding of 'current affairs' made by Patricia Holland in her excellent study of the series *This Week*: P. Holland, *The Angry Buzz: This Week and Current Affairs Television* (London: I. B. Tauris, 2006).

2 A selection of 12 editions of the series is now available on DVD. They span the period from 1967–91 and offer a useful chance for researchers, teachers and students to see how the programmes looked at their full length rather than in the extract format of 'retrospective' specials. The title of the DVD, suggestive of further releases, is *World in Action Volume One*. It is produced by Network DVD and is widely available over the internet (including at networkdvd.co.uk).

3 Jeremy Wallington, speaking in the *World in Action: 30 Years* retrospective programme.

4 The 'Insight' team was developed under the editorship of Denis Hamilton in the 1960s. The list of journalists who worked on it at one point or other in their careers provides something of a roll-call of distinction in investigative reporting. Its way of re-thinking how serious investigation could be given clarity, high readability and strong social and political impact was influential across the range of British journalism, providing a sense of renewed commitment beyond the specific practices (e.g. uses of photography and explanatory page layouts) it introduced. *World in Action*'s adoption of investigative journalism is discussed in Chapter 3.

5 There is a distinguished history of ethnographic filming from within the academic community, specifically from Anthropology. See, for example, P. Loizos, *Innovation in Ethnographic Film: From Innocence to Self-Consciousness: 1955–85* (Manchester: Manchester University Press, 1993), but the form that this mode takes in *World in Action* is necessarily guided by its requirement to be engaging, accessible television rather than academic documentation.

6 Including profiles of General Alexander Haig, Gerry Adams, Nelson Mandela, Ken Livingstone, Derek Hatton, Peter Robinson and Nicholas Hoogstraten.

7 Ray Witney, Conservative MP, speaking in *World in Action*: 'The disarmament man'.

8 There was a general dislike of actors' voices however. In 1980, David Boulton noted that they were often 'too plummy' for the series and tended to over-dramatise, adding: 'Never, never use actors for narration. They can't do it' (*memo to D. Mills, Fitzwalter, Segal, etc., 7 January 1980 (bf. 0720)).

9 See Chapter 1.

10 For more details on this earlier stage of practice and the transition away from it, see N. Swallow, *Factual Television* (London: Focal Press, 1966).

11 The 'riot' was an anti-Vietnam war protest in central London. 'The demonstration' is described in Chapter 3 and discussed in J. Corner, *The Art of Record* (Manchester: Manchester University Press, 1996), pp. 45–6.

12 See, for example, P. Goddard, '"Improper liberties": Regulating undercover journalism on ITV, 1967–1980', *Journalism* 7:1 (2006): 43–63.

13 This device carries echoes of those used in the earlier *Searchlight* series (see Chapter 1), in which Hewat employed life-size graphics in the studio to provide a bold, high impact exposition.

14 Tx. 23 November 1965. *The World Tonight* is discussed in the Interlude chapter.

15 The term refers to a very wide range of practices for combining conventional documentary discourses with professionally acted scenes and dialogue. Derek Paget's *No Other Way To Tell it: Dramadoc/Docudrama on Television* (Manchester: Manchester University Press, 1998) is the best single text offering an account of the history and the definitional problems of this controversial form.

16 Again, Paget's *No Other Way To Tell It* is excellent here, including citation from a number of directors. See also the useful first-hand account offered by Leslie Woodhead's 'Dramatized Documentary' in A. Rosenthal and J. Corner (eds), *New Challenges for Documentary* (Manchester: Manchester University Press, 2nd edn, 2005), pp. 475–84.

17 *World in Action* made 13 programmes wholly or partly in Vietnam and its neighbours, between 1964 and 1980. This was also one of 11 programmes exposing torture in repressive states shown between 1972 and 1974.

18 This edition is also discussed in Chapter 7. For an account of the making of it and the response of the IBA, see Goddard, '"Improper liberties"': 56–8.

19 A discussion of how this edition works in relation to ideas about the 'event worlds' of television reportage (that is, the self-contained units of space, time and action represented within programmes) and the nature of the narrative systems which generate these is given in J. Corner, 'Television's event worlds and the immediacies of seeing' in *Communication Review* 7:4 (2004): 337–43.

20 This expression of collective editorial 'voice' rarely appears after 1965. Its offering of congratulatory comment suggests a strong sense of unified programme identity and positioning as an independent social agent. Early evening news magazines, including the BBC's tremendously successful *Nationwide*, later employed the device in developing their affective relations with viewers and their profile as significant 'players' on the national scene.

21 'Beat the taxman' is also discussed in Chapter 5.

8

Regulation: policy and conflict

It is widely understood that legal, ethical and editorial imperatives routinely operate as limitations on journalism in any medium. But journalists in British television have always been subject to additional obligations imposed through the charters, statutes and licensing agreements that govern the right to broadcast. In Independent Television, a statutory regulator has been responsible for the fulfilment of these obligations, a role undertaken by the Independent Television Authority (ITA), renamed the Independent Broadcasting Authority (IBA) in 1972 and succeeded by the Independent Television Commission (ITC) (1991–2003). In examining *World in Action*, we were surprised to discover how prominent a part regulatory intervention played in shaping and delimiting its journalism. It is no exaggeration to say that, until the early 1970s at least, relations between Granada and the ITA were in an almost permanent state of conflict and that *World in Action* was the principal battleground:

> [N]o single ITV series was the occasion of more discussion between Authority and company, and this dialogue of the 1960s continued unabated through the 1970s. The Authority alternated between sorrow and anger. Granada, valiant for truth, remained aggressively unrepentant.[1]

This chapter examines some key aspects of relations between Granada and the regulatory authorities.

The Act

The ITA's principal obligations concerning programme content were laid down in Section 3(1) of the 1954 Television Act that established Independent Television. Briefly, its seven subsections required the Authority to ensure that:

a. Programmes included nothing that offended against 'good taste and decency' or 'public feeling' or that could 'lead to disorder'.[2]

b. High standards of quality and 'a proper balance' in subject matter were maintained. 'Balance', in this context, refers to the proportion of 'serious' programming that was shown; as a result, current affairs programmes were perceived as a premium product of ITV.[3]

c. 'Due accuracy and impartiality' were maintained in all forms of news.

d. 'Proper proportions' of programming were British in origin.

e. A proportion of output should cater for the particular tastes and outlook of each station's viewers (interpreted as a requirement for regional broadcasting).

f. Programmes preserved due impartiality 'as respects matters of political and industrial controversy or relating to current public policy'.

g. Programmes contained no material 'designed to serve the interests of any political party'.[4]

Conflict between Granada and the Authority over *World in Action* largely turned on definitions of 'due impartiality' and debates over the meaning of subsection f.

Of course, the Television Act contained no definitions of these provisions, so the task of administering them in practice naturally required the ITA to take on a powerful interpretative role, guiding the organisation of ITV and determining whether forms of programming and content were permissible under the Act's terms. In practice, the ITA had established broad principles of content regulation by the early 1960s. By then, interventions over specific programmes had begun to anchor the interpretations and adjudications of the regulator and to inform programme-makers' understanding of the bounds of acceptability. As we have seen in Chapter 2, Granada's current affairs output had already proved troublesome to the Authority but the frequency of interventions relating to the content and form of current affairs programming increased considerably with the establishment of *World in Action* in 1963. The convictions of its first editor, Tim Hewat, and his attempts to develop a livelier, more accessible and more controversial form of television current affairs in imitation of Fleet Street practices played a large part in this. But *World in Action* also enjoyed the support of Granada's senior management, including the redoubtable Denis Forman, who were not afraid to contest the broader issues raised by ITA programme policies as well as its adjudications over particular programmes.

Granada had already proved robust in pressing its case before *World in Action* began. A lucid paper for the Pilkington Committee in 1962 complained that the Act effectively favoured safety at the expense of innovation and likened the inflexibility of the Authority's interpretations to 'the flat-iron of censorship': 'That, as we see it, is the real danger from which television has most to fear – the philosophy of the

flat-iron, smooth, impeccable and deadly dull'.[5] In most respects, however, the ITA saw Granada as 'the good boy of ITV: public-spirited,
adventurous, cultured and generally superior to the other companies':[6]
'[D]espite the fact of living dangerously – or maybe because of it',
wrote Lord Hill, ITA Chairman from mid-1963, 'Granada was live,
vigorous and imaginative'.[7] Differences over the impartiality of its
programmes, and Granada's assiduousness in contesting the Authority's
judgement, were the only serious obstacles to a harmonious working
relationship. But a current affairs programme inevitably yields complaints
from aggrieved parties, forcing the Authority to make frequent adjudications. Naturally, it tended to be more cautious than Granada would
have wished, so disharmony became a feature of its relations with the
regulator for many years.

'A question of facts': *World in Action*, 1963–65

A crisis arose quickly. 'Down the drain', revealing waste and ineptitude
in public spending on defence, was planned as *World in Action*'s ninth
edition, to be broadcast as parliament debated the issue. Its approach
was typically sensational, using the 'Beat the Clock' set and format
familiar to viewers from *Sunday Night at the London Palladium* (ATV,
1955–65, 1973–74):

> This, after Big Ben, is probably the most famous clock in Britain . . .
> Tonight we use this clock to signal its biggest money ever – money paid
> for by the taxpayers. Tonight, every full-circle sweep of the hand takes
> exactly a second, and every flashing light stands for £1 – sixty pounds a
> second, every second. And that's the speed at which Britain is, this year,
> spending money on defence . . .[8]

With this device, the programme catalogued examples of mis-spending
and their cumulative cost. On the day of transmission, Granada referred
the script of the programme to the ITA to ensure that it could not be
construed as undermining 'the primacy of parliament as the forum for
debating the affairs of the nation', in line with an assurance given by
broadcasting organizations when the Fourteen Day Rule ended.[9] ITA
staff judged that it could be so construed but, more importantly, it
was also in breach of Section 3(1)(f) of the Television Act and could
not be transmitted.

All Granada was aghast, Hewat abusively so.[10] The programme's
facts were correct, he claimed, and that should be enough: 'If facts,
objectively assembled, produce a programme that exposes inefficiency,
dishonesty, or simply bad judgement, so be it. We feel such programmes
should be broadcast'.[11] But for the Authority, impartiality required a

balance of views and the programme's 'facts' were one-sided and anti-government:

> [H]owever certain Granada were of the factual accuracy of the programme, this by itself did not clear it of the charge of lack of due impartiality. The whole drift of the programme, we said, was calculated to leave viewers with the impression that defence policy over the years was one long record of waste and miscalculation and that, in the absence of any attempt to show there were other tenable points of view about defence, the programme clearly failed to satisfy the requirements of the Act.[12]

Hewat was in no mood for compromise: as judgements of impartiality were inherently subjective, he argued, journalists were placed in an impossible position by 'the seven-part nightmare' of the Act and 'the blunt instrument' of censorship. He went on: '*World in Action* cannot claim to be truly impartial; for we are human and recognise impossibilities. On the other hand, we refuse to lie, to put up specious arguments or straw men to promote phoney "balance". We do, however, claim to be fair'.[13]

Behind the 'heroic' rhetoric, however, lay a genuine difference of interpretation that was to recur frequently in disputes between company and Authority in subsequent years: Granada's sometimes naïve commitment to 'facts' as guarantors of fairness (doubtless a strategic front at times) was at least an attempt to replicate press practices in television journalism. As Hewat's characterisation of it suggests, Granada found the ITA's approach stultifying – Forman likened it to 'the two-handed lawyer . . . On the one hand, on the other hand'[14] – tending to produce bad programmes and to negate any ability to criticise or evaluate, no matter how clear-cut the evidence. For Hewat, it was futile for the ITA to measure each programme for impartiality because bias was likely to lie elsewhere: 'The style of each programme was set the moment the subject was selected; it was the selection not the writing which mattered'.[15]

Hewat and Forman were also convinced that the ban on 'Down the drain' revealed how the ITA's approach to content regulation differed from that at the BBC:

> At this time there is only one place [such programmes] can be broadcast without risk – at the BBC. The BBC is not impartial today, nor is it balanced; but it is fair . . . And it has no Act of Parliament censoring its programmes.[16]

As if to demonstrate the point, and in a clear snub to the ITA's authority, Forman and Hewat contacted Paul Fox, editor of the BBC's *Panorama*. As a result, the next edition of *Panorama* contained a four-minute extract from 'Down the drain' – a remarkable example, suggests Forman, of 'the freemasonry amongst television producers' overriding channel loyalty.[17] But *Panorama* showed the extract because of the news-worthiness of the ban. Norman Swallow maintained that, whatever the merits of 'Down the drain', it was 'television's equivalent of a [newspaper] leading article' and the BBC's commitment to 'complete impartiality' meant that it could no more have shown the programme in its original context than could ITV.[18] For a despairing Sir Robert Fraser, ITA Director General, the BBC's action was a 'stunt' that 'made me feel sick'.[19]

The 'Down the drain' affair illustrated the contrasting attitudes of Granada and the IBA to regulation. As we have seen, Granada were committed to developing the scope of television journalism to inform the public and scrutinize the powerful, and it was common for it to complain of the constraints it faced in comparison with newspapers. Its commitment to public service broadcasting was sincere, but the company also sought liveliness and sensation, despising the even-handedness of BBC journalism and delighted to cause a stir: 'A good story we defined as something someone doesn't want you to publish', wrote Forman.[20] The involvement of *Panorama* testified to Granada's habitual defiance in the face of authority and sat poorly with the ITA's instinctive caution. It was natural that the majority of *World in Action* editions brought forth some form of adverse reaction or threat, often from those seeking to deflect criticism from themselves. But such responses made uncomfortable reading amongst Authority members, who were likely to be 'safe', lacking expertise in television and jour-nalism, and not always prepared to accept the advice of the Authority's experienced permanent staff. The ITA rejected many complaints against the series; at other times, Granada conceded that mistakes had been made; but the Authority continued to be critical of *World in Action* and easily alarmed by threats of legal action or adverse publicity. Numerous incidents exposed these fault-lines over the next two years.

World in Action began the 1963–64 season with 'The guns', a special 45-minute edition investigating the oppression of the black populations of South Africa and Portuguese Angola. Filmed with tourist cameras and a cover story to facilitate entry, it generated various complaints of bias and inaccuracy, notably from the governments that it criticised and from the Foreign Office. With *World in Action* already a recurring concern at their meetings, IBA members were alarmed and chose to act decisively. Discarding their customary practice of retrospective intervention, they insisted that all future *World in Action* programmes should be vetted in advance, 'the first and only time that the Authority has ever felt it necessary to use this power'.[21] Granada was aggrieved, partly for practical reasons – the requirement to finish programmes, or at least scripts, early enough to allow for approval and then to stick precisely to the approved script went against the very ethos of topical current affairs coverage – but also because the team felt themselves to be the victim of 'a considerable degree of discrimination', especially in comparison with *This Week*.[22] The sense of injustice was compounded by the Authority's investigation into 'The guns'. *World in Action* insisted that the programme was based on extensive research and produced a point-by-point rebuttal of the claims of factual inaccuracy made by the South African and Portuguese governments which, suggested Victor Peers, were politically motivated and based only on small points of detail.[23] Fraser disagreed and qualified apologies were sent to the complainants.

Bernard Sendall implies that the Authority's requirement that programmes were vetted before transmission was not welcomed by its own staff: 'Authority programme officers had the uneasy task of trying to turn that ruling, with its negative and restrictive implications, to good account'. For one thing, he says, Granada insisted that negotiations took place at board level. For another, constraints of time meant that changes could not always be made and '[b]anning or postponement of the programme could easily become the only available options'.[24] Nonetheless, the problem was managed effectively for the most part and at least Granada could count on stronger support from the IBA staff who had passed them for transmission when programmes were criticised. Minor changes were common under the vetting procedure (and occasionally rejected, as when the Authority were informed that a section of a script that they sought to amend was 'entirely accurate'!),[25] but only one programme caused a serious problem. An 'exposé' of the Moral Re-Armament organisation ('MRA') was found to be 'unacceptably biased' and, in a detailed assessment by Fraser, 12½ per cent pro and 87½ per cent anti![26] The programme was postponed by one week for revisions but these were also unacceptable to the Authority, whereupon 'Granada took it entirely to pieces and revised it over the weekend'.[27]

The vetting process was far from welcome at Granada. In 1964, Sidney Bernstein began a meeting with senior executives of the ITA by declaring: 'Rightly or wrongly the general opinion is that the Authority is censorious and that their attitudes have created a restrictive feeling on the creative work of creative people in Independent Television'.[28] Besides its effect on morale and innovation, the policy and the ITA's general approach raised worrying questions among programme-makers about the location of editorial responsibility, a point first raised by Hewat earlier in the year. He likened each *World in Action* to the cover article of the recently-launched *Sunday Times* magazine, except that in Independent Television: 'the Editor would be obliged on Saturday afternoon to send the page proofs to, say, the Press Council and then wait to be told whether or not he could publish his paper'.[29]

Although the ITA's overall responsibility for the content of ITV output was clearly set out in Granada's licence, the bounds of its editorial responsibility were tested again by an incident involving Mandy Rice-Davies, who had achieved notoriety in the Profumo scandal. On 1 October 1963, a disapproving press seized on a complaint from Solihull Education Authority that Granada had filmed Rice-Davies speaking to pupils outside her old school. 'Such a sequence of film would be in thoroughly bad taste', said its chairman, 'if it was linked up with the school'.[30] Dismayed at the negative coverage and following a formal complaint, the ITA sought clarification from Granada. The filming was for a possible *World in Action* profile of Rice-Davies, explained Granada, adding – perhaps disingenuously – that it could not foresee the material being used. The Authority made its 'distaste' known to Granada, describing the incident as 'a serious error of judgement' and adding that 'we found it impossible to foresee circumstances in which we would be willing to transmit such sequences'.[31] Responding for Granada, Peers denied any impropriety (no sound had been recorded, demonstrating that press allegations about schoolchildren being interviewed were false) and asked under what authority the ITA felt it could control material collected by Granada that was not for transmission. In a milder reply, Sendall explained that he was merely offering 'the Authority's view'.[32] But the Rice-Davies programme was abandoned.

Eventually, as Sendall had expected, the script-vetting policy gave rise to the banning of another *World in Action* edition. As with 'Down the drain', the cause was a dispute over the role of facts as guarantors of fairness. The provocatively-entitled 'How to lose the Olympics after really trying' compared Britain's preparations for the forthcoming Tokyo games with those of France and Czechoslovakia, concluding that they were woefully underfinanced. The ITA received the script on the day of transmission, common practice with the programme having been assembled over the previous weekend, and immediately found it to be neither accurate nor impartial: statistical data was incorrect or misleading and no attempt was made to provide an alternative view to balance claims of under-funding.[33] 'The Authority deemed that this was an opinion', explains Forman. 'We replied that it was a fact.'[34] Changes on the scale demanded could not be made in a single day so the programme was not transmitted, with the result that the row became public and Lord Hill found himself having to defend the ITA against charges of censorship. Several amended versions of the programme were made and shown to ITA staff and the Economist Intelligence Unit was commissioned to audit the programme's statistics. But Granada refused to concede the central point that inadequate support for Britain's Olympic team was a demonstrable fact. With despairing irony, Sidney Bernstein told Fraser:

> The programme as we submitted to you yesterday doesn't show any impartiality. We have a blind spot. I don't know how we ever resolve this problem. It's a question of facts. We are not attacking anybody. We are suggesting that we, as a Nation, don't do enough for sport.[35]

Eventually, parts were incorporated into 'Olympics', a much-revised version of the programme, which served as a post-mortem to Britain's Olympic performance a week after the Games were over. Although transmitted, even this edition was deemed by the Authority not to be impartial. But the dispute over the first Olympics programme had one beneficial outcome for the series. Suggesting that 'these disputes and our failure to resolve them are becoming a very real anxiety', Fraser proposed a meeting with Granada.[36] The meeting had little lasting effect in resolving the differences in the interpretation of the Act, but Granada welcomed the Authority's offer that prior vetting of *World in Action* scripts be abandoned as a goodwill gesture.

One of the most acrimonious disputes between Granada and the Authority, and certainly the longest-running, was provoked by the final edition of this first phase of *World in Action*. Following the Thalidomide scandal and the appointment of Lord Sainsbury to enquire into the pharmaceutical industry, 'Drugs' examined the impact of drug companies' promotional and research activities on National Health Service expenditure. It revealed the heavy marketing of expensive branded remedies and showed in some cases that claims about research costs were little more than a façade to justify higher charges to the NHS. Researcher Stephen Prideaux encountered two of the oddest incidents in the series' history while making it and wrote detailed reports of them for Granada. Arriving to film the research effort at the plant of one well-known pharmaceutical company, he was shown three large laboratory buildings each virtually empty. By the time the camera crew arrived, however, they were:

> swarming with staff, each in a white coat. Using back doors and paths, the same staff packed each building as we entered it from the front. The equipment in use amounted to a few bubbling retorts apparently containing

hot water and three freshly-mounted examinations of the effect of certain drugs on animals. I questioned several of the staff and came to the firm conclusion – as did Ken [Ashton, the producer] and the camera crew – that they were secretaries and typists and not laboratory workers as they appeared to know nothing of what they were doing.[37]

Later in the same account, Prideaux claims that, under questioning, the company's public relations officer owned up to this 'simple, though expensive, "con" '. But there was a stranger sequel. Prideaux reports a telephone call a few days later from the public relations officer of the Association of the British Pharmaceutical Industry (ABPI) asking for an urgent meeting. Meeting at a nearby pub, Prideaux says that the man from ABPI

wanted to establish that if I walked out on the show it would be dropped and I confirmed this. Then [he] said he didn't mind telling me he had 'instructions from the top to stop the show' if he could 'at any cost' . . . The ABPI, he said, could do with a . . . book, putting their side of the picture. As Granada were firing me, would I like to write it? How much?, I said. £250, he said. But one condition was that it would have to be begun the next day as it was wanted urgently. I would have to walk out too, he said. Catching on, I asked when delivery was wanted. 'No hurry', and a broad smile was the reply. As it happens, I declined fairly firmly being rather busy.[38]

After transmission, a welter of complaints from the pharmaceutical industry and its lobbyists prompted the ITA to examine the programme in detail. It was certainly highly critical of the industry. Unable to verify the accuracy of the programme's claims, the Authority simply weighed the proportion of critical material it contained against the proportion defending the industry's practices and, as a result, concluded that it was biased.[39] Granada was asked for its comments. Rebutting each criticism, it stood by the programme's findings, was adamant that no apology was warranted and even stated that it would welcome legal action as an opportunity to defend its case.[40] Granada's palliative offer of a follow-up programme in which the ABPI could defend its position more fully was flatly refused by the Association. So Fraser took the decision that the Authority would apologise for the programme's perceived shortcomings on Granada's behalf.

Not surprisingly, Granada's board was 'shocked' and Bernstein pulled no punches in his response:

I suggest that the Authority may have been led into the error of considering facts of an adverse character as a reflection of hostile opinion. In the case of the Drug Industry I submit that the presentation of an entirely objective picture does create a most unfavourable impression. This is not due to any editorial bias; it is a case of facts speaking for themselves ... If for the British public to hear the truth from an independent television company is an infringement of the Television Act, then we admit to such an infringement with pride.[41]

At Granada, a powerful sense of injustice made the 'Drugs' affair into a cause to be pursued on all fronts. 'Should we have suppressed the truth in the interests of impartiality?', asked an internal analysis of the case.[42] Bernstein suggested a meeting with the Authority to discuss the conflict over interpretations of 'balance'. It took place in May 1966 but no consensus was reached. Granada commissioned legal advice that challenged the Authority's interpretation of the Act but the Authority obtained a counter-opinion dismissing Granada's claims. Bernstein's response was to write formally to Fraser asking what right of appeal was open to the company, explaining: 'Our legal advisors give one view; your legal advisors (no doubt equally eminent) give another. This is not a satisfactory position for a programme contractor'.[43] Fraser responded by drawing attention to the terms of Granada's contract, adding:

> I wish that you would accept that, under the Act and the contract, there comes a time when the Authority ... must record its own opinion in relation to those matters which the programme contract submits to the opinion of the Authority.[44]

This represented the end of the correspondence, nearly a year-and-a-half after 'Drugs' had been shown, but while Granada had to accept the Authority's opinion it still refused to accept that it had been just. This impression was intensified when the Sainsbury Report was published in September 1967. Granada found that it 'reinforces all our previous arguments and shows that the ITA had even less justification for apologising than they might have imagined they had previously'.[45]

Being fair ... and seeming to be fair: post-1967 problems

Viewed nowadays, 'Drugs' seems innocuous enough, testing the claims of the drugs industry's critics against evidence that the programme has gathered and the companies' own explanations for their policies. With hindsight, however, the programme's treatment serves to illustrate some of the most significant fault-lines in *World in Action*'s long-running dispute with the Authority, calling into question both the practice of its regulation of due impartiality and the principles upon which its interpretation of its duties were based. We have seen how Granada's claims about the facticity of its programmes conflicted with the ITA's insistence on 'absolute balance', supposedly measurable by lines of script. But as the years went by, the Authority's interpretation of impartiality was slowly modified, becoming less rigid and enabling 'balance-across-series' and, by the late-1970s, the limited acceptance of 'personal view' programmes. Still defending the fairness of 'Drugs' in 1970, Forman acknowledged the effect of this change:

> Over the years the Authority has departed a long way from the concept of 'absolute balance'. At one time they would count the number of lines in a script 'for' and compare them with the number of lines 'against' and tend to use any discrepancy as evidence of lack of balance. In ['Drugs'] they found too little argument in defence of the said firms. I believe that in the light of the Sainsbury Report and other subsequent developments that this show would now be accepted as 'duly impartial'. But the Authority had a point. At the time it did not *seem* fair to the firms in question, who still enjoyed a false and unblemished reputation.[46]

Forman reveals here how 'Drugs' demonstrates another perceived problem with the ITA's operation of the Act – its implicit suspicion of journalism that challenged received wisdom. 'Drugs' *seemed* unfair because its findings did not accord with normative assumptions about the pharmaceutical industry, despite the evidence that the programme was able to offer. The same process seems to have been at work in the Authority's censuring of two later *World in Action* programmes – Charles Denton and John Pilger's 'The quiet mutiny',[47] a report from the Vietnam war front that revealed almost for the first time the widespread disaffection of American troops, and 'The man who stole Uganda', cataloguing the atrocities perpetrated by the government of Idi Amin which had recently seized power. Fraser saw the former as 'outrageous, left-wing propaganda'; a more considered ITA view labelled it 'primarily a statement of a one-sided viewpoint about the Vietnam war'.[48] For Granada, Forman, whilst acknowledging Pilger's left-wing reputation, maintained that he had simply been sent to the front to speak to soldiers and reported 'in a dramatic and rather effective manner that young GIs did not want to fight the war in Vietnam'. This, he said, was not an untruthful or one-sided view, merely one that had yet to gain currency:

> As so often with *World in Action*, what is regarded as a 'personal view' today can become the 'consensus view' tomorrow ... Is it not possible that the situation it describes ... will soon be generally known, and generally accepted?[49]

Furthermore, Forman drew attention to the problems surrounding the notion of 'balance':

Television resounds with the official views of politicians, governments and institutions. Perhaps it is right that it should. But if this is so, surely it is also right that the public should see the other side of the picture.[50]

In other words, the ITA's assessment of 'The quiet mutiny' was a function of the programme's failure to chime with the 'official line' of television coverage of Vietnam, itself an imbalance requiring redress.

The Uganda programme presented similar problems. The ITA considered it in the light of complaints from 'prominent persons with first-hand knowledge of the country', who affirmed that Amin was 'a friend of Britain and a fine man',[51] and concluded that it provided 'an unfavourable picture of that country resulting from *World in Action*'s selection of some discreditable facts'.[52] In reply, Forman noted that a requirement for balance must have limits, comparing the illegality, corruption and brutality of the Amin regime with the treatment of racial discrimination or apartheid:

Such programmes have never included, for the sake of 'balance', arguments against the generally accepted view that such things are to be condemned ... We do not think that the Authority would wish us to interpret the word 'impartiality' so narrowly that for each revelation that is unpleasing to a foreign country we should produce a countervailing programme which dwells upon its merits.[53]

The Authority initially remained unconvinced of Granada's case but, within a year, both the disillusionment of troops in Vietnam and the evils of Amin's regime were universally acknowledged. Granada 'crowed'; it was 'an own goal that the Authority were never allowed to forget'.[54]

In the Authority's response to programmes such as 'Drugs', 'The quiet mutiny' and the Uganda programme, many of those involved with *World in Action* detected a deference to Establishment pressure or to the prominence of complainants. This went hand in hand with perceptions that *World in Action* was unacceptably left-wing. In 1970, Forman wrote:

Amongst a number of rather important people there is an uneasy feeling that current affairs television (not news) lies in the hands of people who are not sufficiently respectful of institutions of government and do not sufficiently reflect what they think are the country's best interests ... From this they deduce that television people, because they are knocking the country's institutions, are perhaps anti-democratic and ... have a left wing bias.[55]

The 'great and the good', the sort of people appointed to be Authority members, tended to be both conservative and well-connected, regardless of their party allegiances. At the time of 'Drugs', for example, Lord

Hill was simultaneously Chairman of the ITA and of a pharmaceutical company.[56] But the ITA's conservatism also reflected the attitudes of its permanent staff, taking their cue from Fraser and later Sir Brian Young as Directors-General. The consequence was an ingrained suspicion of any journalism that challenged the status quo extending, on one notorious occasion, to an accusation from Fraser that Granada's current affairs programmes showed 'a persistent left-wing bias' and 'an undue proportion of communist, Marxist, anti-democratic sentiment', a charge he extended to Forman himself.[57] Forman was staggered, even taking legal advice, and met with Fraser again to demand that he withdrew the allegation. Fraser agreed and cordial relations were restored. For Forman, the 'faults' in Granada's approach that Fraser had sought to identify were a natural characteristic of journalism:

> The point here was that journalism is more interested in looking at the processes of change than at a state of permanence. Therefore traditional policies get less attention than politicians or groups who are trying to change things. Also that journalists tend to be against any regime whether it be conservative, communist or Nixon. They disbelieve the party line, look behind nationalist propaganda, and if they do this in the western world they are likely to be labelled 'left wing'.[58]

Later, Young expressed similar attitudes to the series in, for example, asking a member of the Granada board why 'you accept a situation in which the *World in Action* production team is so heavily slanted to the left'.[59]

Forman assumes that Foreign Office pressure was brought to bear on the Authority over 'The quiet mutiny', 'The man who stole Uganda' and in similar cases ('subconsciously they regard British television . . . as an extension of British foreign policy') but this seems to be conjecture.[60] Indeed, there seems to be very little evidence of clandestine pressure on the Authority except in relation to investigations of official secrets[61] and perhaps this is hardly surprising. More characteristic of government interventions was Defence Minister Peter Kirk's much clumsier attempt to undermine a 1971 *World in Action* investigation into appalling conditions in military prisons ('The sailor's jail'). The Ministry was initially helpful, permission to film was given (though with restrictions sufficiently severe that they amounted to interference)[62] and Kirk agreed to an interview, but his repeated postponements led the production to be severely delayed. After transmission, Kirk complained formally to Granada and the ITA about bias and misrepresentation, made serious and unchallenged accusations against the programme and team in the House of Commons and repeated them widely (including the claim that all those interviewed were drug addicts) even after the Authority had accepted Granada's detailed refutation. Of most concern to the company were groundless and defamatory claims of improper behaviour on the part of a *World in Action* researcher for which Kirk eventually apologised.[63] Kirk's actions amounted to a major irritation but were aimed much more at Granada than at the Authority and were hardly clandestine.

The most extreme suggestion of improper influence on the Authority arose over the banning of a *World in Action Special* exposing the web of municipal and political corruption surrounding the disgraced architect John Poulson. 'The friends and influence of John L. Poulson' was banned not on impartiality grounds but 'as a matter of broadcasting policy' under a rarely-used catch-all clause at the end of the Act.[64] Based on revelations at his bankruptcy hearing but with every allegation corroborated by *World in Action* journalists, it exposed the massive extent of Poulson's payroll and argued for more robust mechanisms for the registration of interests among local and national politicians. Despite prior consultation over the programme with IBA staff, the Authority banned it unseen. They 'rebelled against the programme being shown', suggested Sendall, because it had 'offended their consciences'.[65] Such reasons as were given for the ban barely survived scrutiny: the programme made allegations against people who had no proper opportunity to defend themselves (but all points of fact in the programme had been independently confirmed and those involved invited to respond); the programme risked being in contempt of court (but it had been passed for transmission by lawyers acting for Granada and for the Authority), the programme amounted to 'trial by television' (this phrase had been an Authority bugbear ever since such accusations had been made about the ambushing of interviewees on *The Frost Programme* (Associated-Rediffusion/LWT 1966–74) in 1968, but had never before been applied at second hand to events already reported elsewhere); the extent of corruption revealed would undermine public confidence in local government (but such bodies should surely be accountable to the public). Within Granada, it was widely assumed that the decision was at best an example of the Establishment protecting its own and at worst a form of political censorship, as Forman explained to Young: '[I]t is sometimes felt that the Authority's attitudes reflect the interests of "government" in the widest sense. Authority restrictions on programmes like Uganda, GIs in Vietnam or Poulson fuel this suspicion.'[66] Similar claims were rife in the press, with the *Sunday Telegraph* going so far as to publish details of the close connections between Authority members and those exposed in the programme. Forman's account of a screening of the programme for Authority members seems to confirm the suspicion that they acted out of a concern for the reputations of political colleagues rather than in the wider public interest.[67] Despite this, there is no evidence that external pressure was placed on Authority members and it seems that they merely followed their consciences. The ban was initially presented as 'permanent' and 'irreversible', but three months later, after some cosmetic changes to spare the Authority's blushes, the Poulson programme was finally transmitted as *The Rise And Fall of John Poulson.*

'A monster that sets out to usurp the law ...': The IBA and investigative journalism

As an early but effective example of television investigative journalism, 'Drugs' illustrates a further problem for the Authority's relationship with *World in Action*. Throughout the series' first 20 years, the Authority found it hard to reconcile programmes that were accusatory in nature with its statutory duties, regardless of their public value. It was also difficult for it to exercise effective oversight over such programmes and at times it was clear that the Authority was ignorant of the requirements of investigative journalism and suspicious of Granada's motives. Comments by Young in the aftermath of the Poulson affair encourage perceptions that the Authority regarded this as a form of programme-making that was troublesome and accepted only grudgingly to be necessary. '*World in Action* has developed a *compulsive* attitude to investigative reporting', he wrote, adding: 'I am not of course saying that investigative reporting is frowned upon by the Authority; and Granada have been doing it in *World in Action* with the Authority's consent for a long time now'.[68] Noting the ongoing *Washington Post* investigation into Watergate, Forman responded:

> What seems to be bothering the IBA at the moment ... is that ... there is something mean, low or ethically wrong in adopting the techniques of investigation that have been developed by television and newspapers, that it is unfair to publish facts which may embarrass people in public life.[69]

For programme-makers, this impression was enhanced when Lady Plowden, newly appointed as IBA chairman in 1975, remarked that television was not the right medium for investigative journalism.[70] Nor was Granada much pacified when Plowden explained that she felt that such programmes were overwhelmingly destructive and risked dispro-portionate damage to industrial companies. Reminding Plowden of revelations about Thalidomide, nicotine and asbestos, Forman responded by pointing out that for victims and the public at large such investigations were wholly constructive.[71] Even in 1980, writing to Young to seek clarification of the IBA's attitude to Granada current affairs, Forman was suggesting that: 'Perhaps the problem is that the Authority does not like investigative journalism at all'.[72]

The Authority's apparent distrust of investigative journalism may also have been coloured by the practical problems that it created and by a lack of awareness or sympathy regarding its methods. As early as 1968, the Authority was seeking to curb the techniques of undercover journalism – concealed recordings, reporters misrepresenting their identities – and to oversee investigative reporting, requesting from *World in Action* lists of investigations in progress so as to answer complaints from those worried that investigations of them were about to be screened.[73] Understandably, *World in Action* journalists were unwilling to trust such sensitive information to an external body that lacked journalistic expertise and might unwittingly enable accused parties to conceal their actions and prevent exposure ('as you know', replied David Plowright, 'such lists are jealously-guarded secrets among journalists and programme-makers alike').[74] At a newspaper, with a unified editorial structure, exchanging such information would be commonplace (as it was within Granada itself) but the location of editorial responsibility was more problematic within the ITV system. As Plowright later put it, investigative journalism

> requires diligence, tenacity, dedication, a clear understanding of the law together with integrity and understanding ... Anyone involved in the editorial and other judgements that are essential must either be involved in the constant dialogue with reporters, editors and lawyers or be willing to delegate that responsibility to someone in whom he has trust. It is easy to regard investigative journalism as a monster that sets out to usurp the law ... It is the most difficult area of decision making for a non-professional body and the most difficult to delegate.[75]

In part, Plowright's plea for delegation was an acknowledgement of two recurring problems with the Authority's oversight of *World in Action*. Firstly, as the affair of the Poulson programme illustrates, it was not uncommon for the full Authority or even its senior officers to override the advice of their own staff, especially that of the regional officers who could most easily be consulted in Manchester but had few delegated powers. When the team had been careful to consult fully to ensure that contentious programmes could be passed for transmission, this could be deeply frustrating. Secondly, the slow-moving, inflexible and metropolitan-centred Authority seemed unconscious of the urgency over decision-making that topical journalism required. It was normal for *World in Action* editions for Monday transmission to be assembled at the end of the previous week or at weekends, but consultation at the weekend, even with programme staff, was a near impossibility. As Forman explained in a letter to Sendall:

> It is hard to explain to people who often work three weekends in a row, and sit up through the night editing a film, that the Authority can only consider their work within office hours and in London.[76]

Programme decisions from the Authority's officers could take days, but this could become months when the full Authority was involved because of its inflexibility in scheduling meetings. The Authority generally met monthly and extraordinary meetings to discuss programming issues were almost unknown. So when the Poulson programme was banned on 25 January 1973, the issue could not be raised again with the Authority until its next full meeting on 22 February despite a Granada delegation meeting representatives of the full Authority on 1 February. On 22 February, the Authority merely requested revisions for consideration at its next meeting on 22 March. For Granada, the Poulson case brought into focus numerous long-standing questions about Authority oversight of programmes:

> Are the officers [of the IBA] responsible for executive decisions on programmes or aren't they? ... Is the IBA really not prepared to trust its senior officers and rap them over the knuckles in retrospect à la BBC?,

asked a Forman memo.[77] He also sought assurances that the Authority would judge programmes on the basis of a viewing rather than a script, as had had been the case with Poulson. And he noted how the Authority's inflexibility in meeting compounded the problems caused by programme bans:

> [I]f the full Authority are to be involved in decisions upon a topical programme, should they not be prepared to meet and reach a view at short notice? ... I believe that this apparent disregard by the Members of the Authority for the speed of decision making in current affairs programmes irks our people almost as much as a negative decision. It can also give the press long periods in which to speculate.[78]

The IBA's response failed to address these points directly and was dismissive: 'It is not the system of IBA control itself that has made these interventions so awkwardly frequent over recent months ... We believe that the remedy is in Granada's own hands', replied Young.[79]

'Aiding and abetting the enemy': terrorism

As the 1970s and 1980s continued, the IBA seemed gradually to become more tolerant of *World in Action* and more inclined to support its work in the face of complaints. In part, this reflects increasingly tolerant social attitudes, as well as the longevity of the series and its standing as part of the television firmament. But programme-makers could never predict its attitude with confidence, so its decisions could still cause surprise on occasions. In areas of greatest sensitivity for the British state, the Authority maintained an understandable caution, notably over official secrecy, discussed in Chapter 4, and Northern Ireland.

Programmes about Northern Ireland were subject to additional legal constraints as a result of the Troubles and covered by specific IBA guidelines, as well as attracting periodic public pressure from the Home Office.[80] Controversies arising out of current affairs coverage both on ITV and the BBC were numerous. Despite the sensitivity of the subject, *World in Action*, like *This Week*, felt a journalistic duty to explain and record the actions and motivations of all parties in the Troubles. Northern Ireland was the subject of 44 editions of the series between 1968 and 1998. Many drew comment or censure from the Authority, generally for a perceived lack of balance or for including interviews containing extreme views; several were felt to be unsuitable for transmission in Northern Ireland (although the Authority was most unwilling to take this step); two were not broadcast at all.

The Authority's decision not to transmit 'South of the border', a film exploring the effects of the Northern Irish Troubles in the Irish Republic, had a number of features in common with its later action over the Poulson programme. Four days before its planned transmission date on 1 November 1971, the programme was banned unseen at a meeting of the full Authority, the first time it had acted in such a way. Granada had already consulted extensively with ITA officers and the full Authority's action was not foreseen.[81] As with Poulson, the Authority's slowness and inflexibility manifested itself too. As the programme had been banned by the full Authority, members decided that only the full Authority could overturn the ban. So it was not until its next meeting on 16 November, 18 days after its initial decision, that the Authority actually saw the programme and discussed whether its initial action had been correct. Here the decision not to transmit was upheld.

Granada was dismayed at the ban (David Boulton, the programme's producer, was 'speechless', according to *The Times*)[82] and convinced that the decision was mistaken. Meeting with Young and Sendall at the ITA on the day after the initial decision was taken, Forman found that they too were 'disconcerted with what had happened', agreeing that 'it was a precedent to ban a programme sight unseen'.[83] The press were also critical of the Authority's action. Besides prominent news coverage, it prompted a concerned leader in the *Guardian* and feature articles elsewhere. To the embarrassment of both Granada and the Authority, an unnamed Granada source found by the *Sunday Times* claimed: 'You can practically see the steam coming out of Sidney's ears'.[84] In an open letter to Young, Alan Sapper of the ACTT condemned the Authority, suggesting that its actions foreshadowed a 'blanket ban' on political groups opposed to the government's Northern Ireland policy. 'There is no precedent for such a ban in the entire history of Independent Television', he wrote. 'The Authority considered it unnecessary to take the trouble to see what it was banning.' He further criticised the ITA's failure to explain its decision: 'no doubt because it is difficult to say why a film should be banned if it has not been seen'.[85] After much internal discussion, Granada screened 'South of the border' for the press on Friday 19 November. At the discussion that followed, only one journalist opposed the programme's transmission and then only in Northern Ireland. The 'overwhelming majority' of the weekend's press comment was 'favourable to Granada and critical of [the] ITA'.[86]

The ITA's decision seems to have been swift and unanimous but based on instinct rather than specific guidelines or clauses of the Act, hence the difficulty in explaining it. Granada considered that 'South of the border' was balanced, both in time and weight of opinion, including interviews with senior Irish opposition politicians and footage of the Prime Minister, Jack Lynch, who would not appear in person, but also extracts from speeches by the Sinn Fein president and the Provisional IRA's Chief of Staff recorded at Sinn Fein's annual conference. The conference had been the subject of ITN news coverage and extracts from the speeches had already been shown. Boulton summarised what he considered to be the 'feel' of the programme by saying: 'It is inconceivable that [anyone] watching this programme, even if they are predisposed to sympathise with Freedom Fighters in general, will come away with [anything] but distaste for these particular people' [the 'provisionals'].[87] At the Authority meeting at which the programme was initially banned, Bernard Sendall spoke of the value of giving viewers 'a better understanding of the ideas and attitudes of the IRA and the way they are regarded in the South'.[88] Nevertheless, with only a brief discussion, the Authority decided that allowing the IRA to speak in current affairs television, as opposed to news, 'was tantamount to "aiding and abetting the enemy"'.[89] Somehow this decision had to be conveyed to the public in terms of the Authority's duties under the Television Act. The closest that the Authority came to giving a reason for the ban was its suggestion that the film was 'likely to lead to disorder or be offensive to public feeling' under Section 3(1)(a) of the Act, in the light of the 'present critical situation' in Northern Ireland.[90] Young proposed to Forman that a further reason was that the Authority was troubled at the number of *This Week* and *World in Action* programmes made that were felt to be unsuitable for transmission in Northern Ireland, although he accepted that this had not been raised explicitly at its meeting. Liz Curtis offers other possible reasons as well – pressure from Ulster Television on the Authority (certainly UTV's Managing Director made representations about the programme in advance of the Authority meeting and it was this that led Sendall to feel that he should raise the issue); that criticism of the British Army made by Garret Fitzgerald, the Irish opposition leader, rather than the presence of the IRA, had offended the Authority.[91] Young also suggested that the programme lacked impartiality, but it was hard for the Authority to make this stick – *World in Action* was required only to be balanced across a series. Forman's response was withering:

> We do not understand the banning of the film under Section 3(1)(e) of the Television Act. This section requires that a programme should show *due impartiality*: it is clear, however, that the ban has been applied because the programme is not sufficiently *partial*.[92]

Nearly ten years later, with republican hunger strikes prominent in news coverage, another *World in Action* report on Northern Ireland went untransmitted. 'The propaganda war' sought to examine the propaganda tactics of the IRA and its allies. The programme discussed republican tactics and showed film of several events 'expressly designed to win publicity and influence with either the local community in Northern Ireland or the world outside'.[93] One of these events was the 'lying in state' of deceased hunger striker Patsy O'Hara, who was filmed surrounded by an INLA 'guard of honour' as neighbours filed past. When the programme was shown to the IBA, they considered that 'the sequence crosses the dividing line between reporting propaganda and adding to it'.[94] Granada were disappointed that the Authority took this view, but much angrier when some editions of *The Times* quoted Lord Thomson, IBA chairman, explaining that the film was unacceptable because Granada 'had crossed the line to engage themselves in the making of propaganda for the INLA'.[95] For the *World in Action* team, this represented a worrying escalation of the wording of the IBA statement and such impressions were heightened further by press coverage elsewhere (including a claim by Tom Normanton MP that the programme's producers were 'the type of people who are happy to give publicity to terrorists').[96] Writing to Thomson, Forman felt the need to explain that the 'lying in state' had not been staged for the cameras and to complain that 'our journalists have not been defended [by the IBA]. They have been disowned, and worse: it is alleged they are in league with the enemy'.[97] Thomson claimed that he had been misquoted, but otherwise showed little sensitivity to the enormity of his apparent gaffe.[98]

Initially, Granada was confident of getting the Authority to reconsider their decision, but it soon became apparent that the programme would not be cleared for transmission without the removal of the 22-second 'lying in state' sequence. This Granada refused to do and so the IBA's prohibition stood. Ironically, the sequence had already been shown several times in promotional trails for the programme.[99] Of course, at the heart of the debate over the programme was a much wider dilemma of strategy and principle in the reporting of Northern Ireland: should the same principles of 'free speech' and journalistic scrutiny be applied to terrorist groups in Northern Ireland as were applied elsewhere, or should they be denied what was later called 'the oxygen of publicity'?[100] For Granada's journalists, the former was the only acceptable course:

> Because we felt and showed for embittered critics of the *status quo* in Ulster the same sympathy we had felt for those challenging Whitey in Washington and chanting 'Hell No, We Won't Go' in California, our reporting – all television reporting – from Ulster was subjected to ever closer scrutiny.[101]

The IBA's line was rather different, however. Forman took the trouble to note down an exchange with Bernard Sendall over another *World in Action* programme about Northern Ireland because it seemed to exemplify the IBA's mindset:

> BS: Er – I think we can keep it out of the firing line.
>
> DF: But there's hardly one fact in it that has not already been published in the newspapers.
>
> BS: True. It will come as no news to anyone in Ireland. But the cumulative effect of all that information about British security work coming in one lump will be a shock to many people in this country.
>
> DF: Isn't that the point of the programme?[102]

For all the sensitivity that the IBA displayed, of course, a journalistic belief that Northern Ireland issues deserved exposure and analysis was not a licence to endorse republicanism, let alone terrorism. 'We believe that exposing propaganda as such is the best way of defusing it', said Plowright's draft press statement following the ban on 'The propaganda war', and the commentary read over the offending sequence described the 'lying in state' as 'a potent mixture designed to turn a convicted terrorist into a hero'.[103] Looking back, however, Boulton was anxious to give a balanced judgment on the regulation of programming about Northern Ireland:

> [W]hat is likely to strike the disinterested historian is ... the relative rarity of such head-on clashes between the Authority's watchdogs and front-line reporters. What has been freely reported on Northern Ireland ... far outweighs what has been censored.[104]

Understandably, the issue of terrorism remained a sensitive one for the IBA and a further programme ban was narrowly averted in 1989. But this time, in a programme called 'Playing with fire', the activities of the Animal Liberation Front were under scrutiny. At the beginning of that year, *World in Action* learned that ALF members, already conducting a sustained campaign to bomb premises involved with animal research, were planning to extend this to fast food shops, regardless of the threat to members of the public using them. As well as exposing the ALF's plans, the team sought to 'confront' their perpetrators. Interviews with ALF representatives were sought and, in true 'cloak and dagger' style, Granada's Managing Director, Andrew Quinn explained:

> [O]ur journalists received an anonymous telephone call suggesting that they go to a disused public building where they might see 'something interesting'. When they arrived, they were met by four men who had already put on masks to disguise their appearance. These men then submitted themselves to a rigorous and searching interview.[105]

As part of the interview, the masked men admitted to the fire-bombing of Dingles department store in Plymouth. Granada argued that this 'confrontation with the people directly responsible for such outrages has effectively exposed them as dangerous and misguided'.[106] But, despite agreeing that there was a legitimate public interest in investigating the activities of the ALF, the IBA refused to accept a filmed interview with masked individuals on the grounds that it glorified their military-style efficiency and could be an incitement to crime.[107] Since all remarks made by the ALF representatives were 'effectively challenged' in the interviews, Granada could see no justification for this view.[108] But the Authority did propose a compromise. In rejecting the programme, IBA Director-General Lady Littler suggested: 'running the film sequence mute against a commentary clearly explaining the circumstances in which the interview was obtained. We would then prefer the views expressed to be summarised in commentary ...'.[109] Granada saw this as an unacceptable weakening of the programme and feared that it might have the opposite effect to that intended by the IBA:

After discussions here, we believe that our audience would think it absurd that we should intervene so obtrusively between them and the available facts. They would wonder what the interviewees said which was so dangerous and persuasive that we could not allow it to be broadcast ... This, we believe would risk giving the activists a platform and a status which their arguments do not merit.[110]

The subject of the programme had been first been raised with the IBA in May 1989 with transmission planned for 10 July. But with the dispute still unresolved, it had to be postponed and the issue became public. For the press, Granada described the IBA's objections as 'a fresh infringement of broadcasting freedom'.[111] But behind the scenes, it was simultaneously pursuing compromise and seeking to force the Authority's hand by uncovering precedents and soliciting support from influential figures. Barry Wood, the programme's researcher, discovered that masked ALF representatives had previously appeared on a TVS programme and a 1984 Granada regional programme without objection from the Authority.[112] Copies of 'Playing with fire' were offered to a fire officer injured by ALF activity, police and lawyers who had investigated and prosecuted them, and the judge at the largest ALF trial to date. Their responses, supporting the screening of the programme in its present form, were forwarded to the IBA. In mid-August the stakes were raised considerably when lawyers acting for Devon and Cornwall Police served papers on Granada seeking the handover of 'all untransmitted material, documentation and notebooks' relating to the ALF investigation. This raised grave concerns among Granada's journalists as well as their lawyers, who pointed out:

The basic point of such an order, if granted, would cut across the fundamental working principle of confidence and trust that has to exist between investigative journalists and their sources ... The information obtained in such programmes is available only by virtue of journalistic enquiry. The granting of this order would mean that such information is no longer forthcoming. This would be a loss not only to the general public but also to the police.[113]

Despite its draconian nature, and suspicions that it was 'a fishing expedition',[114] the order was granted and Granada had no alternative but to comply.

Compromise, and a fresh sense of urgency at Granada led by a desire to open the new *World in Action* season with a programme that had become so notorious, finally won the day. A much-amended script, containing stronger public interest justifications for the programme and featuring a much-shortened interview with the 'masked men', was offered to the IBA.[115] When the Authority still refused to countenance any use of the interview, the sequence was re-shot with an actor speaking the ALF's responses and a still from the original interview in the top-right of the screen. This the Authority was prepared to accept and 'Playing with fire' was eventually shown as the second edition of the new season on 2 October. It was well-received, but the affair was hardly a victory for Granada nor for journalism. To get it on the air, it had been necessary to consent to a device that *World in Action's* editor had earlier described to the Authority as 'slightly absurd', explaining 'we are at a loss to understand how, in the light of your own guidelines, the Authority has reached this decision'.[116] In its policy, the IBA appears to have embraced the rationale behind the notorious 'broadcasting ban' (1988–94) then applying to terrorists and their supporters in Northern Ireland. Worst of all, the court order had demonstrated the existence of a form of regulation more powerful even than the IBA and one that showed little sympathy for journalists seeking to safeguard sources of privileged information in the public interest.

As the 1990s began and the IBA's replacement by the 'lighter touch' and less interventionist Independent Television Commission drew closer, it was apparent that that Granada's relations with the regulator had become less confrontational and more constructive over the years. For its part, the IBA had gradually softened its rigid interpretation of 'balance' and accepted 'balance-across-series' and, at least in John Pilger's films for ATV and Central, the 'personal view' as limited exceptions to due impartiality. 'By the mid 1970s', wrote Ray Fitzwalter,

> [t]he Authority became more understanding about the type of journalism that asked more questions and certainly remained steadfast in its defence of public service broadcasting generally. Differences became more sophisticated, bannings became extremely rare, contentious adjustments or delays tended to continue.[117]

The IBA's attitudes to controversial programmes were never so consistent that journalists could have complete confidence in them, and it had never fully embraced the claims of Granada's journalists that facts, rather than a balance of propositions, should stand as guarantors of fairness. Since the 1960s, Britain itself had become a more open society, less deferential to authority and capable of embracing a wider range of perspectives on issues, while *World in Action's* own reputation and its value to ITV had steadily grown. In this light, Fitzwalter felt able to add:

> One thing is clear of all the major milestone programmes which brought great conflict – arms spending [ie. 'Down the drain'], 'The man who stole Uganda', 'South of the border, 'The rise and fall of John Poulson', 'The

squeeze', the Official Secrets Act [ie. 'Secrets], 'Mr Kane's campaign', 'The propaganda war' – one knows that the arguments for cutting, banning or delaying presented at the time did not stand the test of history.[118]

In all, then five *World in Action* programmes might be said to have been banned by the regulator, but this is misleading.[119] Parts of the Olympics and Poulson programmes were shown later in a modified form, and the Authority might legitimately claim that Granada was responsible for the failure to transmit others through its refusal to make changes. Similarly, as Fitzwalter suggests, the Authority caused numerous programmes to be delayed or changed, often in the face of protests from the *World in Action* team. However, it would be wrong to see regulation as a monolithic process. *World in Action* received valuable support on many occasions from the Authority's staff, with programmes such as 'The most widely used drug in the world' or *Who Bombed Birmingham?*,[120] in which the IBA supported Granada in the face of criticism and legal action intended to prevent it from naming the real Birmingham bombers, often held up as examples. As we have seen, the most unpredictable or contentious regulatory interventions often occurred at the behest of Authority members themselves and in spite of advice or support for programme-makers offered by the Authority's staff.

Notes

1 J. Potter, *Independent Television in Britain, Volume 3: Politics and Control, 1968–80* (Basingstoke and London: Macmillan, 1989), p. 116.
2 The passing of the 1963 Television Act removed a further prohibition on the 'offensive representation of or reference to' living persons.
3 See P. Goddard, J. Corner and K. Richardson, 'The formation of *World in Action*: A case study in the history of current affairs journalism', *Journalism*, 2:1 (2001): 79.
4 Television Act, 1954, 2 & 3 Eliz. 2, c. 55.
5 *Report of the Committee on Broadcasting 1960*, Volume II, Appendix E, Memoranda submitted to the Committee, Paper No. 113, p. 691 (Cmnd. 1819–1). The unattributed author of these comments was Denis Forman.
6 D. Forman, *Persona Granada* (London: Andre Deutsch, 1997), p. 214.
7 C. Hill, *Behind the Screen: The Broadcasting Memoirs of Lord Hill of Luton* (London: Sidgwick & Jackson, 1974), p. 20.
8 *World in Action*: 'Down the drain'.
9 Sir R. Fraser, 'Granada and *World in Action*', paper presented to the Independent Television Authority (ITA paper 57/63), 12 March 1963. The Fourteen Day Rule, preventing broadcast discussion of any issue to be debated in parliament in the coming fortnight, had been permanently suspended in December 1956.

10 Forman, *Persona Granada*, p. 216.

11 *Hewat, draft press release, 7 March 1963 (bf. 1154).

12 Fraser, 'Granada and *World in Action*'.

13 *Hewat, draft press release, 7 March 1963.

14 *Forman, 'Due impartiality', draft for paper given at ITA Consultation on News and Current Affairs, Bristol, 6 January 1972 (bf. 1087).

15 *Hewat, draft memoir for unpublished history of Granada Television, c. 1976 (bf. 1437).

16 *Hewat, draft press release, 7 March 1963.

17 *Forman, draft article based on lecture on 'Censorship and Television' given by Forman to Department of Extra-Mural Education, Glasgow University, 14 November 1967 (bf. 1522); *D. Crow, unpublished history of Granada Television, 1969 (bf. 0978). Crow suggests that *Panorama* became involved as a result of a chance meeting between David Samuelson and Fox.

18 N. Swallow, 'Instant Truth', *Contrast*, 2:4, Summer 1963: 226–7.

19 Quoted in Forman, *Persona Granada*, p. 217.

20 Forman, *Persona Granada*, p. 215.

21 *Fraser, letter to V. Peers, 7 August 1964 (bf. 1086).

22 *Peers, letter to Fraser, 4 August 1964 (bf. 1086).

23 *Peers, draft (letter to B. Sendall) [?] (ITA), (no date) (bf. 1085).

24 B. Sendall, *Independent Television in Britain, Volume 2: Expansion and Change, 1958–68* (Basingstoke and London: Macmillan, 1983), pp. 302–3.

25 *Peers, letter to Sendall (1 November 1963), responding to *Sendall's letter (30 October 1963) asking why 'Repairs' had been shown unamended (both bf. 1228).

26 Sendall, *Independent Television in Britain, Volume 2*, p. 303; *Fraser, assessment of 'MRA' enclosed with letter to Peers, 27 September 1963 (bf. 1228) – the numerical precision of Fraser's assessment here hints at the rigidity of the ITA's conception of 'balance'.

27 Sendall, 'Programme Report for September 1963', paper presented to the Independent Television Authority (ITA paper 199/63), 11 October 1963.

28 *Forman, 'Draft notes of a meeting held on the 21 July 1964 at the Independent Television Authority premises' (bf. 1088).

29 *Hewat, draft press release, 7 March 1963.

30 Quoted in *The Times*, 1 October 1963, p. 5.

31 *Sendall, 'Programme report for September 1963'; minutes of meetings of the Independent Television Authority, 17 October 1963 (184/63) and 7 November 1963 (185/63).

32 *Peers, letters to Sendall, 18 and 22 November 1963; *Sendall, letter to Peers, 25 November 1963 (all at bf. 1228).

33 G. Wedell, 'Granada's Olympics programme', paper presented to the Independent Television Authority (ITA paper 106/64), 25 June 1964.

34 Forman, *Persona Granada*, p. 219.

35 *Transcript headed 'Telephone conversation between Sir Robert Fraser and SLB, 24/6/64' (bf. 1376).

36 Sendall, *Independent Television in Britain, Volume 2*, p. 304.
37 *Prideaux, letter to B. Heads, 15 August 1965 (bf. 1085).
38 *Prideaux, letter to Heads, 15 August 1965. The reference to Granada 'firing' him alludes to this being the final programme of the series and, consequently, the end of his contract with Granada.
39 A count of 464 lines of script for the 'prosecution' and 38 for the 'defence': A. Pragnell, 'Granada and political impartiality', paper presented to the Independent Television Authority' (ITA paper 99/66), 20 October 1966.
40 Forman, *Persona Granada*, p. 220.
41 Quoted in Forman, *Persona Granada*, pp. 220–1.
42 *Crow, resumé of events to date, '*World in Action* programme on the British drug industry', 21 April 1966 (bf. 1497).
43 *Letter to Fraser, 5 January 1967 (bf. 1419).
44 *Letter to S. Bernstein, 17 January 1967 (bf. 1419).
45 *Crow, memo to C. Bernstein, Forman, 6 October 1967 (bf. 1497); *Report of the Committee of Enquiry into the Relationship of the Pharmaceutical Industry with the National Health Service 1965–1967* (Cmnd 3410).
46 *Forman, 'Granada editorial policy', draft internal paper, 28 October 1970 (bf. 1522) (original emphasis).
47 See also Chapter 6.
48 *J. Wallington, 'Diary note of a lunch with the ITA', 29 September 1970 (and quoted in Forman, *Persona Granada*, p. 228); *Sendall, letter to Forman, 30 November 1970 (both bf. 1090).
49 *Letter to Sendall, 16 November 1970 (bf. 1090)
50 *Forman, letter to Sendall, 12 October 1970 (bf. 1090; letter quoted in full in Forman, *Persona Granada*, pp. 228–30).
51 Potter, *Independent Television in Britain, Volume 3*, p. 117.
52 *Sir B. Young (ITA Director-General), letter to Forman, 27 April 1971 (bf. 1070).
53 *Forman, letter to Young, 4 June 1971 (bf. 1070)
54 Forman, *Persona Granada*, p. 233.
55 *Forman, 'Granada editorial policy'.
56 See Forman, *Persona Granada*, p. 222.
57 *Forman, 'Aide memoire of a meeting at the ITA, 23.1.70', 26 January 1970 (bf. 1011). Forman gives a detailed account of the affair in *Persona Granada*, pp. 222–7.
58 *Forman, 'Your diary note of lunch with the ITA – 29.9.70', memo to Wallington, 2 October 1970 (bf. 1090).
59 *D. Harker, memo to Forman, 'Brian Young's conversation with Sir Paul Bryan', 8 August 1980 (bf. 1072).
60 Forman, Fleming Memorial lecture: 'TV: Some mysteries of the organism', *The Royal Television Society Journal*, July/August 1973: 231–2. See also Forman, *Persona Granada*, pp. 228, 233.
61 Ray Fitzwalter's reference to Lady Plowden's 'outside source', for example – see Chapter 4.

62 *Fitzwalter and M. Southan, memo to Forman, 'Sailor's jail', 4 July 1971 (bf. 0721).

63 *Fitzwalter and Southan, 'Sailor's jail'; *Forman, memo to S. Bernstein, 'Sailor's jail', 12 July 1971 (bf. 1070).

64 See also Chapter 3 and P. Goddard, 'Scandal at the regulator', *Television*, May 2006, pp. 28–9.

65 *D. Plowright, 'File note of a telephone call with Bernard Sendall on Thursday 25 February 1973', 30 January 1973 (bf. 1071).

66 *Forman, appendix to letter to Young, 'Some general notes on *World in Action*', 18 June 1973 (bf. 1071).

67 Forman, *Persona Granada*, p. 235–8; see also Potter, *Independent Television in Britain, Volume 3*, pp. 131–6.

68 *Letter to Forman, 26 April 1973 (bf. 0964) (emphasis added).

69 *Letter to Young, 7 May 1973 (bf. 0964).

70 In an interview with Michael Charlton on *Newsday* (BBC2), quoted by Peter Fiddick in *The Guardian*, April 14 1975, p. 10.

71 *Forman, letter to Lady Plowden, 14 June 1979 (bf. 1071). This exchange formed part of correspondence over a complaint about 'The invisible risk', a *World in Action* investigation into the safety of microwave ovens. Coincidentally, the complaint was from the Association of Manufacturers of Domestic Electrical Appliances, whose president was Lord Plowden, her husband.

72 *Forman, letter to Young, 5 September 1980 (bf. 1072).

73 *J. Weltman (ITA), letter to Plowright, 30 July 1968 (bf. 0964). For a detailed account of the Authority's oversight of undercover reporting, see P. Goddard, 'Improper liberties': Regulating undercover journalism on ITV, 1967–1980', *Journalism*, 7:1 (2006): 45–63.

74 *Plowright, letter to Weltman, 5 August 1968 (bf. 0964).

75 *Draft document (unattributed but almost certainly Plowright) discussing issues arising from the IBA's treatment of the Poulson programme, no date (1973) (bf. 1208).

76 Quoted in Forman, *Persona Granada*, p. 231.

77 *Forman, 'After Poulson', draft internal paper, 15 March 1973 (bf. 1071).

78 *Forman, letter to Young, 10 April 1973 (bf. 0964).

79 *Letter to Forman, 26 April 1973 (bf. 0964).

80 See J. Potter, *Independent Television in Britain, Volume 4: Companies and Programmes, 1968–80* (Basingstoke and London: Macmillan, 1990), pp. 207–13; B. Rolston and D. Miller (eds), *War and Words: The Northern Ireland Media Reader* (Belfast: Beyond the Pale, 1996). For an account of the problems surrounding *This Week*'s coverage of Northern Ireland, see P. Holland, *The Angry Buzz: This Week and Current Affairs Television* (London: I. B. Tauris, 2006), pp. 111–67.

81 *Forman, '*World in Action* – South of the border', paper for Granada Television Board, 8 December 1971 (bf. 1070).

82 *The Times*, 2 November 1971, p. 1.

83 *Forman, '*World in Action* – South of the border'.

84 *Sunday Times*, 7 November 1971, p. 3.

85 Sapper, letter to Young, quoted in *The Times*, 10 November 1971, p. 1.

86 *Forman, '*World in Action* – South of the border'.

87 *D. Boulton, 'Re: *World in Action*: IRA', memo to Forman, 29 October 1971 (bf. 1070).

88 *Sendall, '*World in Action* – November 1st', notes for ITA meeting, 28 October 1971 (bf. 0721).

89 *Forman, '*World in Action* – South of the border'.

90 *Forman, 'File note of telephone conversation with Brian Young, 17.11. 71', 17 November 1971 (bf. 1070); Potter, *Independent Television in Britain, Volume 4*, p. 209.

91 L. Curtis, *Ireland: The Propaganda War* (London: Pluto Press, 1984), pp. 151–3; *Forman, '*World in Action* – South of the border'.

92 *Forman, untitled draft statement (context unknown), 17 November 1971 (bf. 1071) (original emphasis).

93 *Plowright, draft press statement, 5 June 1981 (bf. 1071).

94 *'*World in Action*: IBA Statement', IBA press statement, 5 June 1981 (bf. 1071).

95 *The Times*, 11 June 1981, quoted in: *Boulton and 9 WIA producers, letter to Lord Thomson, 17 June 1981 (bf. 1071).

96 In the *Daily Telegraph*, 2 June 1981, p. 1.

97 *Forman, letter to Thomson, 17 June 1981 (bf. 1071).

98 *Thomson, letter to Forman, 23 June 1981 (bf. 0720).

99 Curtis, *Ireland: The Propaganda War*, p. 205.

100 See Sir I. Trethowan, 'Should the terrorists be given air time?', *The Times*, 4 June 1981, p. 14.

101 D. Boulton, speaking in the *World in Action – The first 21 years* retrospective programme. 'Listen Whitey' and 'Hell no, we won't go' were *World in Action* editions on American racism and resistance to the Vietnam War respectively.

102 *Forman, diary note: 'Scenes from a broadcasting life – Three confidential episodes occurring on the 7th of September 1973' (bf. 1496). The programme was 'A question of intelligence'.

103 Quoted in Curtis, *Ireland: The Propaganda War*, p. 205.

104 Speaking in the *World in Action – The first 21 years* retrospective programme. NB. Boulton's statement pre-dates the British Home Office's notorious 'broadcasting ban' (1988–94) on the speech of proscribed groups in Northern Ireland.

105 *Letter to Lady Littler, IBA, 4 July 1989 (bf. 0740).

106 *Quinn, letter to Littler, 7 July 1989 (bf. 0740).

107 *Littler, letter to Quinn, 6 July 1989 (bf. 0740).

108 *Quinn, letter to Littler, 7 July 1989.

109 *Littler, letter to Quinn, 6 July 1989.

110 *Quinn, letter to Littler, 7 July 1989.

111 *Granada Television press statement, untitled, no date (bf. 0740).
112 *Wood, memos to Fitzwalter, 5 July and 29 June 1989 (bf. 0740).
113 *Unattributed paper accompanying letter from P. Herbert (Goodman Derrick solicitors) to Fitzwalter, 14 August 1989 (bf. 0740).
114 *Herbert, letter to Fitzwalter, 14 August 1989.
115 *Fitzwalter, letter to C. Mulholland (IBA), 13 September 1989 (bf. 0740)
116 *S. Prebble, letter to S. Elliott (IBA), 26 June 1989 (bf. 0740).
117 Fitzwalter, 'Can the whistle keep on blowing?', speech to Edinburgh International Television Festival, 27 August 1984.
118 Fitzwalter, 'Can the whistle keep on blowing?'
119 'Down the drain', 'How to lose the Olympics after really trying', 'South of the border', 'The friends and influence of John L. Poulson', 'The propaganda war'.
120 Discussed in Chapters 3 and 5 respectively.

9

Conclusion: television in action

This book has offered an exploration of how one current affairs programme developed its identity and its reputation for quality and for social and political impact across four decades. This development involved a process of almost continuous critical review and adaptation in response to change. The Britain within which *World in Action* contributed to public knowledge, debate and dispute, often using its investigations to intervene in spheres of policy, was a country undergoing major transformation, sometimes rapidly, sometimes at a more gradual, incremental, pace. It is a banality of historical commentary to talk of 'change' as the backdrop to a particular focus of inquiry, but the political, economic, social and cultural shifts across which the series sustained its significance require recognition as part of any assessment of its values. To some of these shifts, for instance the move away from the deferential towards the questioning in relation to the discourses and protocols of 'authority', the series acted as a resource and a voice. In describing its task, former members often used that maxim of critical journalism that its mission was to 'comfort the afflicted and afflict the comfortable'. Its commitment to the encouragement of a culture of civic engagement was outstanding, even if not always successfully realized. To other shifts, for instance the opening up of new possibilities for inefficiency and corruption created by larger and more complex state and corporate bureaucracies, it did its best to take up a position of criticism and 'whistleblowing'. To one of the most marked shifts of the 1980s and 1990s, the tightening grip of market relationships on public life, it responded with a wide range of investigative approaches but also, finally, became itself a casualty in 1998, when the intensified pressures of ratings and scheduling effectively closed down its working space.

If there is one word that catches at, even if it does not define, the history of *World in Action*, that word is 'dynamic'. Dynamism is built into the core formula for the series right from the beginning, as the title proclaims. The scope is to be international, the mode of engagement one that registers process, what *is happening*. It is a model of visual journalism in which the potential for the serious also, in various ways, to be *exciting*, is fully explored. *World in Action*'s dynamism of form and address, subject to regular review and revision, came about as a result of three other dynamic relationships. First of all, there was that between the wider society, its politics and the institution of television – a major, transforming relationship for much of run of the series. This relationship was often volatile and frequently controversial, making national life visible to itself in completely new ways and bringing new terms, voices, experiences and attitudes into the realm of 'public debate' so as to create what can be seen as a reconfigured 'public culture'.[1] Secondly, there was the play-off between the series itself and other 'institutions' within the television sector, including Granada Television, regulatory authorities and the activities of the other broadcasting organisations, including the BBC. The various dynamics at work here, sometimes supportive, sometimes vigorously competitive and occasionally adversarial, played a key role in the formation and reformation of the series identity, as we have shown. Thirdly, there is the quite distinctive character of the series as the product of a team, one which quite frequently changed its members and roles. What we might see as the productively 'unsettled' nature of the series, both internally and across the two other axes of relationship we have indicated, is integral to its identity and its legacy.

There has been no hypothesis tested in this book and no implied view of television values that can now be turned into a 'conclusion'. However, we hope that the work of documenting the programme's history, its varied stylings, contexts, modes of working, successes and problems, reveals a pattern of values, some of which are relevant to the present.

In reflecting on this pattern and its significance, we want to give attention to three themes that have threaded their way through many of the preceding pages. First of all, there is the idea of 'documentary journalism' and the kinds of visual storytelling that it involves. Secondly, there is the notion of a critical 'producer culture' and the importance of the combination of skill and value which this entails. Thirdly, there is the idea of television and public life, an idea that has provided the over-arching framework for the whole project. Having looked back at our account in this way, we want to finish with some comments that pick up further on our third theme. What is the situation of 'current affairs' television today, what spaces and forms are closing down and what are opening up for the articulation of 'public issues'? And how does historical scholarship like ours relate to other kinds of attempt to understand what television is and where it is going?

1) Documentary journalism

World in Action is an outstanding example of a particular type of television series, a kind which it did not create but which it certainly greatly helped to shape, refine and expand in range and depth. The most obvious, because most used, label for this is 'current affairs' which we have regularly employed throughout this book. Current Affairs is essentially a description of content and its way of indicating news-related themes carries what has often been seen as a very British ring of the off-hand and the vague.[2]

Documentary journalism is an awkward term too, but it more accurately indicates the two central ingredients which, in intent, approach and form, provided the basis for the category of work in which *World in Action* achieved its success. In several of the chapters we have shown how this combination was often uneasy and always unstable but absolutely vital to appeal and impact. Here, journalism is the core term and the production of investigative, explanatory reports the principal discipline. However, documentary indicates the defining variant, the production of visual narratives through which the reports can be expressed and the significance of what has been found out made available to a popular audience. The strength of the recipe, or in fact various recipes, upon which *World in Action* drew throughout its run lies in the combination of reportorial drive with an engaging 'visual offer', to watch things happen not just to look at people talk. In its extensive use of the commentary over film mode, the series found what was its most familiar way of regulating the immediacy and drama of film sequences with a continuous flow of focused and firmly-voiced reporting, never letting the movement become too relaxed or spacious, never letting what was shown become simply diverting. The series thus has to be seen not only as a significant chapter in the history of broadcast journalism but as a development and expansion of the broad strand of documentary expression. Some of its editions, though inclining towards the 'immediate' and often towards the 'rough' and the 'dirty' in terms of production refinement, displayed a visual design and crafting that are in the best traditions of the rich body of work identifiable under this heading.[3]

2) Critical producer culture

As Georgina Born has recently emphasised in her impressive workplace ethnography of the BBC,[4] not only the resources and skills but the values and morale of those involved in production are an important factor in determining the quality of output. One variable here is the extent to which production staff feel an adequate space for creative originality is available to them. Another is the question of whether the criteria they are working with are shared by their management and by audiences. Once doubt starts to enter in respect of corporate priorities or a gap opens up between production criteria and the criteria used to measure success with the audience (at its crudest, the changing formula for getting 'good figures'), then problems of bad faith and cynicism arise. We have shown that, for most of its run, those who made *World in Action* were able to work with some confidence in respect both of management and of audience and we have pointed to how this confidence broke down in its final years, undercutting the series' sense of purpose and direction and leading to an uneasy sense of 'commodity' value displacing the directness of commitment both in relation to content and approach.

However, our emphasis has been on the 'critical' nature of the culture of production that sustained the series until the final years. To look through the archives is to see regular evidence of debate and dispute about what the programme should be doing. This was pitched not only at the level of general principles but more often at the level of detailed scrutiny and analysis of recently broadcast editions themselves. It is perhaps useful to consider a few phrases, effectively at random, from our notes of the comments made by production team members. We have quoted extensively from the archival record in previous chapters, where we have considered specific editions, aspects or phases of revision and innovation, giving appropriate context and references. Here, it might be best simply to present a few critical points from the archive as 'overheard', anonymous voices, comments quickly typed down and distributed as part of the ferment of interest in making the series better:

> Editing must be even more adventurous to improve pace and transitions.

> If you want to film groovy subjects groovily you are in danger of being seduced to a position of *only* wanting to film groovy subjects.

> We often fail because the original concept is never grasped. As a result the story is muddled, the shooting ratio ridiculous.

> There is a distinction between the kind of 'objective' film-making [being advocated] and impressionism. The latter seems to be very often a smart way of describing shapelessness.

> I have yet to see an interview with a politician who produced a new and constructive thought.

> It goes without saying that every programme must have an attitude – however implicitly it is expressed, even if it becomes apparent only towards the end of the show.

We should be seeking, not a story, but the man or the situation which reflects the story, the singer not the song. (A handwritten comment on the margins of this typed note reads 'you've got to have the story first'.)

It all comes down to ... knowing what you want so say rather than having to mark time for 45 seconds with flare shots and Jazz Bach.

All too often the slightly hectoring, informative voice of the narrator distantiates, alienates.

These various fragments of comment, often expressing very divergent views, point to that broader culture of engagement concerning the function and form of television current affairs by which *World in Action* was regularly re-energised. Permitted by a degree of economic and institutional space, it allowed a special relationship to flourish between professional, industrial and social criteria.

3) Television and public life

The concern with 'getting it right' within the *World in Action* team partly reflected, as we have noted, a sense of the public importance of the project stretching beyond the success of any one edition in terms of its share of the audience. However, a popular audience was always an essential part of the changing formula; the journalistic mission could not easily drift into the kind of self-regarding metropolitanism that was perceived as a risk for some arts programmes. The series project was in many respects a project of *challenge*. It quite often put its challenge to authorities in relation to specific problems and oversights but it also routinely challenged its audience to care. In this sense, it routinely offered a strong and often provocative civic address, one presented to viewers always assumed to be able to watch and respond and make up their minds from a basis in prior knowledge and experience and from their own sense of civic value. There is no doubt that the sheer limitations of the viewing alternatives available for much of *World in Action*'s history contributed to the relative confidence in which it went about the business of being serious and popular at the same time. It was only with the increased availability of satellite and cable channels in the 1990s that a significantly new context for programme design, schedule and audience size emerged, one in which the public visibility of output on any one channel was no longer of a magnitude that allowed routine assumptions to be made about 'being heard'.

The changing, complex and often tense relationships around regulatory issues that we have traced in Chapter 8 confirm not only the difficulties of making the series but the kinds of public significance and public consequences it was able to have. The disputes, sometime heated and often tortuous, around ideas of 'fairness' and 'impartiality' in the context of a journalism of challenge, testify to the existence of what we might call a 'television with teeth', able to cause problems and to threaten, if only circumstantially, the exercise of power and privilege. *World in Action* also operated for the most part in a Britain where, whatever the levels of inequality and prejudice, the expansion of the sphere of the 'private' and rise of consumer identity to the point of challenging and redefining the idea of a 'citizen' had yet to occur. Both the subsequent shifts in the television economy and in socio-political values have to be reckoned with in any comparison of the series' often noisy public presence against the available options for television today.

Current affairs and the new television order

Patricia Holland has shown how current affairs might now best be seen – rather than as a kind of programme, as a 'project' dispersed across a number of different forms of factual output, addressed to different audiences.[5] In a way that usefully challenges the pessimism that follows from using older models as the only reference point, she notes the energy and the accessibility of many new approaches while being mindful of the encouragement towards a thinning out of explanatory contexts that the more competitive television economy has introduced. In her BBC study, Georgina Born, comments on how the generic idea of 'current affairs' came under pressure during the 1990s. She observes that 'the very seriousness, the impartial, authoritative and analytical tone of current affairs were perceived as liabilities within and beyond the [relevant] department'.[6] Additionally, pressure was coming from developments on 'either side' as it were. First of all, there was an increasing interest in occasional long-form journalism (or 'features') from within news departments, sometimes displaying a more attitudinal character than was to be found in core news items. Secondly, the burgeoning of a variety of documentary-based formats led to more frequent visits to the traditional 'current affairs' agenda from this area of work (focusing particularly on consumer affairs and lifestyle topics) even if much of the output was entertainment-led and deliberately 'soft' in approach. Born comments how, in consequence of this, there was a renewed emphasis on narrative values, 'the "story" became a mantra'.[7] Her sense of a growing verdict of 'failed genre' is not in contradiction with Holland's suggestion, informing a more hopeful judgement, that we now have to see 'current affairs' in broader terms, as a programme element dispersed across output. Indeed, the recent review of the Office of Communications (Ofcom) concerning 'current affairs' within the schedules can be read positively to indicate that, when regarded as an element, the treatment of current affairs is as strongly represented on British television as ever.[8] Of course, quite a lot of dispute could surround precisely how the category is defined once a variety of very different formats are seen partially to fulfil the commitment to provide the dimension of output thus described. The redefinition of 'current affairs' will be part of the larger redefinition of 'public service broadcasting' currently under way. This is a process in which the forces of economic convenience will be in deep, if not always open, contest with a perceived requirement to oblige television to fulfil a public role not entirely covered by size of audience or multiplicity of choice.[9]

Television history and television studies

Finally, we want to say something about the business of doing television history. After a long period of relative neglect, it is now clear that historical work across different genres is becoming a defining feature of recent television studies, with a number of monographs, articles, conferences and research awards testifying to this. We noted some of the key contributions to this development in our Introduction.

Television historiography poses many challenges for inquiry, some of which we have explored elsewhere.[10] As remarked earlier, as well as putting chronological development and thematic analysis in tension, it raises questions about the appropriate context for making sense of data and bringing out the significance of the 'record'. The historical story we have told draws heavily from the written archives of the series, complemented by interviews and our own analysis of the programmes themselves. The contemporary written record in many ways offers a firmer base than retrospective interviews, if only because the documents were mostly written to get something done – they are discursive agents in the process of getting a programme made and screened, the series improved, modifications introduced in response to new suggestions, protection from official and legal 'interference' devised and response to such interference promptly produced where necessary. However, interviews introduce a stronger sense of the experience of making the programme, not always revealed in even the most personal of memoranda. Moreover, the retrospective, reflective view can be valuable when recognised as such even if detail may escape it.

Our own engagement with the 'texts' of the programmes has been modest but, we hope, productive, bringing out some of the formal strategies, modes of address and depiction, and to use Raymond

Williams' phrase, 'structures of feeling' within which the communicative work of the series was undertaken.[11]

Our history is bound to be a selective account and its assembly from discrete records will inevitably be inadequate both to the experiential worlds of making the series and viewing it within the shifting public, private and domestic contexts that constituted the settings for its weekly reception in British homes. With these limitations, we nevertheless believe a useful job has been done.

Part of the 'use' is in providing a record of major national achievement for all those interested in television and its bearing on public life. This is material for debate as well as admiration for what was achieved. A good account of the television we once had is a further resource in discussion about the kind of television we have and the kind we want. A more focused 'use' is within the study of television, where attention to policy, production, programmes and audiences develops briskly, inevitably with a contemporary emphasis despite the swing to historical work we noted earlier. Especially if accompanied by easier if selective access to programme material (as we hope it eventually will be), our study opens out a long view of public issue television at work ('television in action', indeed). Such a view can enrich our sense of the agenda for contemporary teaching and research and perhaps even inspire attempts to develop this agenda further, whatever new priorities and perspectives assert themselves here.

Notes

1 'Public culture' suggests the broader pattern of feeling, forms of expression and modes of discursive and aesthetic exchange at work within a society, the basis upon which politically oriented deliberation (as indicated in Jurgen Habermas' influential idea of the 'public sphere') is organised and performed.

2 One of the papers produced for a team discussion in April 1967 has a joke about the current affairs label. In the context of an anecdote about discussions with an East German television executive, the possibility of the term being misunderstood as concerning 'electricity – or the dried fruit trade' is considered. (*R. Spurr, untitled paper for 'What's next' meeting (bf. 1228)).

3 The literature on the problems of definition surrounding the idea of 'documentary' is extensive and growing as a result of the emergence of new factual forms committed more directly to entertainment. Among the most recent publications, Anita Biressi and Heather Nunn's *Reality TV: Realism and Revelation* (London: Wallflower, 2005) is notable for its broad sense of generic shifts within a long tradition of different kinds of 'documentary' practice.

4 G. Born, *Uncertain Vision* (London: Secker & Warburg, 2004).

5 See the 'Postscript' to P. Holland, *The Angry Buzz: This Week and Current Affairs Television* (London: I. B. Tauris, 2006).

6 Born, *Uncertain Vision*, p. 400.

7 Born, *Uncertain Vision*, p. 400.

8 http://www.ofcom.org.uk/media/speeches/2006/03/current_affairs#content. The Ofcom website has regular updates on commissioned research concerning related issues of policy and output.

9 See J. Corner and A. Hill, 'Value, form and viewing in current affairs television', *Journal of British Cinema and Television*, 3:1, (2006): 34–46, for a critical commentary using material from Ofcom research. Sylvia Harvey's 'Ofcom's first year and neoliberalism's blind spot: attacking the culture of production' (*Screen*, Vol. 47:1, 2006: 91–105) is a provocative and detailed review of how 'public service' ideas have fared within the regulatory regime introduced by Ofcom.

10 Our joint commentary on these issues in relation to the research project of this book is J. Corner, P. Goddard and K. Richardson, 'Researching Television History', *Norwegian Journal of Media Research*, 8:1, (2001) 38–49. A broader review of some of the main issues can be found in J. Corner, 'Finding data, reading patterns, telling stories: Issues in television historiography', *Media, Culture and Society*, 25:2, (2003) 273–80.

11 Brought up by Williams at a number of points in his writing to indicate the affective as well as cognitive frameworks within which a culture is 'lived' and cultural change is shaped. See our earlier note above on 'public culture'. For an early and influential use of the idea of 'structure of feeling', see R. Williams, *The Long Revolution* (London: Chatto & Windus 1961, regularly reprinted in paperback editions).

Index of *World in Action* programmes

Each edition of *World in Action* referred to in this book is listed here, in chronological order, together with transmission (tx.) date, name(s) of producers and page references. Occasional collaborative programmes were credited to 'the *World in Action* team' rather than to individual producers. Not all editions were broadcast with titles and those listed here are the titles by which they have most commonly been referred to in various forms of Granada Television documentation. Alternative titles are also given where appropriate. Occasional programmes were broadcast under their own titles rather than as editions of *World in Action*. The authors regret any errors or omissions.

Index